Politics and Public Protection

EMERALD ADVANCES IN HISTORICAL CRIMINOLOGY

Series Editors: David Churchill and Christopher W. Mullins

This series embraces a broad, pluralistic understanding of 'the historical' and its potential applications to criminology. Providing an inclusive platform for a range of approaches which, in various ways, seek to orient criminological enquiry to history or to the dynamics of historical time, the series also offers a platform both for conventional studies in the history of crime and criminal justice, but also for innovative and experimental work which extends the conceptual, theoretical, methodological and topical range of historical criminology. In this way, the series encourages historical scholarship on non-traditional topics in criminology (such as environmental harms, war and state crime) and inventive modes of theorising and practising historical research (including processual approaches and futures research). The series thus makes a valuable contribution to criminology irrespective of disciplinary affiliation, theoretical framing or methodological practice.

Previous Titles

History & Crime: A Transdisciplinary Approach edited by Thomas J. Kehoe and Jeffrey E. Pfeifer

The First British Crime Survey: An Ethnography of Criminology Within Government by Julian Molina

A Socio-Legal History of the Laws of War: Constraining Carnage by Christopher W. Mullins

A Socio-Legal History of the Laws of War: The Birth of International Humanitarian Law by Christopher W. Mullins

Politics and Public Protection

BY
MIKE NASH
University of Portsmouth, UK

AND
ANDY WILLIAMS
University of Portsmouth, UK

United Kingdom – North America – Japan – India – Malaysia – China

Emerald Publishing Limited
Emerald Publishing, Floor 5, Northspring, 21-23 Wellington Street, Leeds LS1 4DL

First edition 2025

Copyright © 2025 Mike Nash and Andy Williams.
Published under exclusive licence by Emerald Publishing Limited.

Reprints and permissions service
Contact: www.copyright.com

No part of this book may be reproduced, stored in a retrieval system, transmitted in any form or by any means electronic, mechanical, photocopying, recording or otherwise without either the prior written permission of the publisher or a licence permitting restricted copying issued in the UK by The Copyright Licensing Agency and in the USA by The Copyright Clearance Center. Any opinions expressed in the chapters are those of the authors. Whilst Emerald makes every effort to ensure the quality and accuracy of its content, Emerald makes no representation implied or otherwise, as to the chapters' suitability and application and disclaims any warranties, express or implied, to their use.

British Library Cataloguing in Publication Data
A catalogue record for this book is available from the British Library

ISBN: 978-1-83753-529-3 (Print)
ISBN: 978-1-83753-528-6 (Online)
ISBN: 978-1-83753-530-9 (Epub)

INVESTOR IN PEOPLE

Mike: For Joe and Margot
Andy: For Eve, Ella, Grace, Poppie, Issy, Maisy and Bella

Epigraph

Our boys did not stand a chance. There were clear warnings of Saadallah's extremist risk and becoming a 'lone wolf' attacker. We have been sat in court demoralised, bewildered and disillusioned by the agencies' failure to effectively communicate, assess the risk and protect the public. It is clear to us that the boys were failed by the agencies that were entrusted to protect them. The failings of the state exposed by this inquest sicken and disgust me. Those who failed in their duties are responsible for David's, James's and Joe's deaths.

Relatives of three men murdered in a Reading terror attack speaking after the Coroner's Inquest. *The Guardian*, 27 April 2024.

Contents

List of Figures and Tables — *xi*

About the Authors — *xiii*

Part One: What Is Dangerousness?

Introduction: Dangerousness, Politics and Public Protection — *3*

Chapter 1   The Dangerous Offender Population — *15*

Part Two: Public Protections Responses

Chapter 2   Legislation: To Punish, to Protect and What? — *37*

Chapter 3   The Agencies of Public Protection: Prisons, Parole and the Police — *59*

Chapter 4   The Probation Service: At the Heart of Everything? — *93*

Part Three: Other Dangerous Groups

Chapter 5   Mentally Ill and Personality Disordered Offenders — *113*

Chapter 6   Terrorism and Terror-Related Offenders — *137*

Part Four: Current Issues and Trends in Public Protection

Chapter 7 Serious Further Offending: Hindsight Bias and Political Scapegoating *155*

Chapter 8 Civilian-Led Public Protection: The Public's Response to Bad Public Protection Politics *185*

Conclusion *209*

References *219*

Index *241*

List of Figures and Tables

Chapter 7
Fig. 1.	The SFO Process (From HMIP, 2020a, p. 18).	160
Fig. 2.	Quality Assurance Rating – Outstanding and Inadequate.	163
Fig. 3.	Number of SFO Convictions 2010–2022.	165
Fig. 4.	Sample Comparison of SFOs – NPS vs CRC, 2014–2019.	168
Fig. 5.	SFO Independent Reviews' Themes.	177
Fig. 6.	Sentiment Markers for SFO Independent Reviews.	178
Fig. 7.	Findings and Recommendations Comparison, Pre vs Post-TR.	180

Chapter 4
Table 1.	TR Proposed Allocation for Different Offender Groups.	106

Chapter 7
Table 2.	Number of SFO Offences, NPS v CRC 2014–2019.	166
Table 3.	Sources of Information Used in the Campbell Review.	172

About the Authors

Mike Nash has been the Head of Department and a Professor of Criminology at the SSCJ, University of Portsmouth. With colleagues, he worked on a range of higher education courses for serving police and probation officers. As a former Senior Probation Officer, he worked in a lifers' prison and a maximum-security category A prison. He worked on the early development of what were to become the multi-agency public protection arrangements (MAPPA). He has written and published on public protection matters for over 30 years.

Andy Williams is a Principal Lecturer in Criminology and Criminal Justice at SCCJ, University of Portsmouth. Having completed his doctorate in 2003, which consisted of an ethnography of the Paulsgrove demonstrations in 2000, he has developed academic courses and practitioner training in understanding risk and dangerousness for violent and sexual offenders. He is the co-author (with Mike Nash) of *The Anatomy of Serious Further Offending* (2008, with Oxford University Press) and *The Handbook of Public Protection* (2010, with Routledge). His recent books are *The Myth of Moral Panics* (2014, Routledge with Bill Thompson) and *Forensic Criminology* (2015, with Routledge). He has undertaken numerous evaluations of public protection systems including an evaluation of the Integrated Management IRIS model for Avon & Somerset Police and Probation services (2014), Hampshire's Violent Offender Intervention Programme (2016 for Hampshire's Police and Crime Commissioner) and Aurora New Dawn's DVA Cars™ initiative (2018 and 2023). His current research is an online ethnography of grooming and online child abuse activist groups ('Paedophile' Hunter).

Part One

What Is Dangerousness?

Introduction: Dangerousness, Politics and Public Protection

This book does not offer a definitive guide to public protection in England and Wales in the first quarter of the 21st century. We do not believe such a book could ever be written. We do not write in great detail about every aspect of the public protection process. Instead, we write about the gaps in between key elements of that process. We discuss a soft, malleable, pliable and loose entity often described as a 'system' but which we would argue is anything but. It is rather like a ball of plasticine, thrown between the public, the media, politicians, survivors and the agencies charged with the onerous task of protecting the public. Each leaves their imprint, and each time the ball is re-shaped, only to be changed again when the next serious event arises. Thus, we believe that public protection does not stand still long enough to be described in detail as a complete entity. We think it better to consider not only the ways in which it changes, but what caused those changes and why. We hope that those who work in the field are given ideas about their working lives, and we also hope that general readers are given new food for thought about what is a very important social and political issue today.

The title of this book has been chosen quite deliberately. We originally considered calling it The *Politics of Public Protection* but rejected this on the basis that there is not a specific 'politics' that relates to protecting the public. Instead, we felt that *Politics and Public Protection* would better illustrate our view that politics, and party politics in particular, has a very considerable impact on the legislation and professional policies of numerous criminal justice agencies. By this we mean that, rather than a carefully thought through agenda, politicians too often find themselves responding to rare, isolated but serious incidents which cause public alarm and media demands for action; whilst attempting to avoid being blamed for very harmful incidents. Inevitably, this response has seen nothing but a ratcheting up of protective measures for nearly three decades. Rather than one political party driving this agenda, it could instead be argued that a consensus has emerged which has left many measures unchallenged, even when considerable issues of human rights are at stake. From the 1990s onwards, the Labour Party has been seen as rarely opposing a 'red meat' conservative public protection measure. Indeed, by not opposing, but supporting and then pushing the agenda forward, the perception is common that Labour has contributed to a repressive and controlling system as much as their political opponents. Yes, undoubtedly, debates in the Parliament and comments to the media have seen a tinkering around the edges of proposed legislative measures, but these roll on, becoming more inclusive and more restrictive with each new headline crime. The impact of this protection roller-coaster on the agencies, which have to deliver it, is rarely debated in public; it is our intention to do so here.

 We should be clear at this stage that the public protection measures we will discuss are not led by or delivered by a public protection 'service'. No such organisation exists. In the UK, we do not have a public protection agency. Instead we have a number of agencies, working together with varying degrees of effectiveness, to operate what might be termed a public protection *system*. We, however, believe that this word implies too much in the way of organisation and coherence and instead prefer the word *process*. For many years now, governments have believed that the way to solve complex problems has been to establish complex systems to deal with them. Words such collaboration, sharing, multi-agency and inter-agency working have become commonplace. Serious failures, usually in the form of a repetition of serious crimes, mean that these systems have not worked. The response, inevitably, has been to look for ways to tighten the system to *ensure* that exchange and cooperation takes place. Within these organisational responses is, we would argue, a lack of attention to the training and skills of those who have to work with unpredictable and potentially dangerous offenders. The huge, politically-driven changes to probation training in the 1990s is one such instance which, we would argue, has led to a significant skills deficit in working with people who have the capacity to cause great harm. Indeed, we are currently in the bemusing situation where the internal training run by the MoJ's Learning and Development team restricts both the method and content allowed. Training is delivered by staff who simply follow pre-designed slides, some of which are out of date in terms of accuracy in policy and practice. The lack of innovation in terms of teaching delivery is astounding at times; however, with Sonia Crozier taking over as lead, we have high hopes that things will improve in the future. Protecting the public from seriously harmful offenders is a difficult task. Offering protection though is something of a chimera. It is very much about preventing something terrible from happening; an act committed by someone who may be unknown or, if known, may or may not do that act. Public protection 'success' may be the absence of the act, but we cannot know if it may or may not have happened. Unfortunately, the drive to include the unknown, to make the future more certain, has the effect of making the process ever-larger and more inclusive. Tragedies will inevitably occur. If so, it is the offender who is culpable, not a supervisor. That said however, there are mistakes, there are errors of judgement, there may be an over or indeed under-reliance on formulaic risk assessments. Drill down far enough and there will be individual errors, so it is important to understand why, rather than simply ratchet-up the system further through ill-conceived policies.

Public Protection – Who Is Involved?

Rather like a sponge, public protection has sucked in agencies and organisations over many years, way beyond what might be seen as core criminal justice departments. For example, the multi-agency public protection arrangements (MAPPA) which we discuss throughout the book, have placed a 'duty to cooperate' obligation on a range of what might be regarded as 'social' services. These include health, mental health, social services, education, the voluntary sector and additionally, private sector companies. All are required to share their information in order to protect the public, so confidentiality comes second to protection. Apart from sharing their information, many of these agencies are required to work alongside those with whom they may share an entirely different ethos. Differing cultural and professional perspectives are meant to bend to the public protection mandate. We would agree that there is great benefit in sharing different perceptions of risks and harm, but think the important word here is 'different'. Singing from the same hymn sheet may sound like an attractive idea, but not if it stops a range of views being heard, with those regarded as being less central to the process, feeling unable to state their opinions. We also think that sometimes the default position of worshipping at the altar of multi-agency working (MAW) might do more harm than good.

Police and Sex Offenders

Even for those core criminal justice agencies, the public protection process has triggered considerable professional and cultural change and challenge, with some of the outcomes being very surprising. The police service, for example, is probably regarded as the epitome of a public protection organisation. It is tasked with fighting crime, apprehending criminals and keeping people safe, in itself a huge task. Added to these however are well established roles in road safety, accident investigation, dispute resolution, keeping the peace, policing crowds and protests to name but a few. It is rare for the police service to lose a role, but in 1997, it gained a massive new responsibility and one which was almost the complete opposite of its normal functioning. The Sex Offenders Act of that year established a register for convicted offenders to be held by the police. Although the term 'register' was something of a misnomer, it being little more than the recording of basic details of personal information, it was a new task and a not inconsiderable one, although a slow start saw only 8,600 by 2000 (Thomas, 2008). The number of registered sex offenders now stands at over 67,000 with everyone requiring at least one home visit each year – more if their risk deems it necessary. As with much in public protection, individual, high-profile incidents can have an immediate and usually strengthening impact on measures deployed by governments. In 2000, the abduction and murder of eight-year-old Sarah Payne, by convicted and registered sex offender Roy Whiting, brought forth the first major revisions to the register. No doubt pushed forward by an emotional victim led campaign (Savage and Charman, 2010) and powerful support from Sunday national Newspaper the

News of the World (NoW), the Criminal Justice and Court Services Act 2000 (CJCSA 2000), made the following amendments:

- Initial reporting to be within three days, with that reporting in person and to a prescribed police station.
- Police were given new powers to photograph and fingerprint offenders at their first registration.
- Offenders to be required to notify police if they were planning to be abroad for a period of eight days or more.

Whilst the tragic murder of Sarah Payne and the contentious NoW campaign had the effect of galvanising efforts to implement MAPPA (through s67 of the CJCSA 2000), the main thrust of the NoW campaign did not come to fruition. This was a demand that public notification of the whereabouts of sex offenders, as enshrined in Megan's Law in the liberal US, be included in a UK Sarah's Law. Widespread professional (but not public) opposition to this proposal would mean that it would be another eight years before four pilot schemes, following the Review of the Protection of Children from Sex Offenders (Home Office, 2007), allowed parents, guardians and carers to seek information from the police about a person's previous criminal record (see Kemshall and Wood, 2010, for an evaluation). This limited form of disclosure, avoiding the worst excesses of the schemes in America (see Leon, 2011; US Justice Department, 2023, for a legal and theoretical summary), reflects something of a British compromise, and, despite some heated debates, this restraint has been evident in at least some aspects of UK policy. That said, the public protection agenda has spread its tentacles wide, with few left untouched by its progress in what Cohen (1985) identified as being the net-widening control culture.

In a resource starved world, the police service has concluded that some of the mandatory aspects of work with sex offenders needed to be modified (NPCC, 2017). In particular, the time taken for statutory home visits has been on an upward trajectory for two decades. The NPCC estimated that very high-risk offenders would receive a visit monthly, high risk, three monthly, medium risk six monthly and low risk annually. In terms of the sex offender caseload, 2% were said to be very high risk, 18% high risk, 30% medium risk and 50% low risk. Based on our 67,000 SOR caseload, this would equate to over 138,000 home visits, including 16,080 monthly visits to very high-risk offenders and 33,500 annual visits to low risk. These numbers prompted police chiefs to propose ending the statutory fixed visit scheme and replace it with a holistic system based on active risk management. The purpose of the plan would be the development and review of risk management plans rather than a visit and a chat. If low risk offenders were offence-free for three years, they could be moved to *reactive management*, which would not require home visits. Populist measures such as the SOR are rarely costed and little thought is given to the skill set required for the work. It is also highly likely, as specialist police officer time is squeezed, that newly qualified and civilian staff will be used to undertake sex offender risk assessment. Making this is a task that 'anyone can do' will undoubtedly detract from the headline promises about protection made by politicians.

Victims and Public Protection Policy

One important feature of public protection policy development since the 1990s has been the growing importance of victims to the process, although not every case ends with survivors having an influence on policy and legislation. It is undoubtedly the case that if survivors are well educated and can handle public speaking, if the victim was photogenic or could be described as 'wholly innocent' and the media decided that the case was newsworthy, then a vigorous campaign may well bring about change, and sometimes, the sort of change not wanted by politicians or professionals. The idea for a widespread community notification of sex offenders was vigorously opposed by senior police officers, a cause that they won in the face of a powerful media lobby. However, as we say further on in this volume, for the last decade or so, we have seen increasing attacks on the very professionals who deliver public protection. Again, these scenarios usually develop following a further serious offence and an inquiry into organisational failures. Governments are increasingly keen to 'pass the buck', the rationale being that they have made the laws and provided the powers for agencies to act, so any failure must lay at their door, not the government's. This position is fundamentally wrong, and, at various points in this text, we hope to highlight where government policy should be directly linked to the public protection process and how well (or not so well) it operates.

An example of this process occurred following the deaths of three people murdered by Valdo Calocane. We discuss this case in detail below, but for now suffice it to say that the perpetrator was found, following an almost unprecedented five psychiatric reports, to be suffering from schizophrenia and, as a result, was allowed to plead guilty to manslaughter. A concerted campaign by the very eloquent, extremely upset and angry survivors has pushed two agendas. The first of these is for there to be a consideration of a charge of murder in the second degree, something which Calocane could have been charged with. The issue here for the survivors was that they did not feel that a manslaughter verdict actually reflected the awful crimes suffered by their family members. This point was picked up by the review into CPS decision-making in the case (HMCPSI, 2024 and *The Guardian*, 25 March 2024), with recommendations that the government undertake (another) homicide review and create the new second degree murder category. The second feature of the families' complaints had been the degree to which they were consulted by the CPS although the review found that it had acted entirely appropriately. The Government has, however, taken the opportunity to exercise further control over its agencies, with new measures proposed for the Victims and Prisoners Bill – at the time of writing, going through parliament (MoJ, 9 April 2024). As always, the new measures were wrapped in typical public protection language with a press release saying, 'Tough new measures to bolster landmark victims' law.' One of these tough measures would enable victims to address a mental health tribunal before the release of serious offenders and make in effect a victim impact statement. The assumption of this being tough appears to be premised on a view that such statements might actually prevent or slow down a patient's discharge – and perhaps that the professionals cannot be trusted to make the right decision. The measures also proposed that the police and other criminal justice professionals would be placed under greater scrutiny through a new statutory duty to not only inform victims of services but also deliver services in accordance with it. Failure to meet the expectations could result in the issue of a 'certificate of non-compliance'.

The Outcomes of Working With the 'Worry Group'

We mentioned MAPPA earlier as an example of how public protection forces agencies to work together in one common cause. Established by the 2000 Criminal Justice and Court Services Act and strengthened three years later in the Criminal Justice Act, it manages a caseload of nearly 90,000 offenders. Not all of these would be considered high risk (see comments on sex offenders earlier), but the totality of the numbers does create a 'worry group' giving a feeling that the dangerousness problem is very much bigger than it really is. When added to nearly a quarter of a million offenders under probation supervision and approaching 90,000 in custody (very close to capacity), it is unsurprising that the public have a sense of fear and demand protection. Attempts to reduce some of these numbers almost inevitably meet with a negative media reaction, fuelling as it does more punitive calls from the public. Recent attempts by the government to reduce the size of the prison population by the early release of some short-sentence prisoners, known as the *End of Custody Supervised Licence Scheme*, was not met with universal approval. Notable among the objections were from organisations representing domestic abuse victims, as domestic abusers had been included in the possible release list, along with thieves, burglars, violent offenders and shoplifters – with the proviso that their sentence was under four years. Those serving more than four years, including sexual offenders, terrorist, Category A prisoners were to be excluded. Although the government sought to reassure the public with the addition of post-release conditions such as tagging and curfews, this measure echoes other blanket measures where simplistic assumptions about risk are made. In this case, the suggestion is that certain offenders and/or certain sentence lengths makes an automatic suggestion of lower risk. This is of course nonsense, with many short-sentence prisoners being not only unstable, but many also having committed quite serious crimes. A three-and-a-half-year sentence would not be given for a very minor matter.

It is interesting to note that shoplifting is included in the list for early release meaning, so it has to be assumed that it is considered a lower-risk crime. Yet, by 10 April 2024, a Prime Minister's announcement (Home Office, 2024) indicated a retail crime crackdown, with assaulting a retail worker becoming a standalone offence punishable with up to six months in prison, unlimited fines and banning orders. Alongside these measures will be a roll-out of mobile facial recognition facilities in towns, cities and other shopping areas. Serial offenders will be made to wear tags, so that 'the probation service will know where offenders have been and when' (Home Office, 2024). Once again then we see the mixed messaging on crime, on one level a crime is effectively labelled as low risk, on another, new measures are wrapped up in tough language to demonstrate that the government is doing something about the problem – it is taking *action*. Undoubtedly retail crime and assaults are an issue, many readers have probably witnessed incidents, but it leads to a confused public message when the same offenders are targeted for early release and new punishments at the same time.

We regard this simple example as embodying the rather formulaic approach to public protection that we see today. By this, we mean that an often-simple logic, for example, put A with B and C and will be the inevitable result. A particular crime committed, allied to a low risk score, means that danger will not be the outcome. This is undoubtedly not the case. Danger is very much about context, meaning that so-called low-level offenders can commit very serious crimes if the context, or conditions are right. Later in this book, we talk about the case of Wayne Couzens, a serving police officer given a whole life sentence for the murder of a woman he abducted and raped before committing her murder; all the while utilising his police status in the planning and execution of the crime. He had a long history of what is, much too often, regarded as a low-level crime – indecent exposure. His crimes were serious of their type, threatening to women and revealing a misogyny which would later feed into the murder he committed. These crimes were not however taken seriously and were not regarded as a pattern of behaviour which was escalating in seriousness. Crimes against the person will often reflect an attitude to the victim or that type of victim in general. By understanding these attitudes, risk assessment may become more meaningful. However, as long as certain crimes remain regarded as non-serious and generate low risk scores, a deeper examination of the offender's motivation is unlikely to take place.

As we mentioned above, the 'worry group', or public protection caseload is significant in size. It shows little sign of decreasing as, very often, the decision about who is *in* is an automatic one, usually determined by the commission of particular listed crimes. Once inside the group, the next decision is of course, will you be allowed to leave? It is at this point that the somewhat automatic process of inclusion gives way to a process of assessment and review, with a number of different agencies involved. Even here though, there are attempts at creating one view, for example, by the use of shared risk assessment instruments. However, despite concerted efforts to bring agencies into one particular line, it is evident that there remains a difference between them. In our view this is a good thing. Why would you want police officers to be thinking in the same way as probation officers or social workers? Their differing perspectives are the fundamental underpinnings of MAW and all can bring their distinct professional knowledge and experience into considering a person's potential for harm. If we are to work with and understand serious offending behaviour, we need to work with and understand human behaviour. Therefore, the skills utilised by a child protection social worker are also those needed to work with serious offenders in other contexts. The rubbishing of social work skills in the 1990s and since continues to baffle us.

Unfortunately, it appears that professional knowledge is increasingly undervalued if it does not accord with prevailing political views. The decision to release long-term and indefinite sentence prisoners has been a function of the independent Parole Board for several decades. As we discuss in the Parole section below, this power is being reduced and removed in some cases, as a result of decisions reached which were not popular with the media and therefore not with the public or politicians. The arguments around parole decisions mirrors much of that concerning public protection more widely. A range of issues are overlaid, meaning that it is difficult to focus on the actuality of events. For example, in discussions on parole, the issue often debated actually refers to the length or type of the original sentence. This is nothing to do with Parole and everything to do with the sentencing Judge. The Parole Board's job is to consider the release of eligible prisoners who have reached the correct stage of their sentence. This is fixed in legislation and is not at anyone's discretion. If the prisoner has met the criteria for release, and these are strict, then the prisoner would be released with whatever conditions are deemed necessary. If the prisoner then goes on to commit a further serious offence, the Parole Board is blamed, even though they have acted in accordance with their mandate. Not to be distracted from the punitive path, the government has pushed forward moves to alter the constitution of the Board by including those who they believe might be like-minded (police officers), restricting the power of probation officers to make recommendations in their reports or lengthening the period in a sentence before parole eligibility kicks in. Even if those who have responsibilities execute them appropriately, in the often-febrile public protection world, that is not good enough for some politicians. If these bodies will not play ball, then a new game will be invented and they will not be invited to participate.

Play Ball or Disappear

The Probation Service is an organisation which has felt the winds of change more than most criminal justice agencies. Since the ending of the post-war liberal consensus, it has been vulnerable to the impact of more punitive agendas, as attempts at reforming offenders gave way to the more certain world of punishing them. As an agency with a Victorian legacy and an original ethos of 'advise, assist and befriend', it is not difficult to see how it became an easy target for change, notably during the 1990s. The first of these came with the 1991 Criminal Justice Act, which established a sentencing framework based on proportionality and seriousness – a term which is familiar to students of public protection. In essence, if a crime was 'so serious' a custodial sentence must follow. If, however, it was 'serious enough' a community penalty could be passed. This placed the probation service firmly within the framework, responsible for orders referred to as 'punishment in the community, whereas at its inception, being placed on Probation required a suspension' of punishment. Rather than befriending, probation was to be concerned with public protection, enforcement and rehabilitation. For nearly 90 years, Probation adhered to social work values and training. During its formative years Home Office Children's Services offered advice, which was welcomed. Ideal probation officers were seen to be men or women endowed not only with intelligence and zeal but also sympathy, tact and firmness. It is within this tradition that probation ran until not only legislative changes but the abandonment of the social work training process, which was deemed not to be a suitable means of expressing the nature of probation work. The then Home Secretary Jack Straw got in on the anti-social work message, deriding the use of the word 'client' by probation officers, insisting it be replaced by 'offender'. He said, in 2009, 'probation officers now routinely talk of the criminals they are working with as offenders - which is what they are - instead of the euphemistic language of clients...' (Canton and Dominey, 2018, p. 43).

Social work training and a social work ethos had no place in the brave new world of punishment in the community. Alongside a more punitive stance came changes in the nature of inquiries undertaken by probation officers for the courts, with much less attention to be given to personal histories and circumstances and more to analyses of offending behaviour. It is difficult to see how one can be separated from the other, but clearly the nature of 'social' inquiry was regarded as looking for 'excuses' for offending rather than explanation (see Canton and Dominey, 2018 for a discussion of probation reports). For many years, probation officers were ridiculed as being the offenders' friend and apologists for the crime. One of the authors is an ex-probation officer and doesn't recognise that characterisation. In pushing probation officers towards a more punitive role, it is evident that successive governments were downgrading the importance of rehabilitation, even though it remains an aim of sentencing. For us though, the elimination of social work takes us to a curious moment in a number of recent serious further offence inquiries. These investigations and subsequent reports are to identify failures that may have contributed to another serious crime by an offender under supervision. Often clad in organisational failings with calls to strengthen systems, recently there has been an increase in findings where staff are said to lack professional curiosity, improvements to which might help reduce incidents of serious further offences (see HMIP, 2022a, 2022b for a comprehensive guide). The skills needed for this, we will argue below, were many of those included in the original combined social work and probation training course. This is underpinned by the fact that the guide contains numerous references to good child protection and safeguarding work. Probation has therefore been shifted into a punishment, enforcement and control ethos for over 30 years. It has become a risk assessment and management service to the extent that it was cut into two sections by the Transforming Rehabilitation revolution (see below), a process decided upon by dividing its caseload on what we believe to be fallacious risk grounds. Like many other public organisations, it has suffered from austerity and now, despite an upsurge in recruitment, suffers acute shortages in experience. Somehow, the bureaucratic demands of public protection on agencies needs to be reduced, so that staff can gain experience and advice in post.

The Structure of the Book

As we were deep in the research and writing of this book, we soon realised two things. Firstly, we could have written a whole book on each chapter and secondly, we would have to make some tough editorial decisions. It was simply not possible to include everything we wanted, or indeed should have, included in a text on *Politics and Public Protection*. Some of these decisions were very difficult to make. The number one driver for our editorial decisions lay in the fact that we didn't want to simply update and regurgitate what was in our previous texts (Nash, 2006; Nash and Williams, 2008, 2010). Therefore, readers might rightly question the omission of some issues over the inclusion of others. For example, we could have written an entire chapter on risk and risk management but decided against it. Risk is of course, central to public protection so we have threaded it through where it relates to this and politics. There are, of course, other very useful texts that are available if readers wish to grasp a more fundamental knowledge of the public protection processes and issues themselves (e.g. see Annison, 2015; Harrison, 2011; Pycroft & Gough, 2019). In particular, for historical developments in criminal justice, we would highly recommend the seminal series by Paul Rock, David Downes and Tim Newburn –*The Official History of Criminal Justice in England and Wales (Volumes 1 to 4);* for an analysis of legislative and organisational changes to prisons and probation try Roy King and Lucy Willmott's *The Honest Politician's Guide to Prisons and Probation;* and for a 'pracademic' perspective see the edited collection by Maurice Vanstone and Philip Priestley entitled *Probation and Politics*. Other excellent texts include Lol Burke and Steve Collett's *Delivering Rehabilitation* and the edited collection by Kevin Albertson, Mary Corcoran and Jake Phillips, entitled *Marketisation and Privatisation in Criminal Justice*. What we have simply tried to do with our text is include what we believe to be some of the important areas linking politics *and* public protection. This is based on our experience, knowledge and practice. As mentioned above, one of the authors was a senior probation officer before changing to an academic career. Both authors have a combined experience of 50-plus years as academic researchers exploring the vagaries of offender management and public protection practice. At times, we may come across as overly critical but we would like to assure readers (and any practitioners out there) that most of this criticism is validly directed towards the various governments and their policies which have impacted upon the day-to-day practice of public protection. On the whole, public sector practitioners have done a remarkable job despite facing what seems like constant change, dwindling resources and attacks on their professionalism and professional organisations.

Our Politics and Public Protection delves into the multifaceted landscape of safeguarding communities from potential dangers posed by offenders. Divided into four parts, the book traverses various dimensions of public protection processes in England and Wales and the links with politics within these dimensions. Part 1 initiates the exploration by dissecting the notion of 'dangerousness' and the intricate process of identifying potentially hazardous offenders. It scrutinises the challenges confronting public protection processes in these regions. In Part 2, the focus shifts to governmental responses to dangerous offenders and the strategies employed to shield the public, as well as the politics that are the foundations to these responses. Chapters within this section scrutinise the roles of different governmental bodies such as the Police Service, the Prison Service, the Parole Board and legislative frameworks in managing risk and ensuring public safety. Part 3 delves deeper into the complexities by examining two specific offender groups: mentally ill and personality-disordered offenders and terrorism-related offenders. Each group poses unique challenges to public protection agencies, demanding tailored approaches to risk management, yet all are based on specific political framing. Finally, Part 4 grapples with the aftermath of serious further offences and contemplates an alternative paradigm to address perceived shortcomings in the existing system. It critically assesses the viability of civilian-led public protection initiatives and explores the potential of a reformed approach. Throughout the text, *Politics and Public Protection* navigates the intricate intersections of politics, legislation and public safety, offering insights into the evolving landscape of offender management and public protection in England and Wales.

Chapter 1

The Dangerous Offender Population

Describing, let alone defining, the dangerous offender population is a challenging, complex and contentious task. However, before even beginning to consider the size or make up of this population, it is necessary to understand what we mean or understand by a dangerous offender. Why though, is this so important? In many ways, there is a simple answer. It is because there is not an offence of dangerousness; rather than an actual and specified crime, it is a *quality* of the individual committing particular crimes and often the *nature* of those crimes. Unlike other criminal activity, dangerousness is not defined by a specific crime, for example sexual offences, burglary, fraud or robbery. People who commit these crimes have broken particular and fairly specific laws. They therefore become known collectively as a type of offender named after the offence, for example a sex offender or a burglar. When we consider the meaning of dangerous in a criminal context, we find that it is not offence specific, instead it might be defined by the *manner* in which any number of offences have been committed, or felt likely to be committed in the future. It is therefore much more about the individual nature and circumstances of the crime *and* the criminal rather than the commission of a specific offence – although, to be fair, from a very broad baseline, this will trigger the process. In other words, it is possible for someone to be classified as dangerous even if they have committed a non-serious offence. As Peter Scott remarked (1977, p. 129), 'the legal category, even murder, arson and rape, is not very useful in determining dangerousness'. In a similar vein, Floud and Young (1981, p. 25) had said, 'it is impossible to divide people sharply into the dangerous and the safe; dangerousness is a matter of degree and the spectrum is wide'. It is however, most likely that offences such as murder, serious sexual assault, terrorism and arson, would most likely attract the dangerous label.

We might then ask, why can't we sentence these people simply for the crimes they have committed, such as violent crimes or other serious offences? The answer to this question is that a number of professionals working in criminal justice and mental health services believe that some offenders are much worse of their type *and* have shown an indication that they will *repeat* their actions. So, what we have so far in thinking about this dangerous offender population, is that a range of offences have been or might be committed, and they may be at the very serious end of the spectrum but equally, may not. Very importantly, a formal risk assessment would have predicted a repetition of their harmful behaviour. It is therefore a very ill-defined collection of individuals based upon a range of variables which, in most respects, defy accurate classification, measurement or prediction. There is however good reason to try to narrow down our definitions, and this concerns what we, as a society, have developed as a means of dealing with dangerousness. Traditionally, the more serious the crime, the more severe the penalty; a system of proportionality common to many Western jurisdictions. As we explained earlier however, within the dangerous context, sentencing is actually based not only on the legal offence itself, but also quality and nature of the crime and its likely repetition. The offender as an individual becomes very significant in the sentencing process. Sentencers are able to consider the imposition of exceptional sentences, often known as protective or preventive sentences, for these very specific offenders. These sentences depart from the proportionality principle, enabling the court to sentence not just for what offences have been committed, but for what offences *might* be committed in the future. The additional punishments can include longer than 'deserved' terms of custody, additional post-sentence supervision and/or additional restrictions upon release into the community, or indeed, no release at all. In other contexts, these additional punishments, unrelated to a specific criminal act, might well be regarded as a violation of human rights – a debate that has dogged the consideration and assessment of dangerousness for a very long time.

If an offender is designated as dangerous, are they dangerous all the time, in all situations and in any place, is it a one-time label that sticks forever? Are they therefore unconditionally dangerous and as a result, beyond redemption? Herschel Prins has previously estimated (1988) that there were 3–400 *unconditionally dangerous* offenders in the UK. Today, our public protection system, which is designed to assess, manage and contain dangerous offenders and those assessed as high risk, is responsible for thousands of offenders in custody, in the community or within the mental health system. What is the difference between a group of a few hundred and one of many thousands, who make up what we term as the 'worry group'? In this chapter, we will be exploring a range of definitions, many dating from 30 or 40 years ago, which nearly all use a similar group of terms, whilst exploring the interplay between them. The fact that these terms have changed little over time, perhaps suggests the enduring difficulty of agreeing upon a definition. One of these terms though has perhaps come to prominence above the others, and that is risk. We will be referring to risk as both a tool for assessment and for management throughout this book, and we will be particularly concerned with exploring what, if any, is the relationship between risk and danger.

Before we move on, perhaps a small example might serve to demonstrate how the arguments may unfold in this chapter. Think of the scenario at a pedestrian crossing. The pedestrian arrives and presses the button. As we all know, they should then await the green man before crossing. The other side of this road safety bargain is the motorist. The driver, on seeing a flashing light should slow and at the red light, stop. If all this happens, there should be a safe crossing. But what if elements change or rules are not followed? What if the pedestrian steps straight onto the crossing, because the green man is visible. They might believe it is safe to do so because those are the rules, and they are in the right; children in particular might have this mindset. However, many people would check first and remember the voices of parents and school safety staff urging caution and looking for certainty. The pedestrian is therefore attempting to mitigate any risk posed by the driver not stopping, even if they should have done so. The driver of course has agency. They may be distracted and not see the light and fail to stop. They may stop too late and hit a car pushing it onto the crossing. The driver may be intoxicated or drugged and therefore compromised or, much worse, the driver may have malicious intent. Therefore, the situation is that the pedestrian, as the person at risk, can mitigate potential dangers by following the rules and exercising additional caution. They also, to a certain extent need to have trust in the driver. At the same time, however, the driver may either wittingly or unwittingly convert a risk managed situation into a dangerous one. The issue is will they or won't they, and how do you know? Grappling with this uncertainty, the efforts made to make situations more predictable and the impact this has on offender and victim rights, is at the heart of this chapter.

Dangerous People

In a 21st century world, 'knowing' dangerous people doesn't seem to be too difficult. For maybe the majority of populations across the globe, it is those individuals who would cause severe harm or death to others. Many people could name notorious criminal cases where this type of outcome has resulted, and the depraved 'beasts' and 'animals' who perpetrate these crimes come to personify the dangerous individual. It is also the case that many of these individuals have offended previously, giving rise to the belief that their crimes should have been *anticipated* and *prevented*. Indeed, repetition and a sense of failure around the idea of prevention, almost makes serious cases much worse in the minds of the public. Failure and blame therefore often accompany descriptions of dangerousness, and it is perhaps this which has led to the dominance of risk assessment and risk management as a means of dealing with the issue. This reflects a view that dangerousness can be 'managed'. For the public, this might offer some comfort and for professionals, offers a way of thinking about and handling the assessment and supervision of those who would harm others. The importance of the risk industry is that if offers the potential to bring some certainty out of the unknown, and as the former US Secretary of Defense, Donald Rumsfeld suggested following the 9/11 attacks on New York, unknown unknowns constitute dangers *par excellence* (Defense.gov transcript: DOD news briefing – Secretary Rumsfeld and Gen. Myers, n.d.).

Were Dangers Always the Same?

Our current and widely held view of what constitutes a dangerous offender was not always the case. As John Pratt (1997) summarises so well, in the 19th century, in jurisdictions as far apart as Australia, America, England and Canada, dangerousness was applied to a *group* of people, namely those who threatened *property and the rule of law.* Indeed, these people were seen as beyond the reach of the law and who took the increasingly severe punishments being handed down as an occupational risk. They were not deterred. Those whom we would now very quickly place into the dangerous category, in particular sexual and violent offenders, were not considered even in the same league as property offenders in the 19th century. Crimes against the person were regarded as being committed in 'hot blood' (Pratt, 1997, p. 26) or as an aberration or a crime of passion or provocation. As such, they were considered to be impossible to predict (this in contrast to a modern risk assessed approach, which is meant to offer at least a passing resemblance to prediction). Contemporary thinking suggested that, on the whole, these crimes were one-off and unlikely to pose a risk to wider society – a reflection of the late modern thinking concerning domestic abuse and violence. Indeed, risk of violent and sexual crime was felt to be minimal for the majority of the population. Pratt (1977, p. 17) cites Anderson (1907, p. 2), in showing how risk was limited by the type of offence, perhaps demonstrating that attitudes have not changed much over time, '[...]a man who murders his wife is not necessarily a terror to the wives of other men. A man who kills his personal enemy excites no panic in the breasts of strangers'. When the notorious killer Jack the Ripper was on the loose, his victims were described as coming from a 'small and definite class' of women and in a 'limited district' of London. As a result, the wider population of London were felt to be 'secure' (Anderson, 1907). These examples encourage us to think beyond the presenting information and narrow attitudes. Partner killing is a classic example of limited thinking, when the death of the victim is considered to bring an end to the violence. As Scott (1977) indicates, if pathological jealousy is a factor in the first murder, then there is a strong possibility of further destructive behaviour. The understanding of motive and context is crucial in any consideration of dangerousness in offenders.

What we now call acquisitive crime was, in the 19th century, regarded as *the* threat to wider society. It was, in essence, regarded as a danger to the social fabric; it was an attack on wealth and the aspirations of those who sought to better themselves through hard work (men of course, as the sex which could hold property). These crimes generated the greatest public alarm, the most significant police response and some of the most severe punishments. People committing these crimes were regarded as beasts preying on society, much as in the same terms now used to describe sex offenders. Yet by 2022, an official report (HMICFRS, 2022b, p. 6) concluded:

> The response to SAC (serious acquisitive crime) from policing isn't consistently good enough. Too many offenders remain at liberty and most victims aren't getting the justice they deserve. Forces are missing opportunities to identify and catch offenders, from the moment a member of the public reports the crime to the point where a case is finalised.

The suggestion was that these crimes were not a priority for police services. As a result, crimes were often attended by untrained or under-trained officers – if officers attended at all (the Daily Mail, 7 April 2022, for example reporting that the police failed to attend up to 120 burglaries a day in 2022). With evidence gathering said to be poor and unsystematic, the newspaper (Daily Mail, 20 June 2022) reported that in half of the country's neighbourhoods, not a single burglary had been solved in three years. This apparent division in seriousness between acquisitive crime and crimes of violence, for example, is belied, in our opinion, by the description of the impact that acquisitive crime has on the victims, '[...]being a victim of SAC can have a long-lasting effect on how safe people feel in their homes and communities. The impact can be far reaching, deeply affecting neighbourhoods and everyone who lives in them' (HMICFRS, 2022b, p. 6). Despite this, the police clearly prioritise resources to what we might call the 'modern' understanding of dangerousness – although there may be a far more nuanced response to some 'dangerous' crimes, notably perhaps, serious domestic violence and sexual offending.

So, What Is Dangerousness?

Working towards a definition, it is evident that perceptions of what constitutes dangerousness and dangerous behaviour vary by time and place. The term is constantly interchanged with seriousness and risk as if they all mean the same. More accurately though, these different terms might reflect efforts to get at a *clearer* understanding of that most 'elusive' term (de Vries and Bijlsma, 2022) – 'dangerousness'. Because being labelled as a dangerous offender can carry such huge legal and punitive consequences, there have been numerous attempts over many years to arrive at a definition which seeks to secure the rights of the offender against exceptional punishment *and* the rights of potential victims to be protected. This inevitably means attempting to 'quantify' danger in an effort to make it more predictable, something by which the state, in the form of courts, can feel justified in dealing with the offender in exceptional and usually preventive ways. This careful, rights-based approach may however come under threat as a result of political expediency or popular unrest. Indeed, to many members of the public, the answer to the question 'who is dangerous?' is an easy one. It is those people who commit the most serious or heinous crimes against the person, usually sexual and violent in nature, with terrorism offences coming increasingly to the fore. In this popular understanding, there appears less concern with identification and rights and more with punishment and prevention. We shall now move on to consider the relationship between risk, danger and seriousness in an attempt to gain a closer understanding of the offender population that the public wish to be protected from, and to see if this is the same group that the government acts against, to offer that protection.

We have already noted that, in the not too distant past, property crime was considered to be far more harmful (dangerous) than physical crimes against the person. However, since the turn of the 20th century, attention has instead focused on crimes which harm individuals rather than groups of people. These crimes threaten lives and can have significant and lasting physical and psychological impact on victims. The fear engendered by these crimes often belies the actual chance of victimisation. Rather than accepting that many of these violent crimes are unique in circumstance and often very personal in terms of victim–offender relationship, the fear is more pervasive. Indeed, it is rare for a headline such as, *'Man arrested on suspicion of murder after woman, 31, stabbed to death by stranger'*, to feed public concern, (Sky News, May 2, 2023). Such a crime is a rarity. The public sense appears, however, to be that the risk of violent assault is everywhere and anyone could be a victim. This matches the 19th century pervasive fear of property offenders; an unknown group who could strike anywhere, almost with impunity. As we have seen, the response to this fear was to impose stronger and more punitive sentences. In the 21st century, this is the position for serious violent and sexual offenders, with those sentences becoming ever more punitive with each new, high-profile case. Fear is then a key player in the demand for a tough response to offenders, a general fear among the public usually unsupported by the facts of potential victimisation. It is with this background in mind that we will explore some of the academic discussions which, over a number of years, have attempted to settle on a definition of dangerousness or what constitutes a dangerous offender.

Can We Define Dangerousness?

Attempting to define dangerousness is an enterprise that crosses a number of boundaries, disciplines and professions although it is not uncommon for the debate to be reduced to the offender being either 'mad or bad' (see the discussion of the Michael Stone and Valdo Calocane cases below to see how this distinction plays out in public and what the answer to that question means for offender and victims). As we noted above, the attempt is important because of the powers that the state can deploy against convicted serious offenders who are also assessed as dangerous. Yet, over many years, there has been limited agreement on a definition of dangerousness. There are a number of elements that appear in these definitions, mostly of a similar nature, but with variations in terminology and changes in emphasis. We will explore a range of definitions which were developed in the late 20th century, mostly, but not wholly, in response to the new protective and preventive sentences being introduced in a number of western jurisdictions. De Vries and Bijlsma (2022, p. 142) in an excellent summary of the literature put the dangerousness debate into context:

> Preventing future crime has become an increasingly dominant function of the criminal law of many liberal democracies. This "preventive turn" has led to a profound debate on the legal and ethical boundaries of the "preventive state." However, the concept at the core of preventive justice – the dangerousness of the offender – has attracted relatively little attention in the current debate.

Before considering a number of definitions, it is useful to consider the five aspects of dangerousness proposed by De Vries and Bijlsma (2022, p. 144) as a framework for the debate. These aspects are (1) the nature of the harm, (2) the probability of the harm, (3) the extent to which dangerousness entails a fact and/or a value judgement, (4) whether dangerousness is a personal characteristic or is based on abstract risk factors, and (5) the temporality of dangerousness. These five points demonstrate why agreement is so difficult to reach in this area. For example, what do we mean by *nature of harm*? Does it concern the amount of violence used in the offence? Was the amount of violence used excessive for the purpose needed? For example, are multiple stab wounds a sign of dangerousness or desperation to complete the act as quickly as possible (Prins, 1988)? Was the victim especially vulnerable? Will the offence have a lasting and significant impact on the victim's life? *Probability* is of course a key aspect of dangerousness. Will the criminal act actually occur in the future? How certain is this and what level of probability is acceptable – 5%, 50% or 100%? (the answer to this aspect may well depend on the political context of the day). When might it happen and how far ahead are we prepared to punish people for events that have not happened? This very much takes us into the murky world of predictions. Whether or not dangerousness is a matter of *fact or judgement* is a significant question in the world of offender rights. The answer to this question very much influences how 'predictions' are made and on what basis. We shall discuss below changes to the parole assessment process in England and Wales which appear to favour the view that dangerousness is indeed a matter of fact, or perhaps worse, a *matter of political fact*. These efforts might be interpreted as a determined effort to rule out or reduce the importance of professional judgement. The notion that dangerousness might be a *personal characteristic* is something that could appeal to many. With this view, the suggestion is that there are 'dangerous people' who pose a threat at any time and in any situation. Such a notion fuels demands for punitive, exclusionary and almost quarantine-like measures. Unconditionally dangerous is a concept which, in essence, scares the population. If, however, it is something arising from a number of risk factors in a given situation or context, it might suggest that the scenario could be manipulated to lessen the potential danger. Finally, *temporality*; under this heading we need to consider if dangerousness is a permanent condition or is it time limited? Again, the answer to this question is intimately linked with the answer to the previous four points.

We would argue that there are clear political efforts to 'harden up' on a definition of dangerousness; an attempt to 'put it in a box' and thus pre-empt the type of disagreements which might prevent the easier imposition of protective sentences, particularly concerning human rights. As far back as 1977 however, Scott argued that, 'Dangerousness is a dangerous concept...it is difficult to define, yet very important decisions are based on it; there is as yet little reliable research in relation to it; it is a term which raises anxiety and which is therefore particularly open to abuse' (Scott, 1977, p. 127). In an attempt to settle a definition and in the context of 'mental abnormality', the British government established a committee in 1975 (the Butler Committee) to consider the handing of offenders with a mental disorder who, having been released from a determinate sentence, were still considered to be dangerous. In considering the idea of a 'reviewable prison sentence', the committee felt obliged to come up with a definition of a dangerous offender. Their answer was an offender who has the propensity to cause lasting physical or psychological harm. They believed that the behaviour of concern was violence because this is what concerns the public. Of course, with what we have already said in this chapter, this definition contains issues over the word 'propensity' and of course, what types and severity of harms would be included – and most importantly of all, it concerned behaviour that was *yet to happen*.

Set up at the same time as the Butler Committee, the Scottish Council on Crime also reported in 1975. Established to consider the problem of increasing violent crime in Scotland, and importantly also considering offenders *not* suffering from a mental disorder, the council proposed a public protection order, a sentence which could detain an offender until assessed as safe for release. As we shall see below, this proposal reflects much of the public protection legislation enacted since the 1970s. The subject of these orders was intended to be a *violence-prone* offender, that is one with a past history of violence. Probability also featured in the Scottish definition, this time *the probability of inflicting serious and irremediable personal injury in the future*. Without certainty over probability, a public protection order should not be made. The question was of course, how could that certainty be brought into the equation and again, in labouring the point, *how* certain does certain have to be? The Advisory Council on the Penal System (1978) proposed the introduction of an 'exceptional sentence' for dangerous offenders. This sentence was to be reviewable, similar to that intended by the Butler committee. Unlike them though, it was intended for offenders with or without a mental disorder. The inclusion criteria were that the offender has caused serious harm in the past *and* is assessed as likely to do so in the future. The council though only spoke about *likely* and not imminent or very likely. The envisaged harms were considered to be serious physical injury, serious psychological harm, exceptional personal hardship or damage to the security of the state or fabric of society. Once again though, we can see terms such as 'likely', 'imminent' and 'very likely' being very difficult to pin down with any degree of *certainty*. Floud and Young (1981) made a determined attempt to differentiate and separate risk and danger, two words which we have already seen as being used interchangeably by a great many people. Dangers were regarded by Floud and Young as 'unacceptable risks' – as such, risks might be managed or not and people may or may not choose to take them. Dangers however, in the committee's view, were to be avoided. In determining dangerousness, a 'predictive judgement' was to be made, and this meant that a purely actuarial assessment was not sufficient. The judgement was to include an assessment of character and recidivism. Dangerous people were disposed to do wilful harm to others, even in the face of social and legal constraints. A key factor in terms of fear is how people perceive the predicted harm or behaviour. Clearly, people have different perceptions but vulnerable individuals may feel greater fear than others, as stated by Floud and Young (1981, p. 6), 'fear converts risk into danger'. In their view, fear is a function of personal vulnerability, which varies inversely with the time and distance from the predicted harmful event.

As we can see from this range of learned debates, commentators use a number of factors in their definitions of dangerousness, which invariably include risk (or recidivism), seriousness, temporality, likelihood or imminence and degrees of harm. A key aspect of much of the above is that of repetition. In other words, the offender already has some history of seriously harmful offending behaviour and the major concern for the authorities assessing them is, 'will they do it again and when'? As we will discuss further below, there are attempts to reduce predictive efforts to manageable equations, which offer a short cut for practitioners. A notable thinker in this field, Nigel Walker, cites one example, *danger = probability x seriousness of the offence* and dismisses it as a misleading cliché, suggesting that offence severity can be distorted by high probability scores (1997, p. 618). Indeed, he suggests that if clinicians offer a probability based on percentages, they should be distrusted. Walker is one of those who suggests that detail (or painstaking detail as Prins (1988) suggests), is essential for the most informed of predictions. Walker suggests four statements concerning the defendant which can be tested out in an assessment of dangerousness.

(1) That his offence shows he is *capable* of a specified kind of serious harm, but that nothing he has said or done at other times suggest he is likely to repeat it.
(2) That he is capable of it, and that what he has done at other times, or said, suggests that *given a similar situation*, he is likely to do the same.
(3) That if (2) seems to be the case and that *he seems to find himself in similar situations* more than could be expected as a result of mere bad luck.
(4) That if his modus operandi, or what he says, indicates that he *seeks out or makes opportunities* for certain kinds of offence.

Walker suggests that when (3) and (4) are true – when the offender has shown something more than mere capacity, a tendency or bent – that the case for precautionary sentencing is compelling (Walker, 1997, p. 619). Of course, abstract debate can help in furthering discussion and attempts to arrive at a workable definition. However, it is interesting to note some of the real-world examples where offenders have been declared dangerous by Judges. The following accounts come from newspaper reports, so do not include full details of the offenders' backgrounds which, as we have seen, is a crucial element of the assessment process. What the following reports have in common though is a focus on the severity and callousness of the violent act, and it is interesting to see how cases such as these shape and construct public notions of dangerousness.

Three accounts from the Manchester Evening News, (Bardsley, 2023), refer to the *nature* of violence in determining a dangerousness judgement. In the first, a woman's former lover let himself into her home where she was in bed with a Tinder date. The perpetrator started punching the victim but left when his ex-lover asked him to stop. However, he simply left and returned with a large kitchen knife and slashed the victim's face, causing a very serious wound. The offender had previously been in court for attacking his girlfriend, with whom he had a relationship lasting eight years. The Judge summed up by saying, 'there is nothing in your past that can possibly begin to explain how you have turned out in terms of your violent and controlling behaviour'. He was declared dangerous and sentenced to 13 years in custody and 5 years on licence. Aside from the brutal nature of the attack, this offence has a feature of a violation of a safe space, a feature of the following reports. The second case involved a 38-year-old woman who got into a fight with her friend, with whom she shared a crack cocaine habit. The fight ended and the victim returned to her home. However, the perpetrator was raging, because she believed her friend had stolen her credit card. She followed the victim to her home where the fight resumed and she bit off a large piece of the victim's nose. A few weeks later the perpetrator attacked another woman with a glass mirror, causing permanent disfigurement. The Judge described this as an act of 'appalling, vicious, deliberate and calculated violence'. The offender was declared dangerous and received six years in custody and four years on licence. In another report, a man received 11 years for rape plus 6 years on licence, having been declared a dangerous offender. In this case, a 35-year-old homeless man had knocked at the victim's door asking for a coffee and a cigarette as he had been outside all night. The victim let him in whereupon he attacked and raped her on her own bed. She repeatedly asked him to stop but he refused. The police described the attack as 'incredibly harrowing, violent and on a vulnerable woman in her own home'.

The final case we will mention at this point was where the offender was described by police as 'dangerous' but was *not* declared to be so in court. The incident concerned a sexual assault in the women's toilets at Birmingham New Street station. A woman entered the toilets and found a man wearing a high visibility jacket. Although thinking it was odd, she assumed that the person worked at the station. The offender made a beeline for her whilst she washed her hands, knelt down as if to pick up something and sexually assaulted her. Having assaulted her he calmly walked away from the toilets. The victim saw him sit on a bench, quickly took off the jacket and donned a beanie hat. He later claimed in court that he was in the toilets because he now identified as female. The police said '[...]he is a dangerous individual (who) deliberately changed his clothing this morning in order to loiter in the female toilets undetected[...]a vile, premeditated assault[...]in a space she had every right to feel safe in'. His sentence was 16 months in prison to sign the sex offender register (SOR) for 10 years and a ten-year sexual harm prevention order, preventing him loitering near women's toilets or wearing a high visibility jacket. He was not declared dangerous in court and was not given a protective sentence. It is perhaps the lack of fit between popular ideas of dangerousness and the more specifically defined definitions used in court, which can lead to the public believing that dangerous offenders are far more numerous than they actually are; or indeed wonder why this person was *not* considered to be legally dangerous. It may be that the actual offence committed was not considered as serious as the others. However, the planning and motive may be very worrying, again showing how offence categories may not be the best starting point for dangerousness considerations. The public's impression may then be an accurate reflection of how dangerousness is portrayed by the media rather than by the law.

There are a number of features which link these attacks. A key aspect of each case is the violation of what might be termed 'safe spaces', such as the individual's own home or indeed the ladies' toilets. In each of these spaces, the offender either let themselves in, engineered an invitation to enter, followed the person to their home or was in a place they should not have been. On each occasion, the offender persisted with the attack despite opportunities to leave and pleas to stop – there was a determination to complete the assault. There were also high levels of serious violence and intimidation in the attacks. We will be exploring the legal definitions of dangerous and key aspects of legislation below; however at this point, we find the criteria used by Canadian Courts (R.S.C. Criminal Code, 1985) to be very helpful in bringing into focus some of the points raised so far. Sections 752/3 state that the offender must be

- Convicted of a serious personal injury offence and constitute an ongoing threat on the basis of 'repetitive behaviour', showing a failure of restraint and 'likelihood' of causing injury or worse.
- (Commit) serious personal injury and show a failure to control his or her sexual impulses and a likelihood of causing injury.
- (Have a) pattern of persistent aggressive behaviour that shows a substantial degree of indifference to the reasonably foreseeable consequences.
- The 'brutal nature' of the offence – not likely to be inhibited by normal standards.

These criteria reflect much of that identified earlier in academic and legal texts. Severity of the behaviour, impact on the victim, violation, brutality and a lack of restraint all feature and are terms which the public may understand. However, one of the more contentious topics, temporality, is mentioned only once, using the term 'likelihood'. As we know, deciding if and when a future violent act is to occur is fraught with difficulty and potential legal challenge. It is our contention that, at times, political expediency overrides legal caution and the bar is lowered.

Dangerous Offenders – Problems With Counting and Classifying

The size of the prison population offers us an understanding of the extent of serious sexual and violent offending although by no means all such offenders receive a sentence for public protection. For example, in the year ending September 2021, there were 11,873 sexual offenders in the custodial population (18% of the total) and approximately 25,000 violence against the person offenders (30% of the total population). Not all of these groups however were serving purely public protection sentences. There were for example, 6,272 serving Extended Determinate Sentences – a longer custodial period plus a lengthy period on licence. There were 9,254 indeterminate sentences, which included Life Sentences and Indeterminate Sentences for Public Protection (IPP, abolished in 2012). There were 6,971 unreleased lifers and also 1,661 unreleased IPP prisoners who were more than eight years beyond their tariff. A life sentence is of course mandatory in cases of murder and discretionary for a range of other serious offences, but in itself is not perhaps a reliable indicator of dangerousness, being in many cases absolutely fixed by the crime rather than the offender. There is of course the ability for the Judge, in determining the minimum tariff to be served, to give a strong indication of some of the more 'personal' aspects of the case. Crime seriousness also reflects tariff length but so too does *political will*, as governments can legislate for mandatory minimum tariffs, or indeed whole life sentences.

The imposition of a 'whole life' tariff may offer a better indicator of perception of dangerousness, but equally may reflect a Judge's view of 'exceptional seriousness'. The whole life tariff was introduced by Conservative Home Secretary Leon Brittain in 1983, but the power was reserved for the home secretary, until the 2003 Criminal Justice Act, when it became available to Judges. The first was imposed by Douglas Hurd in 1988. There have been approximately 100 such sentences imposed since then, some following appeals against earlier tariffs. The Sentencing Code (Sentencing Council, 2020a, 2020b) suggests that the level of seriousness must be 'exceptionally high' and eligibility criteria include the following:

- The murder of two or more persons, substantial premeditation, abduction and sexual and/or sadistic motivation.
- Murder of a child, abduction, sexual and/or sadistic motivation.
- Murder of a police or prison officer in the course of their duty (since April 13, 2011).
- Murder for advancing political, religious, racial or ideological cause.

If the preceding criteria are not met, a whole life order may still be given if seriousness is exceptionally high. For example, in 2021 serving police officer Wayne Couzens was given a whole life order for the murder of Sarah Everard, with the Judge justifying this by saying, 'The misuse of a police officer's role such as occurred in this case in order to kidnap, rape and murder a lone victim is of equal seriousness as a murder for the purpose of advancing a political, religious or ideological cause' he told the Old Bailey. 'All of these situations attack different aspects of the fundamental underpinnings of our democratic way of life'.

Similar sentiments were expressed by the sentencing Judge following the murder of Jo Cox MP in 2016 (see BBC News, November 14, 2016). This case was significant in terms of whole life sentencing as the perpetrator, Thomas Mair, was aged 53 and had no previous convictions, therefore little evidence on which to make a prediction based on repetition. Again, the Judge's comments offer us a good insight into the determination and justification for a whole life sentence. Mair's actions were matched to the fourth bullet point above, in that they were described '[…]as being done for the purpose of advancing a political, racial and ideological cause, namely that of 'violent white supremacism and exclusive nationalism'. Determination was highlighted as a feature of the attack when the Judge remarked, 'when it appeared, after your first assault, that Jo Cox might survive, you returned to inflict further fatal blows upon her'. He concluded 'that this offence[...]is of such a high level of exceptional seriousness, that it can only be marked by a whole life sentence[...]because of her position as an MP, her death was both a personal tragedy and a crime with great public significance' (R v Thomas Mair). This sentence, as with other whole life orders, appears to be imposed more for punishment and retribution than any sense of imminent risk of repetition, sending out a message that the most heinous crimes will receive the most severe penalty available. It is from this high bar that other serious sexual and violent crimes descend and with each step down, deciding who is or who is not 'dangerous' appears to be more difficult.

It is probably clear by this stage that 'getting at' or narrowing down who constitutes the dangerous offender population is no easy task. We have seen that there are key terms which feature in a number of definitions although by no means do all definitions include all terms and the emphasis placed on each of them can vary considerably in terms of significance. Seriousness is a common facet of almost all definitions, but is not one which is universally understood in the same terms. In the infamous IPP sentences, the commission of *serious* crimes was not a necessary precursor for the imposition of an indefinite sentence. Many jurisdictions have relied upon offence classifications as the basic sorting mechanism, but the problem here is that these offence lists are very inclusive. It seems almost as if legislators are afraid of leaving something out, so tend to be 'all-inclusive'. For example, the 2003 Criminal Justice Act divided offences into specified sexual and violent offences, serious offences and relevant offences. In total, 88 sexual offences and 65 violent offences were included as possible sentences for dangerousness. As we have suggested, these very large groups feed into a 'pool of worry' for both professionals and the public, and all offenders convicted of any from these very long lists of offences can be considered potentially dangerous. This is a very simple A leads to B mentality which can both blur real danger and inflate and escalate people into a category that may not be appropriate for them. Of course, it is widely acknowledged that not everyone who commits one type of offence will automatically go on to commit another of a more serious nature. Seriousness therefore, should be more about the nature of the offence, the degree of impact and harm it has for victims, rather than just another offence committed from a list. This takes us into the 'nature' of the harm that may be suffered and, importantly, what the victim *thinks* might befall them. Fear thus becomes a key component and, as mentioned above, it could be argued that fear turns risks into dangers. Fear may therefore lead to an inflated concern with what *could* happen, but equally might not. Fear is linked with a sense of threat which may be felt by individuals or large sections of the population. Threats may be made directly to an individual or it may be *inferred* from the offender's previous *behaviour* (we would stress here that we think previous behaviour is probably a better indicator of future harm than simple offence classifications). Recognising, knowing and understanding that behaviour, may take skills and knowledge which appear to be increasingly tangential to criminal justice (see probation service and parole board discussions below).

Another key term for us to consider is *imminence* – quite simply when will the anticipated harm occur? Again, we would suggest that determining when an act might occur requires a good understanding of the offender's personality and in particular, what are their offence triggers? Let us consider an example of a sexual offence often taken to be of low seriousness. Indecent exposure has a history of receiving scant attention, with cases not treated seriously by the police and rarely ending up in court. Yet important issues may lie behind the somewhat jokey face of this sexual offence. For example, and this is usually a male offence, was the penis erect? Who was the offence targeted at? Was it children? What sex and age were they? Was threatening behaviour attached to the indecent exposure? Where did the offence take place and was there evidence of planning? Is it possible to understand the offender's motivation in committing the crime and is that motivation likely to lead to repetition, or worse, escalation? Simple offence classifications are, in our view, inadequate to establish dangerousness and may in fact be more exclusionary than inclusionary. There is always likely to be a concern, in law, not to over-include offenders into the dangerous category, but, in going the other way, highly risky individuals might be missed. We touch on the Wayne Couzens' case in more detail below as an example of how criminal behaviour can be disregarded, underplayed or colluded with by police colleagues. However, these offences contributed to an escalating pattern of criminal behaviour that was missed, with tragic consequences.

Dangerousness Is a Risky Business

So far, in this short review, we have only briefly mentioned perhaps the most commonly used term in public protection and that is risk. We shall be commenting on the problematic nature of risk throughout but at this point would like to begin the discussion with considering *why* the concept has become so influential. Risk has been constructed as a quantifiable commodity, in large part as both a reaction to and rejection of, the negative perception of looser clinical judgements – and perhaps as an indicator of the ebb and flow of the fortunes of psychiatrists and psychologists (see mental health chapter). Quantification means that scales and tables are constructed so that risk can be high or low and indeed, all points in between. It can therefore be *measured* and resulting from that, appropriate measures and resources can be deployed to mitigate concerns. In more dramatic terms, it brings tomorrow into today. We would argue that this system is too rigid and reduces opportunities to get closer to an offender's thinking and intentions; are those intentions malevolent and is the offender determined on a course of destructive behaviour? What we think is important to stress is the context in which any trigger events might occur; the what, the why and the when? What are the relationships which come together, in a given place and time, which might both foster and spark dangerous behaviour?

There have been recent developments within the academic literature which might help us to reconsider the dominance of the risk agenda and make clearer perhaps the main object of concern; dangerousness. In 2011, Bonholm and Corvellec, wrote about the 'relational theory of risk', stressing the importance of understanding the relationships between the various elements of risk considerations. They used the word 'simultaneity' to describe how risk arises from the relationship between a 'risk object' (say a potential perpetrator) and an 'object at risk' (say a potential victim). Bonholm and Corvellec (2011, p. 176) claim that if this 'risk relationship' is linked in a causal and contingent way, then the risk is considered in some way and under certain circumstances to threaten the valued object at risk (a victim). An important point here is that of vulnerability which, if present, can lead to a state of being 'at risk' from a given threat. To mitigate this risk, the object at risk, or victim, needs to have knowledge, choices and agency. A risk can be modified or mitigated if it can be controlled or avoided. If it cannot, Christofferson (2018) states that the relationship of risk becomes one of danger. In other words, risk coming from an external source which cannot be mitigated becomes a danger. In the alternative, it is argued that a possible harm may only be reduced to a risk if the potentially injured party has a significant degree of knowledge and agency. The absence of these leads to a relationship of danger. We might draw from this that, in many criminal cases, the potential victim is often unaware of the potential risks they face, and as such, they actually face a danger. Is it therefore unhelpful to assess potential harms within a risk framework unless the relationship with danger is at the forefront of thinking? Thus, a risk becomes a danger under certain conditions, notably when the potential victim is unable to help mitigate the threat they face (if indeed they know of the threat). So, is it right to assess risk when knowledge is really needed of potential danger – or a clearer understanding of what the risk is actually of? What might a potential offender do, why and when? Finding out this information would take assessors into the more immediate and dynamic nature of threat rather than static risk. Beck (2009) believed that the 'new' terrorism which emerged following the 9/11 attacks in New York, annulled the rational principles of risk calculation, because purpose replaced chance, and maliciousness replaced good. Risk might be related to positively oriented human decisions (albeit with occasional dysfunctional outcomes), whereas threats may also be marked by agency but with negative intentionality – intentional harms. A threat is an intention to harm but requires the presence of a hostile actor. There may be a reluctance to publicly speak of threats as they tend to lead to public fears, a situation that governments are keen to avoid. However, it may be very important for criminal justice professionals to understand the nature of the threats posed by the offenders they assess. A strict focus on risk assessment may well determine that an offender is a low or medium risk of harm and can be managed at that level. But to what extent is agency and intentionality regularly assessed? Has the offender's motivation for certain types of offending behaviour been fully explored? Has what is in the offender's life *now* been considered alongside what was in their life previously – the realm of protective factors which form part of probation officer practice?

There is no easy way of defining what the dangerous offender population actually consists of or indeed what size it is. In general terms, those included would have been convicted of very serious offences, particularly of a sexual or violent nature and increasingly for terrorist crimes. As we have suggested, although crime classification can act as a filter, it might lead to a considerable inflation of the numbers included as a 'population of concern'. This in turn can lead to an increase in public worries, beginning the cycle of action and reaction by governments. Of course, a considerable downside is that the numbers requiring assessment are huge which, in turn, leads to a search for quick methods. Actuarial methods, based on fixed data, require much less in the way of active, current investigation and therefore take much less time. 'Shortened' versions of risk assessment tools further reduce the opportunities to get at some of the motivational dynamics we have tried to stress in this chapter. The question is less that of who is and who is not included in the dangerous offender population, but more a case of who *actually* poses an imminent danger to others from all those that are included. In other words, how does one sort the wheat from the chaff? As we shall see in the chapter considering a number of serious case reviews, a common feature of several is that of a seemingly incorrect risk classification (and hence an inappropriate risk management plan). Such a scenario implies a lower level of surveillance or control leading to fewer opportunities to spot warning signs of imminent threat and therefore danger. By getting the level of risk wrong, the relational theory of risk is impacted. If the risk object is regarded as less of a threat, then it is likely that fewer mitigation efforts will be taken on behalf of and by the potential victim. The outcome of this, as we have seen, is that the relationship becomes one of danger. As efforts to assess risk are simplified, not least due to time pressures on professionals, there is a chance that both support and control systems are automatically shut off by an incorrect assessment. More importantly perhaps, a lower risk classification may have the unintended consequence of producing a less inquisitive mindset among criminal justice professionals and, as we shall see below, a lack of 'professional curiosity', is becoming an increasingly common finding in inquiries into tragic events.

Summary

It is extremely difficult to pin down hard and fast numbers when it comes to dangerous offenders. Perhaps one thing that can be said is that the numbers rarely go down as the systems and measures put in place to combat and manage the risks posed by this group have a habit of being inclusive rather than exclusive. In other words, governments have found it easier to include more offenders committing a wider range of offences rather than clearly focus on the nature of individual risk of harm posed. It is an attempt at a safety-first approach, one where chances of harm are said to be minimised or at best assessed and managed. At the same time, there are occasions when elaborate systems of public protection fail to '*include*' potentially dangerous offenders *or* inappropriately releases them from the system or declassifies their high risk. These events undoubtedly contribute to a cycle of

The Dangerous Offender Population 31

fear, anxiety, caution and punishment which is the hallmark of public protection in so many jurisdictions of the world. An example of this is the case of Wayne Couzens, a truly modern folk-devil whose crimes and history reflect a number of the issues discussed so far.

Couzens, an off-duty police officer, was responsible for the abduction, rape and murder of Sarah Everard, a 33-year-old woman walking home during the mid-evening in March 2021. The case caused nationwide concern and anguish and thus matches those cases which influence policy and practice almost immediately, such is the publicity and public reaction. For our purposes, the case has similar features to many of the issues described in this chapter, notably the importance of previous behaviour (this man had no previous convictions) and how seriousness was calculated. The Anglioni Inquiry Report (HMSO, 2024) covers Couzens' background in great detail, notably the numerous times that he engaged in various forms of sexual behaviour, most of which constituted criminal activity, but was allowed to carry on in his career as a police officer, even moving between jobs. Naturally, huge questions have been raised over the efficiency of vetting for public office (HMICFRS, 2022a), not least due to another police officer case of multiple rapes. This time the officer concerned was named as David Carrick, who stood accused of a 17-year spree of at least 85 sexual offences and 48 rapes. The Couzens' case is important for the attention, or total lack of it, given to what was regarded as low-level sexual offending. In particular, Couzens committed numerous acts of indecent exposure in public, and often very pointedly directed at specific female victims. Despite a number of internal investigations, in effect, nothing came of these incidents, or misogynistic messaging between him and his colleagues. Rather like Carrick, his career of criminal sexual behaviour (although never charged or convicted) lasted many years – 20 in his case. As noted in the Anglioni Report (2024, p. 2), 'the evidence of his preference for violent and extreme pornography and history of alleged sexual offending dates back 20 years; victims of his indecent exposures were not taken seriously and the police were not adequately trained'. In commenting on police culture, the Report continued, 'as long as vile behaviour and deeply abusing language are normalised and accepted as 'banter' in policing culture[...]people like Couzens will be able to commit atrocious crimes undetected'. It is often said in the assessment of dangerousness that previous behaviour, unlike convictions, is not easy to detect and therefore to be considered. Yet in Couzens' case, it was well known by many of his colleagues, including his seniors; indeed, his nickname was 'the rapist'. The Report concluded that masturbatory fantasy and rehearsal practice is commonplace prior to serious sexual offending and is critical in the commission of the most serious acts. In a chilling comment, the Report said that, 'an increase in the frequency of sexual offending can be deadly serious and needs to be treated as such' – in the case of Couzens, it was not (2024, p. 74). In police terms such behaviour is known as a 'red flag', whilst other agencies may describe it as a warning sign or a trigger. Whatever it is known as, this case underlines, absolutely, the importance of knowing and acting on 'behaviour'. We know we have laboured the point, but any system which is over-reliant on previous convictions is not, in our view, fit for purpose.

The final point we wish to draw out of the Couzens and Carrick cases is the final sentencing outcomes. Both offenders received life sentences, the difference being that Couzens' was a whole life order and Carrick's a 32-year tariff. For the public, it may be difficult to differentiate between these two extremely serious cases, but a distinction was made by the courts. In receiving a whole-life tariff, Couzens' sentence was outside of the criteria used to determine this disposal. Lord Justice Fulford justified his selection of a whole life sentence as follows, 'the misuse of a police officer's role such as occurred in this case in order to kidnap, rape and murder a lone victim is of equal seriousness as a murder carried out for the purpose of advancing a political, religious, racial or ideological cause'. His crime was construed as an attack on the fundamental underpinnings of 'our democratic way of life' (Fulford, 2021). In the Carrick case, in which the Judge considered the Couzens' judgement, it was not found that either his crimes or misuse of his police role was enough to warrant a whole-life term. The Judge did however consider that he would present a danger to women in intimate situations that would last indefinitely (Rex v Carrick, 2023). He received a life sentence with a minimum tariff of 30 years for a total of 36 life sentences. Clearly, it is a considered legal consideration and understanding of criteria which differentiates these sentences, but maybe the overall severity of the crimes does not appear to be that different in total. One (Couzens) did include a lone female victim and murder was the outcome. She was also a stranger chosen by Couzens after considerable planning. In the case of Carrick, there was technically a relationship of sorts in all cases, with virtually all offences occurring in his flat or other premises. There was therefore, a 'hint' of a relationship (albeit frequently coerced) and, as we have seen, this does tend to cloud the seriousness issue for the courts.

If there is one theme which has emerged from this chapter, it is likely to be that of uncertainty. This is something of a paradox in that the pursuit of a definition of dangerousness, certainty is what is sought after. As we have argued, there is a lack of certainty at all levels. There is some, but not unanimous, agreement over what factors should be included in an assessment of dangerousness. Key terms such as severity and imminence are frequently included but may be given more or less prominence. Seriousness and severity are other terms on which there is not widespread agreement: the Couzens and Carrick cases show this in recent light. As dangerousness looks to the future, so notions of imminence and likelihood come into play, but again, *how* imminent and *how* likely are less often discussed and certainly not agreed upon.

Throughout our discussion we have alluded to the interplay between seriousness and dangerousness, with both terms too often, in our view, used interchangeably. This discussion often plays out in considerations over the length of life sentences or whether or not a whole life sentence should be given. With much of the argument about indeterminate sentences having been concerned with the risk of *future* offending, the two judgements just described appear to put seriousness over and above dangerousness, although to be fair, decisions are never as simple as this. Perhaps because of a lack of certainty and agreement, politicians feel the need to step in and establish clarity for the public. However, even in this particular area, there may be a variety of motives for intervention. Elsewhere in this book we have referred to the use of 'wedge' politics in criminal justice to establish political differences. The area of violent and sexual offenders has been a fertile ground for this approach. However, since the 1990s, there has been no wedge, no gap or difference that would be noticeable to the public. Instead, a consensus around harsher punishment has seen measures become more punitive, restrictive and controlling and indeed included significantly more offenders (and potential offenders) into the dangerous category than early committees on this subject would have foreseen. Politicians have felt the need to respond in vigorous terms to rare and mostly exceptional offending, with the result that this is normalised in the minds of the public and exceptional measures are seen as essential. As we have said, establishing the size of the dangerous offender population and who should be in it is a difficult task. The uncertainty however concerning who and why means that a void is filled with an increasingly inclusive policy with a huge impact on offender rights, prison numbers, probation caseloads, the work of the parole board and how the crime problem is constructed. The rest of this book is concerned with how this problem is tackled.

Part Two

Public Protections Responses

Chapter 2

Legislation: To Punish, to Protect and What?

In a book with 'public protection' in the title, it may come as a surprise to readers that there is not an act of Parliament which is solely concerned with this subject. Instead, measures are most commonly included in broader criminal justice acts, or those concerned with policing or the probation or prison services. We would argue that a lack of clarity over the meaning and understanding of public protection may be a reason for this, as would the somewhat reactive nature of many measures designed to protect the public. Thus, governments are able to use a number of legislative opportunities to bring forth measures, often demanded by and well-received by the public, at short notice, rather than as an outcome of a considered legal and policy process – what Downes and Newburn (2023, p. 271) described as 'initiativitis' under Prime Minister Tony Blair's criminal justice policies. Public protection measures therefore frequently result from rare but high-profile criminal events, which governments feel obliged to respond to. Politics therefore plays a key role in these measures by which politicians prove their 'toughness' to the electorate and attempt to demonstrate their listening qualities. However, as we have noted elsewhere in this book, there is a lack of consistency concerning which causes, or issues, are responded to as a matter of urgency. For example, it has taken until 2023 for any government to legislate for parity in the murders of women within and outside of domestic relationships (MoJ, 3 August 2023). Public protection legislation is therefore often a response to a profound sense of shock among the public. The rarity of the events underpinning these emotions is often overlooked, in what can become an extremely fraught situation where fear and blame can dominate the emotions. As we indicated, legislation in this field can often follow the commission of a single, but often heinous, crime. In the United States, official responses to these crimes have led to the creation of what collectively have become known as 'apostrophe' acts (Fanarraga, 2020), with the name of a victim featuring prominently in the title of the legislation. This very personal response often follows long and high-profile public campaigns from the victims' families and enables governments to show their responsive and caring side. It can also, if viewed cynically, enable tougher legislation to be introduced which impacts on a much wider group of people, entailing a much deeper erosion of rights, riding on the back of the emotions triggered by single cases.

As we have seen however in chapter one, the rarity of these cases makes legislating for either their prevention or punishment a difficult task. Underpinning much of the legislation in this area is a desire to regulate and control in a sense to reassure a frightened public that the situation is in hand. The legislation frequently aims to create certainty out of uncertain and unpredictable events; indeed, acts committed by very often unpredictable people. However, what this 'certainty' means in action is another matter altogether. Does the public want to know who all so-called dangerous offenders are? If so, what would they do with that knowledge? Do they want all dangerous offenders incarcerated – and for how long? Do they believe that dangerous offenders can change for the better and that rehabilitative work is important? Do they want the return of the death penalty? In essence these issues are rarely discussed in a rational manner. Instead, they are all too frequently framed by fear, failure and blame. In a legislative framework, pinch points occur at sentencing (usually identified as being too lenient), at consideration for release (parole) where it is thought to be too early, or at the point of supervision in the community (not strict enough and based on poor risk assessment). Wendy Fitzgibbon (2011, p. 82) admirably summarises the tensions involved in working with those labelled as dangerous, when she describes the work of the Aarvold and Butler Committees.

> ...the notion which preoccupied the Aarvold (1973) and Butler (1975) Inquiries, that the protection of the public and the rehabilitation of the offender are equally valid and important aspects of policy which pull in different directions, and between which some balance must be found, has been displaced by public protection as the overwhelmingly dominant task of public protection.

The question is though, how is this dominant task to be achieved? As we have already noted, the rhetoric around public protection can be frenzied, frenetic and impassioned, replete with generalised accusations and bold promises. It is, essentially, highly political, having become a more focussed aspect of the politicisation of criminal justice since the 1970s (Downes and Newburn, 2023). Yet, one must ask if this is one problem that the government, any government, cannot solve – cannot 'win'. Promises made in respect of so-called dangerous offenders will always be of tough action, of longer sentences, of indefinite sentences, of more control and monitoring and a quicker and firmer response to supervision violations; but what comes next when these promises are not kept? Perhaps one very discernible and seemingly irreversible trend at the moment is the squeeze on any discussion of human rights. This issue had so preoccupied the committees described in chapter one but, in the early 2020s, appears to have well and truly slipped behind a rhetoric of punishment. Recent developments over forcing the attendance of convicted offenders to face their victims in court at sentencing (or indeed to be told NOT to attend) has been framed in a language to denigrate offenders and draw the general public onside. It is difficult to know when a trend for offenders to refuse to attend court really took off, but it does appear to fit in with a more generalised NO culture of the early 2020s (i.e. I will not go to work in the office, I will not send my children to school etc.). Forcing offenders into court followed a high-visibility campaign by Farah Naz and Cheryl Korkel among others. The government responded by describing these offenders as 'cowardly' and who 'try to evade the final moment of justice'. These most 'horrendous criminals cannot be allowed to take the coward's way out' they are 'vile offenders' (Ministry of Justice, August 30, 2022). Eligible offenders will be those committing crimes where the maximum sentence is life, including serious violent and sexual offenders. Prisoners may be 'forced' into the dock by custody staff or face an extra 2 years in custody. The proposal has not been without its critics however. A former prison officer, Bryn Hughes, whose police officer daughter was killed, warned against a 'knee-jerk, headline grabbing response', saying that such a policy offered an opportunity for abuse to be shouted at families and that use of force and restraint would be problematic. There were also objections from legal quarters (see HoC Library, October 24, 2023).

Another interesting example of bringing legislation down to 'street level', is what has become known as 'apostrophe laws' as mentioned above. These laws bear the name of victims; the most famous of which perhaps might be Megan's Law in the United States. These laws are often not aiming to introduce 'new' legislation, but more to toughen up aspects of existing legislation of introduce additional variants to it, or increase the available penalties. Apostrophe laws emerged in the United States in the early 1990s, reflecting the punitive turn taking place in their criminal justice system. Fanarraga (2020) offers a very helpful theoretical framework through which to consider these laws and their rationale. He suggests, particularly building on the work of Roach (1999), that there might be three ways in which apostrophe laws can be viewed. The first is as an attempt to honour victims, the second is as an exploitative strategy and thirdly, as a purely symbolic piece of legislation. These ideas are set within a wider model based around Punitive Victims' Rights where aims are similar to a crime control model, emphasising punishment as the fundamental goal of the CJS but in which victims play a central role. Petitions and advocacy play an important role in the legislative process. Often, following an horrendous crime, victims demand protection in strong and emotional ways, support punitive interventions and want to mobilise grass roots support to pressure politicians (Roach, 1999).

Honouring the victim is meant to represent the state's response to victims' families and to address the harm done to a loved one. In the face of concerted and high-profile pressure, legislation is proposed that memorialises those who have suffered the harm. Importantly however, the legislation should not be merely symbolic but have an impact usually in terms of prevention and protecting from future harm. The exploitative law-passing strategy (Garland, 2001), suggests, perhaps cynically, that governments use the emotions and powers of these very individual victims' stories, to push through their own personal and political agendas. Fanarraga (2020, p. 5) suggests that apostrophe laws are more to do with lawmakers' political goals, than an actual attempt to address the demands of the victim's family. Finally, it is worth considering the potentially symbolic nature of apostrophe laws. Rather than producing impact or change, they are characterised by empty gestures, instead making a point to the public that something is being done. Attaching a name to these laws makes this symbolism more powerful and at the same time renders the political opportunism very unpalatable. One very interesting aspect arising from Fanarraga's examination of 47 US apostrophe laws was that, on average, it took 4.86 years from the crime or event before a name was attached to a bill, but only 278 days for that bill to pass into law. Men and women as named subjects were split fairly evenly (to the surprise of the authors who had been expecting more females meeting the 'ideal victim' category), but it took until 2004 before the first non-white victim featured on an apostrophe law. As with many of its crime policies, the UK has imported the idea of apostrophe laws. Examples of these include the following:

- *Tony's Law* – the maximum sentence for causing or allowing the death of a child raised from 14 years to Life.
- *Harper's Law* – introduced a mandatory life sentence for anyone killing an emergency worker whilst committing a crime. This followed a campaign by PC Andrew Harper's wife, Lissie, who wanted the sentences handed down for the manslaughter of her husband, 16 years, 13 years and 13 years for three individuals, increased.

Away from increasing sentence length, the UK has seen slight variations in the provisions.

- *Jade's Law* – provides for the suspension of parental responsibilities for those who kill a partner or ex-partner; this to take place at sentencing.
- *Daisy's Law* – whereby children born as a result of rape will be officially recognised as victims of crime.
- *Clare's Law* – is the informal name given to the Police Domestic Abuse Disclosure Scheme, which allows the police to disclose information to a victim or potential victim of domestic abuse about their partner's or ex-partner's previous abuse or violent behaviour. The two core principles of the scheme are a right to ask and a right to know.
- *Sarah's Law* – the Child Sex Offender Disclosure Scheme, which allows those with children to ask police if a person is a convicted or suspected child sex offender.

The Tone and Trends of Public Protection Legislation

When legislating for public protection, a core focus is the seriousness of the crimes committed or suspected to be committed in the future. As a minimum, these crimes are very serious, with lasting physical and emotional damage to victims, or of course, death. Very serious crimes against the person invariably invoke the most severe penalties. In the UK, the crime regarded as the most serious of all, murder, must receive a mandatory life sentence. However, this has meant the evolution of a 'scale of seriousness' over the years, whereby all other crimes are compared to murder and therefore, anything other than that crime becomes, by default, less serious and not deserving of the mandatory maximum penalty. Even within the murder category however, there are degrees of seriousness, with the 'worst' types earning the longest tariff – the time to be served before release can be considered. The question is, how is the difference between one murder and another decided? When death is the outcome, it may appear to be a simple decision for the public and that is that the offence must be murder. However, murder may well not be the verdict of the court, not least because it may not have been the subject of the charge (see below discussion on the Calocane case). Clearly, the ultimate decision is that of the sentencing Judge, but, as we have seen, the public and victims' families, can have a significant impact on perceptions of certain crimes and perhaps on sentence length and ultimate release decisions.

It is clear, from using a range of indicators, that criminal justice in the UK has been getting tougher. The prison population has been steadily rising for many years and at the time of writing (early 2024) stands at a record level. Yet, the reality of both sentencing and prison numbers appears to be lost on the public. The Prison Reform Trust (PRT), in their Summer 2023 Bromley Briefings, reported that their surveys showed that two thirds of people believed that sentencing was not harsh enough and that although average sentences were much higher than 25 years previous, 56% of those asked believed that they were shorter. Life sentence tariffs, for example, have risen from an average of 12.5 years in 2003 to 20 years in 2020 (PRT, 2021a). What though, has fuelled this increase? One answer could of course be that murders are 'getting worse' – but is this really possible? Murder by stabbing is the same act at all times, but of course it is acknowledged that the unique circumstances surrounding the act can make it more or less awful. This has however always been the case and degrees of severity, or 'awfulness' have been reflected in minimum tariffs since procedures were introduced in 1983. If not an increase in severity, then perhaps it is a growth in numbers, fuelling a public panic, which has led to an increase in minimum tariffs. Again though, the evidence does not support this claim. Since 1898, the population of England and Wales has increased by approximately 87% (31.5 m–58.7 m), whilst the number of murders has increased by approximately 100% (300–600 – with a spike to 696 in 2022). On average then, the increase in murders is roughly in line with population growth and there is nothing to suggest that the problem is out of control or that additional or stronger punishments are needed. Finally, despite the lurid headlines, murders by strangers remains a very rare event. In the year ending March 2022, 301 victims from a total of 696 (43%) were killed by someone known to them; family member, friend or acquaintance. Only 85 were officially recorded as a stranger perpetrator (12.2%). That said, the relationship of 84 was unknown and 226 cases had not seen anyone charged (ONS, 2023a, 2023b).

It is therefore hard to see a pure crime reason for the increase in severity of punishment in recent years. This is well summarised by Appleton and Gilman (2022, p. 6) when they say '...increases in the minimum terms to be served by life-sentenced prisoners in England and Wales in recent years have been driven by punitive political trends and legislative changes. They are not necessarily ... a direct consequence of shifts in the severity of murder or caused by broader increases in the overall prison population' (which rose by 24% between 2000 and 2010 whilst whole-life orders rose disproportionately by 187%). As we have noted previously, politicians have been keen to demonstrate their tough credentials *and* to show that they are listening and responding to the public. The setting of minimum tariffs in life sentences has been an enduring battle ground between the Courts, most recently the European Court of Human Rights (ECHR), and the UK Parliament. This battle has taken two forms: the right to set a minimum tariff (the Home Secretary or the Sentencing Judge) and the right to impose a whole-life tariff (a life sentence with no minimum tariff and therefore no prospect of release). As we discussed earlier in this book, these issues have very much centred on control, with politicians increasingly wanting to demonstrate that it is them, rather than the courts, who have authority. As we also mentioned in the section on parole, this debate about minimum tariffs also centres on release decisions, risk and what is considered to be the appropriate punishment. As a baseline, life sentences prisoners were serving between 10 and 13 years by 1939.

Tariff setting procedures were introduced in 1983 by Conservative Home Secretary Leon Brittan (Hansard, 30 November 1983). The history of this is tortuous and complex, with arguments put forward by politicians, the Judiciary, the Houses of Parliament and the ECHR. Suffice it to say that these arguments have rarely, if ever, been concerned with reducing the length of tariffs, but rather who has the power to set them and how to increase the minimum terms. British politics has of course demonstrated a decidedly anti-European trend for a number of years, culminating in the decision to leave the EU via the in-out Brexit vote in June 2016, with final withdrawal in January 2020. We will not rehearse the Brexit arguments here, but it can be said in relation to this book that much of the debate centred on the control exercised by European institutions over UK sovereignty, and in our particular case, the role of the ECHR in influencing criminal justice measures such as prisoner release and whole-life sentences. Indeed, the Government has increasingly taken to referring to the ECHR as a 'foreign' court – part of the anti-European and disparaging rhetoric that has so marked Conservative Party politics since the Brexit vote.

Fanaragga (2023) offers an excellent summary and detailed review of the legality and morality of whole-life orders and we recommend this article to readers. Blick (2023) makes a few telling points concerning the power relationship between courts and politicians and concludes, for example, that 'by any metric, the prospect of release for WLT/WLO prisoners in England and Wales has become vanishingly small'. It is the prospect of a sentence without any hope of release which has exercised the courts now for a several decades. Such sentences, known as 'irreducible', are regarded as inhumane by the ECHR and much recent history has been about the UKs efforts to convince the ECHR that its provisions are compatible with human rights. The current position of the UK government is that it may leave the ECHR to avoid what is regards as obstruction. For many British commentators, offering the prospect of release was *incompatible* with the punishment handed down for exceptionally serious crimes; for prisoners regarded as the worst of the worst. The British House of Lords had already asserted that there was no reason in principle why a crime, if sufficiently heinous, should not be regarded as deserving of lifelong incarceration for the purposes of pure punishment (Appleton and Gilman, 2022, p. 5). This followed on from decisions to increase the minimum term to be served by the so-called Moors Murderess, Myra Hindley, from her original Lord Chief Justice recommended 25 years, subsequently increased to 30 years by the Home Secretary and, as this neared its end, to a whole-life tariff. As Home Secretaries lost the power to set the minimum tariff for adults in 2002, governments have attempted to seize back control by setting minimum tariffs for particular crimes within primary legislation. For example, the previous way of calculating tariffs in discretionary life sentences, set at one half of the 'equivalent' determinate sentence, has been increased to two-thirds by the Police, Crime Sentencing and Courts Act, 2022. A whole-life order has been set as the starting point for the premeditated murder of a child. Whole-life orders are now the 'appropriate' starting point for a range of murders where the seriousness is 'exceptionally high', this can include the murder of two or more victims, where murder includes substantial planning or premeditation, abduction of victims, sexual or sadistic conduct, the murder of police or prison officers in the course of their duty and where murder is committed to further political, religious or ideological causes. What has happened here is a two-pronged assault; a reduction of Judicial discretion in the types of sentence they can impose and at the same time, the length of those sentences.

As we describe in the section on Parole, politicians have been busy wresting control back from professional decision-makers in sentencing. Parole was of course a relatively secret process but has become increasingly exposed to media and public scrutiny. Sentencing has always been in the public eye, but in recent years, has become disputed territory between Judges, legal commentators and 'tough' minded politicians. Sentences offering no prospect of release, except perhaps in the case of a terminal illness, deny any belief that the people who commit these more serious murders can be redeemed, or can be rehabilitated. The sentence is purely for punishment and retribution, going against one of the stated purposes of the prison service to look after prisoners 'with humanity and help them lead law-abiding and useful lives in custody and after release'. No-one has yet been released from a whole-life sentence in the UK and numbers are steadily growing as the new mandatory criteria bed in, with numbers in excess of 70 in 2023. WLO prisoners describe their sentence as a 'living death sentence, and Vannier (2021), in Appleton and Gilman (2022), describing WLO sentences in California, identifies three sociological dimensions of death identified by WLO prisoners; (a) *procedural death*, with no chance of review, (b) carceral or social death, with exclusion from rehabilitation activities and (c) *embodied death*, which involves the ageing process and associated illnesses which receive limited care from prison and health authorities. Blick (2023) concluded his article by expressing a desire for a 25-year review to be re-introduced into while life orders, based on a free vote in Parliament, and a survey of British public opinion on the issue of release of WLO prisoners. In the present political and penal climate, however, there appears little likelihood of this, as ongoing measures to strengthen legislation and limit the rights discussion, appear only to meet with public approval. The ongoing dialogue concerning life imprisonment epitomises an age-old debate over the importance of punishment and retribution as against reformation and rehabilitation. This is not a discussion played out in a small legal bubble however, but one in which media and public take great interest. Their interest ensures a continuing role for politicians to push their view of the best way forward and to demonstrate that they are in tune with public opinion. As with most political ideas the time-frame is generally short, ensuring that public protection policies are rarely well thought out and usually given little time to prove their effectiveness before the next measure, usually in response to the most recent serious case, is introduced. We will now briefly pause in our description of contemporary developments to review how the legislative process has evolved since the early 1990s, putting a context around recent measures and proposals, to identify key themes, some of which endure whilst others do not.

The 1991 Criminal Justice Act

This huge Act offers an excellent starting point for many of the issues raised throughout this book. It is a clear attempt to clarify and perhaps 'make real', the aims of sentencing. It also represents attempts at reducing judicial discretion, at creating framework which might ultimately reduce the size of the prison population and also clarify understandings of dangerousness and its application in criminal law. A hugely ambitious task. The 1991 Act attempted to achieve one of its main purposes, reducing the use of custody, by building provisions around proportionality. This was a clever ploy in that it offered something for the 'red meat' wing of the Conservative Party, but also for the more progressive members. Essentially, under the tougher banner of longer sentences for *some* offenders, it was hoped that more liberal measures aimed at stopping the ratcheting up of sentences by a number count of previous convictions, could be achieved. The proportionality principle aimed to ensure that the more serious the crime, the more severe the punishment. The clear intention here was to avoid a situation where a relatively non-serious crime met with a severe penalty because the offender had a particular number of previous convictions – even if these were unrelated to the instant office. This attempt to place controls on sentences was, as ever, balanced by another provision, section 28 of the Act, which allowed for the use of previous convictions if their circumstances revealed a *pattern of behaviour* which aggravated the seriousness of the present or instant offence. It was almost a case of give with one hand and take with the other.

Another departure from the proportionality principle was evident in section 1 (2) (b) of the act which permitted the imposition of a custodial sentence even if the instant offence did not merit it. In these cases, the sentence would be imposed because only custody would achieve the aim of protecting the public *from the offender*, a switch from the overall offence focus of the act. In similar vein, section 2 (2) (b) of the act allowed for a departure from a proportionate sentence, up to the maximum available for the offence in question, *if* the offender was considered potentially dangerous. In these cases, the courts could impose a sentence up to the maximum for the crime, even if the offence did not merit it – *but the person did*. The Act in a way included an interesting paradox. It was clear that offenders should not be punished again, or twice, for crimes for which they have already been punished. Yet, the Act also allowed for punishments for crimes which had not yet been committed, or indeed, for behaviour which might, or might not occur in the future. This position is very well summarised by von Hirsch and Ashworth (1996, p. 176) when they say, 'Since punishment involves censure, its amount should fairly reflect how wrong the conduct is – that is, how serious it is. Proportionate sentences are designed to reflect the conduct's blameworthiness, whereas sentences based on prediction have no such foundation'. The 1991 Act can therefore be viewed as a pragmatic attempt to reduce the costs of imprisonment in financial terms, not least to keep open the door for the tax cuts so beloved of Conservative politicians. It might also be regarded as one of the last attempts to keep a lid on more punitive sentencing. However, the more populist punitive agenda, now rapidly gaining ground, was given space to grow with measures which kick-started the process of focussing on the behaviour of certain offenders, with a view to predicting their future seriousness or dangerousness. This meant allowing for *longer than desert* sentences, or custody where it wasn't justified, or for longer periods of custody beyond that which the offence merited.

Much of the rest of the 1990s was taken up with ongoing battles between Conservative and Labour politicians, frequently over law and order issues. Downes and Newburn (2023) offer a thoughtful and detailed analysis of this period, leading up to Tony Blair's ascendancy not only on law and order, but more generally with the electorate. Before that, fortunes ebbed and flowed between the major parties, but in 1995 Home Secretary Michael Howard seized the initiative, at least within his own party, earning the longest ovation of the party conference that year. He promised a much tougher agenda, including the ending of the early automatic release for all prisoners, restrictions on parole, automatic, minimum sentences for certain types of offender and mandatory life sentences for rapists and other repeat violent criminals. It was acknowledged that these proposals would lead to an increase in prison numbers (and expenditure) but it was felt this would not occur for 1 or 2 years or longer (Downes and Newburn, 2023, p. 153). Downes and Newburn (2023, p. 152) report on a briefing for the Prime Minister before the 1995 conference shows very clearly what many might describe as the cynicism of short-term success in politics over a more considered, long-term strategy. The briefing said:

> ...the Home Secretary has a package of measures which should result in tougher/longer custodial sentences being awarded by the courts. The upside of all of them is huge popular appeal...greater importance to retribution and punishment...and greater deterrence. There is also a chance, with luck, of a decent row with Labour on law and order...downside is a probable increase in the prison population with resource implications (although not this year or next), and a row with the judiciary (although that has upsides too if you really go for them as wimps.

This briefing very much reflected the repeated words of Michael Howard, a populist Home Secretary, who was keen to seize the law and order ground from Labour and worked tirelessly to put 'clear blue water' (Dunbar and Langdon, 1998), between the two parties. In the White Paper, *Protecting the Public* (Home Office, 1996), the government put together the public, victims and a distortion of crime figures as a means of justifying their (new) tough approach. The Paper stated that:

> ...too often in the past, those who have shown a propensity to commit serious or violent sexual offences have served their sentences and been released only to offend again...Too often, victims have paid the price when the offender has repeated the same offences. The government is determined that the public should receive proper protection from persistent violent and sexual offenders. Home Office (1996, p. 48)

There was no reference to the fact that repeated serious further offences were and remain to this day, a comparatively rare event in statistical terms. What was attracting Howard and many more politicians, Conservative and Labour, were the policies unfolding in the United States, particularly those related to mandatory, fixed penalties. These became known, collectively, as 'three strikes and you're out' legislation, mirroring baseball terminology. The utter injustice of this legislation centred on the fact that the 'third strike' did not have to be a serious sexual or violent crime and could just be a felony. Skelnick (1995, p. 5) noted, 'The third strike is any felony. In some California counties more than half of the 'third strike' cases have involved such non-violent offences as shoplifting and auto burglary, theft of cigarettes and in one Los Angeles case – theft of a pizza'. The penalty for the third offences was 25 years to life without parole. Interestingly, the UK was not quite so punitive in one sense as no one faced a life sentence equivalent for a minor theft, but three strikes were reduced to two where serious crimes against the person were concerned. From a list of qualifying offences – a list that was to grow considerably with the 2003 Criminal Justice, see below – the second such incidence would trigger an automatic, mandatory life sentence. Qualifying offences included attempt, conspiracy or incitement to murder, manslaughter, soliciting murder, wounding or grievous bodily harm with intent, rape or attempted rape, intercourse with a girl under 13, possession of a firearm with intent to injure and robbery using a firearm or imitation firearm.

Legislation such as this is an obvious attempt to reduce or remove judicial discretion and ensure that sentencing is at or near the maximum available for the crime. However, what it also achieves is to squarely place the aims of sentencing in the punishment/retribution camp. Fixed, mandatory penalties leave no space for the offender's personal circumstances or history, or indeed the unique circumstances of the crime itself. It is contrary to what many commentators, practitioners and academics, believe to be central to an understanding of and predictions for dangerousness. Three and two strikes legislation punish offenders purely on the commission of certain crimes having been committed in the past (or not, in the case of much US legislation). These measures therefore reflect a significant attempt by government to seize control of sentencing; a major incursion into the independence of the judiciary. They reflect a populist message to a public, misinformed by the media, that crimes of violence and serious sexual offending were spiralling and, not only that, were not being dealt with appropriately by the Courts. The evidence did not support this assertion however. As Tonry (2004, p. 124) notes, 'the evidence does not therefore appear to be present to suggest a considerable increase in the numbers of serious offenders or indeed that courts were becoming softer'. Lord Ackner, speaking in the House of Lords, said that:

> ...the Home Secretary is putting forward proposals in a manner which shows irresponsibility that I would not expect to go with that office...he is exploiting for party political gain the misapprehension of the public that judges are too soft on crime...the Home Secretary...has an unerring populist streak which sadly the Opposition wish to emulate. HL Deb (1997, col. 1013)

Michael Howard had not succeeded in establishing the clear blue water with Labour that he had sought. The Crime Sentences bill was enacted by the New Labour government in 1997 almost in total, but during its passage through the Lords, significant amendments were made so that an 'exceptional clause' meant that Judges could avoid the mandatory sentence if they saw fit. An appeal by five people serving life sentences under the 1997 Act saw Lord Justice Woolf declare that if an offender was not felt to present a significant risk to the public, then this could count as an exceptional circumstance and allow a court NOT to pass a life sentence (Jones and Newburn, 2006, p. 787). Cavadino and Dignan observed that the decision would 'presumably allow sentencers to avoid passing life sentences in many-perhaps most-of these 'two-strikes' cases' (2002, p. 106). The mandatory life provision for second violent and sexual offenders' provision was repealed by the Criminal Justice Act 2003.

New Labour

The CJA 2003 was the first with a real Labour Party stamp on it in terms of crime legislation. In many ways, its most significant achievement was in removing the Crime (Sentences) Act, or at least its worst aspects, in terms of removing discretion and the perceived unfairness and injustice of fixed penalties. Thomas (2004, p. 702) noted that 'the sound and fury which accompanied the enactment of the Crime (Sentences) Act 1997, forms a strange contrast with the total parliamentary silence which surrounded the removal of this penological aberration from the statute book'. The new act did not however throw the baby out with the bath water, in many ways it represented a continuation of the same trends but with a whole range of new words and concepts. There was still an element of life sentences having to be imposed in certain circumstances, but those circumstances might be regarded as more pertinent to the potential harm posed by the offender rather than simply 'adding up' previous convictions. The Act introduced a new set of terminology, 'specified offence', 'specified violent offence', 'specified sexual offence', 'serious offence' and 'relevant offence'. The actual offences are listed in Sch. 15 (1 and 2) and total 153; 65 violent offences and 88 sexual offences. The seriousness classification kicks in if the offence is punishable with a life sentence or a determinate sentence of 10 years or more. Perhaps, the major departure from the 1997 Act was that a further assessment of the risk to the public of serious harm from the offender was necessary, in addition to the specified serious offence, for a mandatory life sentence to be passed. The 2003 Act had then brought the offender back into the sentencing equation.

The Act did however bring in a significant new development with Imprisonment for Public Protection (IPP), for cases which fell outside of the life sentence qualification, but met all other requirements. This was a sentence square in the middle of protective and preventive sentencing provisions. It would be a sentence very similar to a life sentence in that it would be indeterminate and release decided by the Parole Board. However, there was a significant, if not huge, difference to a life sentence. This concerned the nature of the instant crime which *did not* have to be serious enough for a life sentence. The indeterminate nature of IPPs was based upon the perceived *future risk* posed by the offender and therefore largely unrelated to the current offence. For example, a 22-year-old man was given an IPP for stealing a phone from a man in the street, his tariff was 30 months but he was still in prison after 16 years (*The Economist*, March 25, 2022). Offence seriousness remained the baseline for inclusion in the IPP category, with commission of one of 95 serious violent and sexual offences, carrying a minimum of a 10-year sentence, opening up the near certainty of an IPP being imposed. In addition to the actual crime committed, offenders had to be deemed to be seen as posing a significant risk of serious harm in the future. This differentiated the legislation from the flawed automatic life sentence provisions in the 1997 Act, but even these additional safeguards were themselves problematic. The Act stipulated that a previous conviction for any of the 153 qualifying offences triggered an automatic presumption that the threshold of serious risk of harm had been reached. There was in effect a presumption of dangerousness. These provisions significantly expanded the scope of dangerousness whilst simultaneously lowering the threshold. By the time of a significant review in 2010 (Prison Reform Trust), the average tariff was 3 years and 5 months, suggesting that offences were not at the highest end of the seriousness scale. Indeed, a thematic review of IPP sentences reported one tariff being as low as 28 days (HMIPPS, 2008).

The IPP provisions proved to be much more popular with the Judiciary than the automatic life sentences they followed on from, with over 8,700 passed between 2005 and their abolition in 2012. By June 2022, there were still 2,926 IPP prisoners in England and Wales, 1,492 of whom had never been released and 1,434 of whom had been recalled to prison, most commonly for violating their licence conditions. Real problems developed for the IPP regime in that, the sheer number of prisoners allied to a lack of resources in prisons, meant that many were unable to undertake the programmes necessary to try to prove their fitness for release to the Parole Board. Cuts to the system which managed the lifer population of 18%, added to the delays faced by long-term indeterminate prisoners, allied to severe pressures on the parole board and probation service, all caused delays for IPP prisoners and a continued growth in their numbers. It was something of a perfect storm – a sentence popular with the Judiciary, a prescriptive element which amplified assessments of dangerousness and for those sentenced, a real difficulty in proving that they were safe for release. Speaking to the BBC in 2014, David Blunkett who had overseen the introduction of IPPs said, 'We certainly got the implementation wrong. The consequence of bringing the Act in had led in some cases to an injustice and I regret that (HMIP, 2016)'. In an attempt to alleviate some of the problems caused by and suffered by the IPP prison population, the original measures were modified by the Criminal Justice and Immigration Act, 2008. This attempted to reduce overall numbers on two fronts. The first was to introduce a new minimum duration for minimum terms (tariffs) or 2 years, ensuring that more serious offences should be the starting point for an IPP. The new Act also removed the presumption in favour of dangerousness based on certain previous convictions. There was also a provision for sentences not to be imposed if information on the offence and the offender's pattern of behaviour meant that a Judge could be satisfied that the risk could be lowered. This information would largely be derived from the probation officer's pre-sentence report (PSR); an additional task for the probation service and one made all the more difficult by risk averse cultures fostered by populist punitive law and order agendas. The IPP sentence was eventually abolished in the Legal Aid, Sentencing and Punishment of Offenders Act, 2012. It did not, however, retrospectively abolish it, hence the considerable numbers continuing to languish in prison, years beyond their minimum tariff. Calls from a variety of organisations for a re-sentencing exercise have so far been ignored by the government. However, in November 2023 (MoJ, 2023), it was announced that there would be changes to the automatic licence period which was subject to a minimum of a ten-year review in the community. New proposals would set the minimum time for review at 3 years, with a presumption that it would be terminated after 5 years, if not at 3. For prisoners already released, this would signal the end of their indeterminate sentence.

So far in this chapter, we have focussed on various measures to increase sentence lengths, to make sentences mandatory and introduce and increase minimum tariffs in indeterminate sentences. Much of this has centred on reducing the discretion of criminal justice professionals by increasing the powers of politicians to set more punitive measures – measures which they believed Judges did not exercise sufficiently. There were, however, also a number of measures which attempted more than increased sentences, and these might be thought of a concerned more with control and regulation in the community, in particular in respect of sexual offenders. We will now consider the development of these initiatives since the early 1990s.

Controlling the Monsters

There is no doubt that since the 1990s a number of very high profile, sexually violent crimes against children, have brought to public attention the idea of *predatory* offenders. These were characterised initially as strangers who loiter in public spaces, making them unsafe spaces with their inclination and urge to sexually abuse 'innocent' children. The stranger predator became the personification of evil and the subject of numerous attempts to punish, control and regulate their behaviour, notably in the USA and the UK. Much of the legislative activity was concerned with what to do with these offenders post-incarceration, as they were regarded as posing an ongoing, if not never-ending threat. It was perhaps in the area of the controls placed on sex offenders in the community that the UK has seen the greatest policy transfer from the USA. We should note, however, that sexual offending against children remains a hugely under-reported and under-recorded crime, so its true extent is, in part, guesswork. What we do know, however, is that 'stranger' perpetrated child sexual abuse might be as much as 20–30% of the total, with 'known' individuals, from parents and siblings through to other family, friends, neighbours and people in positions of trust, accounting for more than 70% of all child sexual abuse (Karsna & Kelly, 2021, p. 25). The monster predator is a powerful image to be used for those keen to push a tough, no-nonsense law and order agenda, not least because to argue against it renders the critic liable to being labelled as 'the peaedo's friend'. For some time then, this agenda has been used to carry through broader penological measures and it is perhaps only in the 2020s that adult women have come to be seen increasingly as victims and received more media and indeed political attention. The stranger predator trumps a domestic murderer every time – but the end result is still a death. The way in which sex offenders have been dealt with by criminal justice systems around the world, but notably the USA and the UK, have reflected their pariah status; a status that has allowed the creation of a range of 'exceptional' measures with only limited opposition. Janus (2010, p. 317) describes the outcome as 'radical prevention', a process that claims exemption from the normal rules governing state interventions and intrusions. He suggests that (the US) government had taken a wrong turn in not taking the public health approach to a number of behaviours falling under the dangerous label. He believed that:

> ...a public health approach to prevention would have produced comprehensive and systematic, empirically based campaigns to understand and change the root causes of violence. Instead, we have adopted counter-empirical, interstitial laws designed to identify and remove risky persons before they can cause harm. (2010, p. 316)

Public protection legislation is therefore 'prevention' legislation; a clear attempt to stop something (unpleasant) happening in the future – most often a repetition from a known offender. However, prevention is based less on a notion of harsh punishment for the crime under consideration, but more, a potentially massively distorted punishment, for crimes *yet to be committed*. Risk, and its assessment, lies at the heart of this process. Risk assessment is seen as being able to unlock the future. This may sound a fanciful phrase, but, considering the potential loss of liberties involved by offenders subject to this process, then it can be assumed that there has to be great faith in its ability, if used in a democratic society. Before we consider some of the measures deployed against sex offenders in the UK, it is worth briefly digressing to consider the United States (a template for many of the UK efforts anyway) and in particular the work of Janus, noted above, to try to understand the dominance of risk assessment and exceptionalism. Filmgoers will undoubtedly remember *Minority Report*, starring Tom Cruise, a film based on use of psychic 'pre-cogs' to apprehend criminals before they commit their crimes. This may, to some, be a popular idea – stop crime before it happens. But the issue at the heart of this idea is the basis on which the prediction is made – whether psychics or risk assessment algorithms – and how accurate they can be. The simple answer is almost certainly, not very accurate at all. The prediction of rare, human behaviour is an extremely difficult task and when it becomes the basis of legal and moral judgements, the difficulties multiply. Rather than seeing risk as dynamic, it becomes embedded as a fixed quality, justifying measures that reach many years into the future. In the words of Janus (2010, p. 328):

> ...the reification of risk turns risk itself into the kind of taxonomic difference that satisfies the principle of exceptionality. The demand for exceptionality pushes us to think of risk not as a circumstantial statement about a person in a particular context, a particular stage in his or her life, in a particular set of relationships and personal circumstance.

Instead of this wider consideration of the risk context, Janus believes that assessment is focussed down onto the individual and therefore *one person* is singled out, rather than everyone, in terms of a progressive loss of rights. It is as if the risk, or dangerousness, is a characteristic of the person rather than of behaviour. The *person* therefore becomes exceptional, rather than their behaviour. This is explained by the fact that the same two behaviours can result in fixed or indeterminate sentences, depending on the degree of risk attached to the offender. Risk is conceptualised as a stable trait and therefore it is not surprising that detention for life can be a common outcome. Janus (2010, p. 324) identifies three characteristics of radical prevention:

(1) Risk replaces guilt.
(2) The legal regime relies on some assertion of exceptionalism for legitimacy.
(3) The politics of prevention.

Janus makes a telling point about assessment tools when he argues that the tools seek to rank risks, searching for the riskiest, which in turn distracts attention from the root causes of behaviour. He believes that risk assessment tools look for the factors correlated with – rather than which cause – risk. In summarising the wider project to prevent future harms, Janus gives us thoughts to ponder on:

> ...the project to insure safety, to take every last precaution, is never fully complete, because it is based on an impossible task – the prediction of rare events. Each time there is a failure, the politics of prevention seeks to locate blame, and the cycle of prevention politics is re-energised. (2010, p. 330)

Although not fully copying some of the worst excesses of US preventive legislation, the UK has taken on board a number of key features, invariably to engage in a contortion act to get through the legal obstacles in place against punishment without a crime, longer than deserved punishment and continued detention at the end of lawful custody. One key element developed in the US and the UK is the move towards 'civil' measures rather than criminal – in other words the commission of a crime is not necessary and instead, *worrying behaviours* become the focus of intervention.

Registration and Collaboration

The Sex Offender Register (SOR), was established in England and Wales in 1997, under the Sex Offender Act. The word register is something of a misnomer, as there was not a single source or a physical (or electronic) register. It meant, instead, a system whereby convicted sex offenders, post the Act, had to register their details with the local police. Other than this, registration of personal information, the process was initially *passive*, in that there was no obligation to report to the police or indeed be supervised by them. It was not until the 2003 Criminal Justice Act that a system of home visits to registered sex offenders was introduced, with frequency initially based on risk levels, with the lowest risk offenders, level 1, set to receive one home visit per year, with more for higher risk offenders, on a set pattern related to level. It is clear that, the police force, suddenly finding itself responsible for a whole new level of community protection, were not adequately funded for these new tasks. By 2017, the national police chiefs' council (NPCC) decided enough was enough and that a mandatory number of visits did not match individual's risks and, perhaps more importantly, were a huge resource drain for those offenders at the lowest level, 1, which formed 98% of total MAPPA cases (see below). The NPCC (2017) decided that in future, visits would be decided by a tailored approach, rather than one size fits all. Officers would determine the frequency of home visits as part of a holistic risk management plan. Success in future would not be judged simply on the completion of a visit, but on the quality of the risk management plan.

There were some early concerns about the SOR. One of these centred on those convicted sex offenders NOT to be included on the Register because they were convicted before the 1997 Sex Offender Act. There were approximately 110,000 sex offenders in the community not eligible for registration, but any retrospective action was rejected in the parliamentary debate on the bill (Thomas, 2008, p. 87). At the opposite extreme, another concern was that a caution for a sexual offence would qualify the person for registration, even though this was not considered in the original bill. Gillespie (1998) had concerns over this development. In his view offences are either atypical (therefore cautionable) or they are typical (therefore not cautionable). He did not believe they could be both. In similar vein, Thomas (2008, p. 89) suggested that they were arguably for people thought unlikely to re-offend and therefore not needing to be prosecuted. Registration, he believed, was premised on precisely the opposite idea, that sex offenders *will* reoffend. There have been a number of changes to the registration process since its introduction. These have inevitably followed a strengthening trend; for example, reducing the time allowed to first register (Sex Offenders Act, 2003), reporting in person, annual risk assessment of all registered offenders by MAPPA and police allowed to force entry into offender's home for purposes of risk assessment (Violent Crime Reduction Act, 2006 – for a summary of changes see Thomas, 2008). One notable absence from the changes, although small steps have been taken towards it, has been that of community notification. It was the abduction and murder of Sarah Payne in 2000 that really brought this issue to public attention. Her murderer, a convicted sex offender on the register, was Roy Whiting. It might be argued that this fact enabled the police to narrow down their investigation and catch the killer more quickly than they might have. For many campaigners though, it was almost the opposite – the killer was on the register but still managed to abduct and murder a child. The News of the World (then a newspaper with a large circulation) ran a *For Sarah* campaign (see Savage and Charman, 2010, for a review of this case), calling for widespread community notification of sex offenders, i.e. those on the register. It might be said that this campaign met with limited success in the face of a good deal of opposition, notably from those among the police, who foresaw vigilante violence being an outcome. A notorious example of this occurred in a housing estate on the outskirts of Portsmouth, where residents had formed themselves into a group known as Residents against Paedophiles (RAP). For a few days in August 2000, these people protested outside of the homes of a list of 20 people said to be paedophiles, one of whom was a paediatrician. A known paedophile, living on the estate for 2 years, was 'outed' by the News of the World campaign, his flat burgled and damage caused to cars and the local housing office (see Golding, 2010 and Williams & Thompson, 2004a, 2004b). Following this and disturbances elsewhere in the country, the NoW stopped its campaign for full community notification, although Thomas (2008, p. 92) argues that it remained a 'spectre at the feast' for many years. In its place came a provision in the 2008 Criminal Justice and Immigration Act that allowed the police to reveal information about offenders on the SOR, if requested, to parents or guardians (known as Sarah's Law). There was also a presumption to disclose if there were children known to be in a household. This might be viewed as British compromise.

It is extremely difficult to know if the SOR actually works, as it is a near impossibility to demonstrate that something *has not* happened and that this was a result of offender registration. Although writing the best part of two decades ago,

Thomas (2008) described the SOR in these terms: 'it is arguably a prime example of criminal justice policy made at a political level in response to perceived populist demands and with no real supporting experience or research to support it'. This is, in our view, a reasonable description of most public protection legislation. The SOR is essentially a passive measure. It mostly requires offenders to produce information about themselves or to refrain from certain activities, although these types of requirements are nothing like those routinely issued in the United States, particularly self-identification through bumper stickers or a particular colour of paint on the front door. Residence requirements may see offenders having to live miles away from many urban settlements. It is important to remember that registration is not in itself a punishment of the court, it is a consequence of that punishment. It is a fairly weak monitoring system with little in the way of active involvement from state agencies. One way of adding to the control of sex offenders is the creation of a number of *civil* orders, not requiring the commission of an offence, but more the display of risky behaviour. The first of these followed on from a Home Office (1997) document called, *Community Protection Order: A Consultation Paper,* and was initially referred to as a community protection order. This was quickly renamed a Sex Offender Order (SOO) and was introduced in the Crime and Disorder Act, 1998. The order was intended for those who had fallen outside of the provisions of the Sex Offenders Act, 1997, and one assumes in particular, the requirements to register. The orders could be requested by the police or other official agencies and may well reflect the concerns of the public. The terms of the Order had to be negative, that is, to refrain from certain activities or keep away from certain areas. These types of measures, mirror many of the community notification laws in the United States. There were early concerns with this Order, notably that an offence was not required to trigger a potentially substantial infringement of liberty and that conditions could be drawn very broadly and be expansive in scope. One example, from Avon and Somerset Constabulary (Shute, 2004) demonstrates the point. An order was granted with the following conditions on the offender:

- Not to seek contact with any child or young person under 16.
- Not associate with or befriend a child under 16.
- Not reside in a private dwelling where a child under 16 is present.
- Not to undertake any activity (paid, voluntary or recreational), which is likely to result in contact with a child under 16.

Cherie Booth QC appealed against the conditions in the High Court, but the Appeal was dismissed by Lord Bingham who said, in effect, the measures sought to avoid the suffering of future victims – allowing action *before a crime could be committed.* Any loss of offender rights was, in other words, offset by a gain in the greater public good. These orders, requiring a civil standard of proof or the balance of probabilities, are not regarded as a punitive disposal, but it is clear that the conditions themselves can prove very onerous for the offender. Part of the Appeal mentioned above is that conditions were so restrictive that a breach was almost inevitable. As we have seen earlier, a criminal penalty is the likely outcome in breach cases, with up to 5 years in custody, a very significant sentence for not committing a crime. In 2014, SOPOs disappeared from the statute books, to be replaced by Sexual Harm Prevention Order (SHPOs). These two orders are very similar in their provisions, with one notable exception. The three-part test for SOPOs was 1. Is it necessary? 2. To protect the public? 3. From serious sexual harm? With the introduction of SHPOs in the Anti-Social Behaviour, Crime and Policing Act, 2014, the word 'serious' was dropped from the sexual harm criteria – at a stroke lowering the threshold and therefore including many more, less serious behaviours. The same Act also introduced a Sexual Risk Order, which can be made by a court in respect of an individual who has perpetrated an act of a sexual nature and who, as a result, is reasonably believed to pose a risk of harm to the Public in the UK or to children or vulnerable adults abroad. For an SRO to be imposed, the individual does not need to have committed a relevant (or any) offence.

Themes emerging from the growth of protection orders are an increasing use of a criminal standard of proof or the balance of probabilities, in many cases a conviction is not required (risky behaviour instead), a previous history is usually necessary, orders cannot require engagement in activities, orders are therefore largely prohibitive and restrictive and finally, any breach of these orders is a criminal offence carrying a maximum of 5 years in prison and can last from 2 years to an indefinite period of time. These orders can represent a massive intrusion into a person's life and, to make the point clear, are largely based on *anticipated* behaviour or offending. However, a major departure from this trend occurred in the Police, Crime Sentencing and Courts Act, 2022. This Act allowed for both prohibitions and positive requirements to be included in orders. In essence, this puts the civil orders, often not imposed for a crime but, to put it crudely, for a suspicion, on the same footing as a criminal, community penalty by allowing for a requirement to attend an offending behaviour group for example, or be subject to electronic monitoring. The number of protective orders, as outlined by the College of Policing in 2021, covers an extensive range of behaviours and it is worth listing some of these which have caused public and therefore political concern in recent years.

- Domestic violence protection notice order (Crime and Security Act, 2010)
- Female genital mutilation protection orders
- Forced marriage protection orders
- Non-molestation orders (Family Law Act, 1996)
- Restraining order (Protection from Harassment Act, 1997)
- Sexual harm prevention order
- Sexual risk order
- Slavery and trafficking prevention and risk order
- Stalking protection order
- Violent offender order (VOO) (Criminal Justice and Immigration Act, 2008)

In many respects, all roads in the public protection area lead to different types of detention, from indeterminate sentences, to extended sentences, to mandatory minimum sentences and as a penalty for breaching civil (non-criminal) sanctions. There has also been a significant impact on orders supervised and managed by the probation service, which we will discuss further in Chapter six. However, we cannot conclude this chapter without mentioning one of the most enduring public protection developments and one which, almost at a stroke, made public protection everyone's business, the Multi Agency Public Protection Arrangements (MAPPA). We talk a little more about the formation of MAPPA in the terrorism chapter, as the government now regard multi-agency working as the default response to all serious crime. It was the 2000 Criminal Justice and Court Services Act which made the police and probation services 'responsible authorities' with a mandate to work together, share information and work towards the risk assessment and management of known serious and high-risk offenders. The initial model was very much based around well-established child protection conferences, which had brought agencies together and also served as a model for embryonic potentially dangerous offender (PDO) conferences (Nash, 1999a, 1999b, pp. 114–121). These two distinct services might not have been expected to work well together but the history of MAPPA suggests that collaboration and information-sharing have not been as problematic as anticipated. We do, in chapter eight, refer to work which examines the cultural transference between these agencies, in contrast perhaps to concerns expressed by the intelligence services over sharing with those lacking security clearances. In the 2003 Criminal Justice Act, the MAPPA family was considerably extended to include the prison service as the third responsible authority and additionally, a range of other agencies were added under a 'duty to cooperate'. These included housing, education, health and youth offending teams among others. In fact, almost anyone who could contribute useful information could be invited. The bottom line appeared to be, many agencies with one brief – protect the public. In our view, the idea of MAPPA is an excellent one, but the sheer size of the caseload renders at best superficial, the degree of involvement and oversight that can be given.

Summary

It is difficult to see a carefully thought-through, evidence-based approach to public protection sentencing since the 1990s. Laws are increasingly passed as a response to rare, but nonetheless awful and tragic crimes. Unfortunately, each new law is passed on a wave of public emotion and sometimes real fear, with, often unsubstantiated promises offering greater security and safety for the public. Each new measure claims to be tougher than the last, closing loopholes (which had been missed because the previous legislation was rushed and ill-thought out) and cracking down, in seeking to eliminate, rare but scary behaviour. So-called errors are equally met with changes in policy and legislation, even though dealing with dangerous people is a very difficult process. Errors, if that is what they are to be called, are more likely to be a result of overwhelming work pressures and the sheer unpredictability of human behaviour. The significant expansion of those eligible for whole-life sentences leaves little room for the government to manoeuvre, short of bringing back the death penalty. It remains to be seen how much more widely these eligibility criteria can be drawn, or how much more release can be curtailed for fixed sentence prisoners or even 'normal' indeterminate sentences. At the time of writing, the Conservative government is threatening to leave the ECHR. Although this is mostly connected with its Rwanda migrant policy, the ECHR has been seen as an impediment to the government's more punitive desires and leaving it would remove one more obstacle. As ever, financial conditions will be instrumental as the prison population continues to spiral and nearly all the developments described in this chapter result in one certainty. This is that more people will spend longer in custody as they are unable to secure their release and the result of that, is a population heading towards 90,000 and beyond. Public protection has truly replaced community rehabilitation in a world dominated by risk assessment and in which the risk is all bad.

Chapter 3

The Agencies of Public Protection: Prisons, Parole and the Police

Prisons – Keeping In or Letting Out?

There can be little doubt that a majority of the public would support the use of imprisonment for those convicted of seriously harmful crimes against others. The rationale for this is that by taking away the liberty of these offenders and removing them from the streets, public safety would be ensured. At its simplest level, this view is difficult to argue against. Not only is there a safety element to this line of thinking, there is also a matter of punishment for awful crimes, of retribution and just desserts. It is impossible to imagine a politician going before the electorate to argue for shorter sentences for violent or sexual offenders, or indeed for sentences other than custody. Punitive demands are constantly fed by very often prurient mass coverage in the media of every serious (personal) crime. This exacerbates the over-simplified 'us and them' rhetoric, backed by strong moral underpinnings – morals that these offenders allegedly do not have or share. Prison is, since the abolition of the death penalty in the UK in 1965, the most severe sentence available to the courts. The gravity of crimes is marked by the severity or length of the sentence and increasingly, in the most serious cases, by sentences without end. Prisons therefore have a crucial role to play in protecting the public from seriously harmful offenders, by keeping them safely contained for as long as required. Yet fewer questions are asked about what should happen to these long-term prisoners whilst they are in custody. When the place of prison is debated publicly, it tends to be concerned with the length of sentences or the 'soft' nature of regimes. Politicians, in public, find it difficult to present an alternative to the generally punitive prisons agenda, although official statements do more frequently discuss reformative and rehabilitative intent. That said, where dangerous offenders are concerned, there are very few prepared to depart from a preventive and punitive rhetoric. In this section, we will briefly outline the purpose of prisons and in particular, the role they play in public protection.

Place and Purpose

What is clear from the history of punishment, is that debates about the purpose of prison are not new. However, before considering historical events, let us begin in the modern day with a speech from then Secretary of State for Justice, David Gauke at the Royal Society of Arts (6th March, 2018). He said, 'I am clear that offenders go to prison *as* punishment, not *for* punishment...I want prisons to be places of humanity, hope and aspiration'. Two years earlier, a speech from Prime Minister David Cameron, made clear that (prisons) 'must offer chances to change...we should offer hope'. Going further back to 1910, but still with the Conservative Party, Winston Churchill famously said '...there is a treasure, if you can find it, in the heart of every man' (Flynn, 2002, p. 3). The Gladstone Committee of 1895 had endorsed the twin aims of deterrence and rehabilitation, suggesting that more individualised programmes of treatment should be followed to maintain, stimulate and awaken the higher susceptibilities of prisoner (Flynn, 2002, p. 32). The committee's report drew a sharp dividing line with much of the history of prisons in the 19th century where, regimented and harsh regimes played out what were regarded by many, as the twin aims of imprisonment, punishment and deterrence (see Potter, 2019, for a detailed and lively historical account). Potter makes clear however that the 19th century was not bereft of reforming, or even humanitarian, sentiment towards prisoners. Rather, that this 'soft' approach had been seen to fail, not least in the face of a number of serious prison riots. Edward Du Cane, who became chair of the three prison commissioners in 1873, believed that prisons were for punishment and not reform. His slogan, 'hard labour, hard board and hard fare', epitomised his attitude (Flynn, 2002, p. 131). He also believed in solitary confinement, short-cropped hair and a distinctive uniform covered in broad arrows with the same pattern on work boots weighing 14 pounds. An arrow pattern was hammered into the soles so that the prisoner left his mark everywhere. Du Cane used scientific knowledge to establish how much hard labour could be extracted from a prisoner for the minimum input in terms of food and rest. It was established and rolled out in prisons across the country that a prisoner could spend six hours on the treadmill, ascend 8,640 feet, on curtailed sleep and a scientific starvation diet of oatmeal, bread and water (Potter, 2019, p. 308).

The 19th century also reveals another current trend in terms of the interest, if not passion, the media has in all matters penal. They had targeted Sir Joshua Jebb, who as Chairman of the Board of Convict Prisons, had established a humane regime philosophy which was heavy on gratuities, remission and release without supervision. However, a riot at Chatham prison shifted opinions (although ironically it was not an establishment following his more humanitarian regime) and Jebb's response was regarded as too lenient. The press lampooned him as the convicts' friend (a slur once commonly said of the probation service); *The Examiner* urged him to put on a Fat Prisoner Show (like Fat Cattle shows) demonstrating the generous jail diets, whilst a cartoon in *Punch* depicted a feast in Jebb's Pen of Pet Lambs. As Potter (2019, p. 295) explained, ridicule, not reason, became the most effective weapon against rehabilitation and reform. We do not have the space in this volume to consider a full history of prisons, indeed, it would shift us from our focus; we would commend Potter's (2019) work for those interested in this subject. What does emerge from any reading of prisons' history, is the rise and fall in importance of words such as punishment, deterrence, soft regimes, rehabilitation and reform. It is to the ideas underpinning these words that we shall now turn, specifically in the context of prisoners committing the types of crime that are the subject of this book and whether, or not, they should have any of the hope expressed by David Cameron. It is of course a mistake to believe that behind the simple word 'prisons', lies a uniformity of purpose and shared aims. For example, the prisons estate is made up of a variety of establishments which differ by security classifications, by age of inmates, by sex (but note the range of issues arising from transgender women prisoners) and with huge differences in the quality of the actual buildings, with a large number of poorly maintained Victorian establishments still in operation. Drake (2012, p. 2) suggests that prisons serve five purposes; rehabilitation, incapacitation, deterrence, general prevention and the delivery of justice and we should remember that these purposes are delivered (or attempted to be delivered) to an extremely wide offending group, a broad age range, with huge sentence length variations and with patchy provision of rehabilitative programmes. We, however, are interested in prisoners who have committed very serious crimes, usually of a personal nature, for whom the public has nothing but contempt and would prefer the key to be thrown away – or at least, this is what the media want us to believe. What should be done with these people, if the nature of their crimes render notions of rehabilitation seemingly meaningless?

Former Secretary of State for Justice, Dominic Raab, announced in the Forward to the Prisons Strategy White Paper (2021) that 'Prisons keep people safe by taking dangerous criminals off our streets, but they can only bring down crime and keep the public safe in the longer-term, if they properly reform and rehabilitate offenders'. This is an interesting statement in that it contains two contradictory tendencies. Firstly, we see a conflationary depiction of all prisoners as 'dangerous', but then, having said this, promoting the need for a reformative regime. Incapacitation is also cited as a major factor by the former Director of Rehabilitation and Care in the Scottish Prison Service (Spencer, 2007) who said:

> ...there are dangerous offenders, those who perpetrate murder and violence, sexual offenders, terrorists and those responsible for serious organised crime, for whom prison is an appropriate response in order to protect the public from their brand of menace and reduce potential victimisation. It is a legitimate use of custody to incapacitate those who would otherwise continue to seriously harm the public.

In yet another strategy document, Labour Home Secretary Charles Clarke announced that:

> ...we must keep the public safe from violent and dangerous people. We need to make sure that we are keeping the right people in prison and that dangerous people are imprisoned for as long as necessary, that we are protecting the public effectively and that prisons are fit for purpose. Home Office (2006)

The introduction of Indeterminate Sentences for Public Protection, discussed in the legislation chapter, were intended to meet Clarke's plan to keep dangerous people 'inside' for as long as necessary – however this period has grown and grown over time without clear, unambiguous evidence, that it remains 'necessary'.

There is no doubt that prisons have huge, symbolic significance. They serve as a physical reminder that it is a place for 'them' and not 'us'. Prisons serve as a means by which, because some people have been 'removed', the rest of society can feel different and apart from these 'others'. Drake (2012, p. 6) makes the point that these others are regarded as posing threats to security and safety and that the use of imprisonment for some, will enable the law-abiding to gain higher levels of security and personal safety. Drake argues in her book that the increasing state focus on security, forecloses many of the discussions about the reforming possibilities of imprisonment; instead increasing the stress on deterrence and punishment. By focussing on dangerous individuals, the state is more easily able to justify the expansion of imprisonment, but with the majority of prisoners not falling into the seriously harmful category, but rather, as authors such as Bell (2014) argue, coming from a much larger group of social and economic causalities of neo-liberal economic policies. She argues that penal policy aims more at rallying the rest of society around the neo-liberal project by constructing (criminals) as a suitable enemy and scapegoat for the social fallout of the neoliberal project (2014, p. 10). Incarceration, rather than an expansion, or even maintenance, of the welfare state has become the normal response to social and crime problems. In Bell's words, 'the security state has replaced the welfare state' (2014, p. 10). Ian Loader (2006) described what he termed three *public* philosophies of punishment; Doing Harm, Making Good and Doing the Necessary Minimum. For our purposes, the first of these appears to fit most aptly the approach to serious offenders, acting as a flagship for criminal justice policy. As Loader explains, in his view the public are conceptualised not as actually wanting to do harm, but as in favour of the system being harsh, austere and expansive. Punishment is (or should be) pain; crime-related emotions are anger, fear and vengeance and the response should be public protection policies. This philosophy, Loader argues, has escalated the size of the prison population and seen a growth in indeterminate sentences, criminalisation of young people, public distaste for parole and the offender framed as a 'dangerous other', the rightful object of exclusion and banishment.

In the chapter on legislation, we have described the broad trends over the past three decades as: increasing the length of sentences, introducing mandatory minimum sentences, indeterminate sentences for public protection, extending the scope of life sentences and introducing compulsory whole life tariffs. If these developments are added to the changed emphasis in parole deliberations towards much greater caution, then it is easy to see that the prison population will increase, regardless of any change in crime rates. Many of these changes are aimed at high risk and potentially dangerous, serious offenders. However, in the wake of these policies, other offenders, crimes and sentences, are dragged upwards in a huge symbolic show of the might of the security state.

Dangerous Offenders – Getting What They Deserve?

Within the move towards a more expansive and punitive penal state, also lies an attack on rights, an attack that is often justified by the alleged moral status of the offender or prisoner. By categorising offenders who commit the most seriously harmful crimes in this way, it is but a short step to argue that their 'otherness' implies a lack of the moral code possessed by the rest of society, i.e. those who are not offenders. This lack of morality implies that these offenders are not deserving of the same rights as others. It is this rationale that has been taken into the debate about the legality of whole life tariffs and, in particular, their introduction as a mandatory disposal in particular situations. In simple terms, a life without parole sentence means that there is no review period for release and is, in effect, what is termed in the US, 'sentenced to death' in prison rather than 'sentenced to life'. In recent years, British governments have been keen to expand the use of life imprisonment and in particular, the use of those sentences without a hope of release. In certain respects, however, their ambitions have been thwarted by the European Court of Human Rights and in particular Article 3, 'No one shall be subject to torture or to inhuman or degrading treatment or punishment'.

Alongside the question of who goes to prison and for how long is the fundamentally important issue of what needs to happen to them if their future potential for harm is to be reduced? As we have seen, seriously harmful violent and sexual offenders, alongside terrorist related offenders, are seen as a prima facie justification for long sentences of imprisonment. And, as we have also seen, this focus on the extremities of serious offending can escalate the nature of the response to all offenders by, for example, increasing sentence lengths and restricting early release. As for the people who commit these crimes, they are invariably labelled as 'monsters' and considered almost to be non-human. As such, they do not merit the same considerations and rights as the law-abiding majority, or even perhaps, as other 'normal' offenders. In her excellent book, Drake (2012) explores the word that often accompanies the epithet 'monster' and that is 'evil'. Drawing on a range of sources, she describes how the concept of evil acts as a short-cut into penal concepts such as punishment, banishment and exclusion. Furthermore, she explains how, in her view, this idea precludes any discussion of the reformative potential of imprisonment, instead upping the importance of imprisonment *for* punishment. Implicit in this approach is the belief in the personal, or character-based causes, of seriously harmful violent crime at the expense of any exploration of the impact of social conditions and structures. This focus on the individual, sees evil as a trait in some people, but not others, a trait which is not, according to many, amenable to treatment or change. Drake (2012, pp. 6–10) argues that the concept of personal evil may well serve other purposes in the wider deployment of state power, for example enabling the symbolic function of prisons and punishment to be justified rather than discussions of structural inequalities as a causal factor in violence. She also suggests that as people find extremely harmful behaviour difficult to process as a human action, it is easier to believe that it is the monsters and others who are to blame.

The Containment of Long-Term Prisoners

If some offenders are cast as so different from others that extraordinary means become justified, then the issue arises of how they should serve their sentences and in what conditions? Not only are internal regime discussions very important, but equally, another prime rationale for custody is very important, namely the desire to keep these potentially dangerous prisoners from escaping. How this might be achieved has been an enduring discussion among penal practitioners for years. For example, should a massively secure perimeter permit a more liberal, reforming regime 'inside'? Or should the regime itself be highly restrictive; essentially punitive in nature, with a strong emphasis on deterrence and indeed, pure punishment? If the latter is chosen, will the regime become increasingly brutalised and if so, what are the likely effects on prisoners? As Gilligan (2000, p. 767) remarks, 'when people are actively dangerous towards others we may need to confine them for a period of time in locked facilities – but to punish people only constitutes further violence on our part and causes further violence on the criminal's part'. We are back then, to considering the balance to be struck in prisons between reform and punishment.

In the UK, periodic, but very rare, high profile prison escapes are always a trigger for major introspection over the nature of regimes and security. Drake (2012, p. 33), summarises the period 1968–94, as a continual grappling with the tensions of implementing a liberal regime (the hopes of Loader's Platonic Guardians perhaps) aimed at rehabilitation, minimising the negative effects of long-term custody, whilst attempting to establish security and control. These discussions were not solely internal navel gazing, however, as debates took place under the gaze of penal reformers, penal populists, a sensation driven media, victims' lobbies and a private sector anxious to gain a bigger slice of the penal pie. Just as the awful child murders committed by Ian Brady and Myra Hindley (the Moors Murders) reignited the debate over the suspension and abolishing of the death penalty, then so high-profile escapes have a similar impact on public views about prison security. The mid-1960s saw the escape of two Great Train Robbers, Charlie Wilson in 1964, from Winson Green in Birmingham (very unusual in that three men *broke into* the jail to release him) and Ronnie Biggs from Wandsworth in 1965, more mundanely using a rope ladder. George Blake, a spy working for the Secret Intelligence Service (MI6) but also working for the Soviet Union, escaped from Wormwood Scrubs in 1966; three high-profile escapes which severely dented public confidence. As a response to this, the government set up a Committee to Report into Prison Escapes and Security (The Mountbatten Report, Home Office, 1966). This report contained a number of recommendations, some of which have endured and others have not. For example, an increase in dog patrols and CCTV would not seem unusual today, but the two main recommendations received a mixed reception. Mountbatten's key point was that a fortress style prison should be built to house *all* dangerous prisoners in one place. He suggested this be called *Vectis* and be built on the Isle of Wight. This idea did not find favour at the Home Office – nor one imagines, among those living on the Island. It was felt that the risks from a mass break out were too great in one place and that staffing, control and design would prove difficult. The other main recommendation did find favour, to the extent that it has remained unchanged until this day. As Price (2000, p. 1) suggests, Mountbatten is more famous for a proposal that *did not* become policy (Vectis) than for one that did – a system of security classification. The system proposed four categories, essentially based upon the risk posed to the public were the prisoner to escape. Category A would become maximum security and was aimed at those whose escape would pose a serious risk to the public or security of the state. The next category, B, was intended for those who did pose a risk but were deemed not to need maximum security, but should still be securely detained. Category C was felt to be those who lacked the resource to escape but did not have the stability necessary to be kept where there is no barrier to escape. Finally, Category D was for those who could be reasonably trusted to serve their sentences in open conditions; this to include higher category prisoners nearing the end of their sentence. Sitting alongside the risk of escape criteria, was one which stipulated that prisoners should be kept in the least secure category that was warranted – prisoners should not be kept in high security conditions unnecessarily. A decision still needed to be taken as to exactly where these newly classified prisoners should be housed. The government's response was to set up a sub-committee of the Advisory Council on the Penal System, under Sir Leon Radzonowicz which reported in 1968. His main recommendation was that high risk, category A prisoners should be *dispersed* among a number of high security establishments, the opposite of Mountbatten's concentration policy. In essence, this would mean a small number of category A prisoners living among a larger number of category B prisoners. Both the dispersal system and security classification are still in use today, the only difference being that the prisons being used as dispersals have changed slightly.

It is not difficult to anticipate that mixing two groups of prisoners in one establishment, with different security needs, could pose problems and difficulties for the type of regime offered. Would all prisoners be subject to the same level of security and at what level would that be pitched? In a sense this took the discussion back to secure perimeters or secure regimes. Optimistically, it was felt that the majority of non-category A prisoners would exert a positive influence on those tagged as needing maximum security, but clearly if all were subjected to a restrictive regime, this would have been unlikely to be successful. Although in principle, the plan was to mix prisoners and thereby modify behaviour, in reality Category A prisoners were often housed together in what was in effect, a prison within a prison. As Drake (2012, p. 46) notes '...the dispersal policy proved to be fraught by seemingly irresolvable problems of order, control and safety, as well as the persistence of punitive practices, which undermined attempts to create humane and liberal prison experiences'. It was to be continuing problems with disorder, rather than escapes from dispersal prisons (at least until 1987), that kept discussions about security and therefore the nature of regimes, high on the prisons' agenda. In an environment fuelled by law and order discourses, the notion of 'war' inspired by politicians such as Nixon, Reagan and Bush in the US, the rhetoric of Margaret Thatcher and her Home Secretary Michael Howard, all combined to render any attempt to provide liberal and constructive regimes in prison, extremely difficult. As Drake succinctly summarises this period, 'the problems with disorder would not be recognised as a symptom of the contradictions and failures associated with the practice of imprisonment, but would instead, come to be constructed as the result of liberal policies' (2012, p. 49). There were no escapes from dispersal prisons for the first 19 years but they were beset by control problems such as riots, fires and hostage taking.

The audacious helicopter aided escape from HMP Gartree of two category A prisoners in 1987 was not only a shock to the public but also to prison authorities and the government. An inquiry under the chairmanship of the Deputy Director General, G. Lakes, recommended a range of measures to strengthen day to day security. These included regime changes making it difficult for prisoners to know their exact whereabouts at given times, high-level observation platforms and strong cables to prevent helicopter landings. As Home Secretary Douglas Hurd reported to the House of Commons (HC Deb., 1988), 'The current system of dispersal prisons was designed to contain highly dangerous prisoners securely. It also has to provide satisfactory regimes which allow control to be maintained'. This apparent tension between security/containment and safe/positive regimes has in many ways been determined by the long-term prison population, but has ramifications throughout the prison estate. Just as the publicity given to serious crimes can increase demands for severer sentencing, then prison escapes or disturbances fuel the calls for tighter security and harsher or less permissive regimes. Scott (2007, p. 53) summarised this ongoing process as '...dispersal policy led to a heightened focus on security (which) impacted perimeter and regimes, security was privileged at the expense of humanitarian goals. Prison life was characterised by a profound intensification and vigorous enforcement of the priorities of discipline, surveillance and control'. We do not have space in this volume to examine in detail the myriad of Inquiries and Committees formed from the 1960s onwards, although it is probably fair to say that these were almost exclusively *reactive,* a response to the latest crisis rather than a seriously long-term vision for custody in this country.

We have already briefly discussed the Mountbatten and Radzinowicz Reports, and should also mention Woodcock (1994) and Learmont (1995), both of these coming in the wake of escapes from Parkhurst (three prisoners) and Whitemoor (six prisoners). The Whitemoor incident was particularly disturbing because the prisoners escaped from a Special Security Unit. As the subsequent Inquiry revealed, the prisoners were able to manufacture a range of tools to facilitate their escape as well as accumulating a large sum of cash. Most disturbing of all was the subsequent prison search which revealed the presence of the explosive Semtex.

The liberal regime within Whitemoor was cast as the villain of the piece resulting, it was argued, in confusion among prison officers concerning what their role was meant to be. This confusion should not have been unexpected given the contents of other reports from that period. For example, the May Committee (1979) was established to consider pay and conditions of staff, the size of the prison population, capacity for control, security and treatment; a response to what was described as 'concerted indiscipline'. There was an indifferent response to the May Report, not least because the actual committee almost totally lacked any experience of prisons. The Committee did however push the idea of 'positive custody', arguing that treatment and training had had its day. In evidence to the committee, academics King and Morgan (1980) had championed 'humane containment', an idea that was unceremoniously rejected. In retort, King and Morgan (1980, p. 25) made their frustrations clear:

> Prisons have always been human warehouses and in some sense always must be. What the May committee appears not to recognise is that prisons have sometimes been *inhuman* warehouses. For our part we think that the difference between inhuman warehouses and human warehouses is important.

By 1985, another initiative, one might almost say catchphrase, entered the lexicon. In his report, A Sense of Direction, Ian Dunbar, coined the term 'dynamic security', which entailed, among other things, prison staff *talking* to prisoners as a way of gaining intelligence. In 1988, HMPS described themselves as '...serving the public by keeping in custody those committed by the courts. Our duty is to look after them with humanity and help them lead law-abiding and useful lives in custody and on release'.

Tough Talk, More Prisoners

The huge Woolf Report (1991) was, according to Home Secretary Kenneth Baker, to provide the blueprint for penal policies for the next 25 years (Scott, 2007, p. 59), yet, within 2 years, had been 'blown out of the water' (Scott, 2007, p. 62). Woolf had been keen that prisoners did not leave prison embittered and disaffected as a result of an *unjust* experience. Looking to develop positive and educational regimes, the committee had to be clear that they were not looking to mollycoddle prisoners, 'we are not seeking to achieve more comfortable surroundings or increased privileges for prisoners for their own sakes'. What did the damage to Woolf was a hawkish Home Secretary in Michael Howard, declaring that 'Prison Works' in his 1993 Conservative Party conference speech. Tuning into, or more likely shaping, the public mood, Howard wanted the end of 'holiday camps' (prisons) and their replacement by tough, decent, but austere regimes. For those who doubt the power of politics to shape policy, the rise in the prison population by 52% from 1992–1996 is evidence of how the words of politicians may be more powerful than the actions of some criminals. This idea was well expressed by the Prison Reform Trust (PRT, 2021b, p. 5) when they said:

> ...it seems reasonable to conclude...that changes in sentencing have not been driven by a change in the actual incidence of serious sexual, violent and drug related crime during the last 20-30 years. That is not to say there may not have been changes in levels of public concern, simply that such concern derives from other factors. These may include the publicity given to exceptional cases and the desire on the part of political parties to signal their stance on serious offending to the electorate.

Scott (2007, p. 64) suggested that 'the highly objectionable visions of Learmont, Woodcock and Howard (now) shaped the contours of imprisonment'. These views influenced both the nature of imprisonment and the numbers of people experiencing it. The legacy is a population which is massively larger, virtually doubling from the 1990s to 2010, older with those over 50 increasing from 7% in 2002 to 17% in 2023, and serving longer, with 40% of determinate sentences being 4 years plus in 2013 rising to 56% in 2023 (Sturge, 2023). The PRT (2023a, 2023b) reported that 43,000 were sent to prison in 2022, with 61% of those being for a non-violent offence and 38% for less than 6 months. In essence, everything to do with imprisonment was getting longer and larger. The average sentence for serious indictable offences is now over 62 months, 2 years longer than 20 years earlier. The average period served in custody by mandatory lifers was 13 years in 2000 and 21 years in 2021. The minimum term imposed (the tariff) had increased in average from 13 years in 2000 to 21 years in 2021. There are nearly 8,000 prisoners serving life sentences, with 7,150 yet to be released, and 22% already beyond their tariff. Overall, there are twice as many serving indeterminate sentences as there were 20 years ago. The replacement for the IPP sentence, the Extended Detention Sentence, introduced in 2012, has already exceeded the numbers of former IPP sentences (PRT, 2023a, 2023b).

Despite violent crimes involving serious injury falling by 44% between 2009 and 2019 (ONS, 2017), the ever upward punitive spiral shows no signs of abating. Rather than the numbers of serious crimes, it is the excessive attention given to particular crimes that feeds an anxious public and fuels ever-tougher measures. At the time of writing, this penal journey has ended in a total prisons crisis over numbers and resulted in some fanciful ideas to solve the crisis and others more familiar to students of history. *The Guardian* newspaper reported (6 October 2023) that the UK government was in negotiations with Estonia to rent surplus prison places from them. This idea was mentioned by Justice Secretary of State Alex Chalk, at the Conservative Party Conference in October 2023. No doubt a popular idea at conference, a likely less popular measure was delayed until after the conference. This entailed a number of early release schemes for certain classes of prisoners to reduce numbers with immediate effect. This idea had not been mentioned at Conference as it was considered redolent of measures introduced by Tony Blair in 2007, which had met with claims of his government being 'soft on criminals'. The new proposals were outlined in 'The Government's Approach to Criminal Justice; presented to Parliament by Justice Secretary Alex Chalk on 16 October 2023. Early release would apply to those due to be released between 16 October and 12 December 2023, who had not been convicted of serious offences such as violence, sexual offences or terrorism. The Government did not put a figure on possible numbers but the Guardian speculated that it would be in the thousands. Those released would be liable to strict supervision including GPS tracking and extended curfews. Those who failed during their albeit brief licence period would be returned to custody to serve the entire period of the original sentence. Initially announced as a temporary scheme responding to a temporary crisis, the measure was made permanent in March 2024. At the same time, provision was made to extend the 35-day early release to a maximum of 60 days. Concerns were immediately raised about the possibility of domestic abusers being released without adequate risk assessment (*The Guardian*, 11 March 2024). Interestingly, the election of a Labour government on 4 July 2024 neither changed the policy or rhetoric of the previous Conservative government. To tackle what was regarded as the total collapse of the prison system and leading to a breakdown of law and order, eligible prisoners would be released after serving 40% of their sentence, rather than the 50 under the Conservatives. The conflationary Conservative rhetoric described earlier, however, has seemingly been continued by the new Justice Minister Shabana Mahmood, when she described van loads of prisoners circling the country with nowhere to go and looters running amok, robbing shops and setting neighbourhoods alight (BBC News, 12 July 2024, https://www.bbc.co.uk/news/articles/crg5vp0296eo).

This latest policy development, fuelled as we mentioned earlier by a prisons numbers crisis, epitomises the difficulties for politicians in this area. The Conservatives, always keen to proclaim their law and order credentials, were seen as the cause of the crisis by Andrea Albutt, President of the Prison Governors' Association, when she described prison places as 'bust', because of a lurch to the right by Ministers, 'we have a government intent on locking up more people for longer and making it more difficult for them to be released' (The Guardian, 9th October 2023). She regarded the Government's negotiations with Estonia to rent prison places as 'mindboggling'. The conundrum for Government was to seek ways to reduce the population whilst not appearing to be too soft, or too much like Labour. The chosen method was interesting if not shot through with contradictions. The plan was to wrap up the so-called softer measures in a package of more traditionally tough changes, with the target being rapists, who would now serve the whole of their sentence in prison House of Commons (4 December 2023). In his speech to Parliament on 16 October 2023, Alex Chalk reaffirmed a familiar message that 'the first duty of any government is to keep people safe'. He went on again to argue that those who pose a danger to society must be locked up – the worst offenders shall be locked away for as long as it takes to protect the public. He went on to remind Parliament that sentences had been increased for knife crime, dangerous driving and causing or allowing the death of a child. The extension of whole-life tariff sentences was mentioned along with the point that it would become the default sentence for 'the most depraved killers'. Having outlined these previously announced measures, he then came to his major point, which was that rapists or their equivalent sexual offenders, would serve the entirety of the custodial sentence handed down to them – a 15-year sentence would mean 15 years in custody. No doubt this message went down very well with the majority of Conservative Party in Parliament and with many members of the public, as indeed did the plan to remove, at 18 months before sentence end, rather than 12 months, foreign nationals serving their sentences in British jails. The reality of making this plan a success remains to be seen. Undoubtedly, these more traditionally 'red meat' measures were needed to act as a cover for not only the number-reducing measures outlined above, but others which could well be portrayed as the Government being soft on crime.

In essence, the government had an absolute need to urgently reduce the prison population, and aside from early release, other measures were included in Chalk's speech. These entailed the possibility of giving a larger sentence discount for an even earlier guilty plea; many custodial sentences under 12 months would have a legislated-for presumption of being suspended, and there would be a drive to reduce the numbers of prison recalls for breach of licence conditions, unless for a further offence. There were broader statements in the document which perhaps reflect a more liberal ethos, in particular the point that 'prisons should not ruin the redeemable'. Acting perhaps as a mission statement for the Justice Ministry, the document claimed that:

> …we must reform the justice system so it keeps the worst of society behind bars, rehabilitates offenders who will be let out, and gives the least serious, lowest risk offenders a path away from a life of crime. And that matters because intelligent reform means less crime.

Section Summary

There is no doubt that the majority of people believe that prison is the right disposal for serious crimes and that for the most serious of those, very long or indeterminate sentences should be the norm. However, the media has almost an obsession with rare crimes and are prurient in their chasing down of personal information from victims and the police. When one of these crimes can be (however tenuously) linked to a 'professional' failing, then the intensity of media scrutiny is raised several notches. The response to serious further offence cases (SFOs – see Nash and Williams, 2008 and Chapter 7 in this volume) has seen a marked increase in personal blaming and indeed scapegoating of professional staff. The record size of the prison population is witness to the enduring popularity of punitive measures which includes much longer sentences, more indefinite sentences, restrictions on release and zealous recall practice. A prolonged focus on serious and high-risk offenders has inflated the prison population by making prisoners serve longer – if prisoners can't get out, the size of the population has to increase. The period we have reviewed has been marked by tortuous debates about the purpose of imprisonment, about the nature of regimes and the seeming competing demands of rehabilitation, security and control. The two main political parties in England and Wales have spent an awful lot of time criticising the measures of their political opponents, whilst introducing the same or even harsher when they come into power. The political needs of politicians will always ensure that criminal justice and perhaps the place of prisons in particular, will serve as a mainstay for ideas to separate blue from red. What we have reviewed shows that the same ideas do come around again (and again). Unfortunately, the continual rehashing of old (and new) measures merely serves to keep the penal rhetoric at a high pitch, with a punitive ethos seemingly constantly winning out over the long-term rehabilitation of offenders.

Parole – The Windsock of Public Protection?

The parole system, like many institutions in public life, quietly goes about its business with little interest from the public, until that is, something goes wrong. Success for the Parole Board doesn't make the news. Prisoners technically released early from their sentence who do not commit further crimes are not of interest to the public. Therefore, by definition, parole systems are measured and judged by their failures, especially if the case is high profile or notorious. In such instances, the Parole Board is blamed by a range of interested parties, in particular politicians, victims, the media and those of a penal populist stance, for released prisoners offending when they should still have been 'locked up'. This is of course an entirely simplistic and naïve view of what is a detailed, considered and evidence-based process. In this section, we will explore the parole process by considering its origins and relationship to a range of penal philosophies. We will then explore a number of key issues and challenges of recent origin; a period in which parole has become a key element in the public protection process. As former Minister for Justice Dominic Raab (2022) expressed, 'Public protection is the fundamental and overriding function of the parole system'.

What Is Parole?

For fixed-term, or determinate prisoners, parole eligibility kicks in at certain points in their sentence – these points being subject to quite frequent alterations, invariably at the behest of the government of the day and often as a response to external pressures. Typically, release may be considered as part of the parole process from the half-way or two-thirds point of sentence. Reasons for early release may include a pressing need to *reduce* the size of the prison population, parole acting as a safety valve at times of severe overcrowding. In such instances, Ministers can introduce new rules which can see the accelerated release of whole groups of prisoners. Parole is also a possibility for indeterminate prisoners; those whom do not have a fixed date for release. Indeterminate sentences are the Indeterminate Sentence for Public Protection (IPP) and the Life Sentence. IPPs were introduced in the Criminal Justice Act 2003 and first used in 2005 and abolished only 7 years later. In these indeterminate sentences, parole eligibility starts with the end of the 'tariff' imposed by the sentencing Judge. The tariff is the minimum term which must be served to meet the punishment element of the sentence. Within life sentences, the tariff term is often misunderstood by the public to be the time that *will* be served to be followed by release. In other words, an 8-year tariff in a life sentence is seen as an eight-year sentence. This is most clearly not correct. In the case of IPP sentences, there are still many prisoners without any indication of their release date, many years beyond their tariff and over a decade since the sentence was abolished (HoC Library, April 24, 2023). For those prisoners rejected in their applications, a further attempt can be made 2 years later.

Where Did the Idea Come From?

The early release of prisoners from their sentences has a long and somewhat chequered history. Interested readers are referred to Guiney (2018) for a detailed account of early release and parole schemes and we are indebted to him for the short summary that follows. As we indicated above, releasing a prisoner early from their allotted sentence is something of a bargaining situation, for those being released and for those making that decision. It needs to offer something to both 'sides' if it is to be effective. For the prisoner, the benefits are obvious. They 'get back' their lives earlier than anticipated in exchange for promises of good behaviour in the future, *provided* they have behaved well during their sentence. For the authorities, there is more than one rationale. Prison Governors might come down on the side of good order and discipline. Here we have a 'carrot' offered to the prisoner in exchange for early release. In other words, a further and non-punitive control measure is added to the prison regime and one which holds out the tantalising prospect of keeping the inmate population quiet. For governments considering the introduction of early release schemes, there is the very real and pragmatic prospect of lowering the size of the prison population if over-crowding becomes a pressing problem. This can quite easily be achieved by lowering (or indeed increasing) the period of the sentence that must be served, before early release can be considered. A codified early release system might also enhance the liberal credentials of government, *if* that is politically important at the time.

A brief delve into history reveals that there have been two main variants of early release, namely automatic and discretionary. The former is where release is triggered at fixed points of a sentence and *will* be authorised if the offender has been of good behaviour. It is therefore an unconditional release. The other method requires approval from the authorities if certain conditions have been met and its extension is dependent on continued good behaviour in the future. One system then looks to the past, and one very much to the future (Guiney, 2018, p. 8). The evidence suggests that early release schemes originated in the British colonies, when men transported there could earn a 'ticket of leave', enabling them to work and enjoy a modicum of freedom. Codified by the Select Committee on transportation in 1837–8, it was proposed that different sentence lengths could earn degrees of freedom following differentiated qualification periods. For example, a sentence of 7 years would see qualification after 4 years, a sentence of life would see qualification kick in at 8 years. These periods, linked with original sentence length, have endured ever since in terms of when automatic release is triggered or prisoners become eligible for consideration for parole release. The word parole is linked with the French chivalric tradition and in this context refers to *'parole d'honeur'* (word of honour), whereby the prisoner gave their word not to try and escape in exchange for certain freedoms in captivity. The notion of consent has also been central to much of the work of probation officers for many years, until its abolition for both practice and political reasons (Raynor, 2014).

It will not have gone unnoticed by readers, that any form of early release is fraught with potential difficulties for governments and prison authorities. The major concern, of course, is the risk that any released prisoner will go on to commit another offence at a time when they *could,* or some might argue, *should* have been in custody. It is at times such as these, that release schemes come under threat from critics of what is seen as a weak and liberal response to punishment. Cases involving serious further offences are notably problematic for governments but also for parole boards, where public confidence can quickly erode. As we noted earlier, the public is largely unaware of what the Parole Board does and how many prisoners are released on licence. They do however get to very quickly hear when cases 'go wrong'. As Sparks (2000) notes, risk comes into public focus in forensic moments. Guiney (2018) observes that, the Parole Board acts as a lightning rod for public anger. We used the word 'windsock' at the beginning of this section to indicate how the parole process reflects prevailing penal and criminal justice climates. We could equally have used thermometer, barometer, bellwether or temperature to demonstrate the fluid nature of early release and the response to it. It is very much a reflection of prevailing trends and its modern origins (parole was formally introduced in 1967) were a product of what Garland (2001) called 'penal welfarism' led by 'liberal elites' (Loader, 2006). Penal optimism had characterised the 1960s, building on a post-war consensus that crime should be administered by experts, away from politicians. This optimism brought forth a view that prison could and should be geared towards rehabilitation, rather than punishment. Home Office officials were heavily influenced by what they saw as the success of the Borstal system, in which young offenders received training and education leading to an early and supervised release into the community (as a former probation officer, one of the authors can attest to the numbers of plasterers and plumbers in the community who learned their skills in borstal). The unconditional release of less serious offenders – a process known as remission – was regarded as a long way from the rehabilitative ideal. Instead, it was an administrative convenience, enabling authorities and politicians to manipulate the prison population as and when required. Parole, however, was seen to embody a rehabilitative leaning and would represent a drive towards individualised punishment based upon indeterminacy (Guiney, 2018).

Shifting in the Wind

The past 50 years has seen ideas about punishment and rehabilitation on something of a rollercoaster. It would be easy and somewhat foolish to link these fluctuations with political parties or political ideals. For example, the 1979 Conservative government of Margaret Thatcher was elected on a strong law and order agenda; one based on a belief in deterrence, in the use of custody to a greater degree and scepticism over the benefits of rehabilitative measures. At the same time, she was an avowed supporter of a smaller state, cutting taxes and economic liberalism. These ideals clashed with the costs of building more prisons, increasing numbers of police officers and funding all the associated structures and processes necessary to deliver a punitive agenda. Talking tough costs nothing but delivering toughness is expensive. A recent example of rapid policy shift helps explain the febrile world that parole has been drawn into and how difficult it is to conceptualise criminal justice policy as a consistent idea, even within the same political party. On 18 July 2019, Conservative Justice Secretary David Gauke spoke of the need to move away from custodial sentences, whilst only weeks later (11 August), his replacement Robert Buckland, spoke about more and better prisons (Guinney 2022, p. 1159). What had caused such a shift? None other than the election of Boris Johnson as Prime Minister on 24 July. Johnson soon took aim at left wing criminologists and their influence on penal policy. He launched a 'Crime Week', promising to free the police for more stop and search, planned a new sentencing framework and 18,000 additional prison places. By September, Robert Buckland had announced a *Smarter Approach to Sentencing* based on robust sentencing intending to keep the most dangerous offenders in prison for as long as possible. It is not difficult to see how the Parole Board would be impacted by this rhetoric and rapidly changing policy. The decision to release John Worboys by the Parole Board in 2018, a notorious sex offender, brought together a range of issues, such as the role of professionals, the independence of the Parole Board, the involvement of politicians, the engagement of public sentiment, the position of victims in prisoner release and in subsequent parole debates and the role of the European Court of Human Rights. It is worth exploring this case in a little detail to unpick some of the ideas raised earlier.

John Worboys (now known as John Radford) and more infamously as the Black Cab Rapist was sentenced in March 2009 for 19 sexual offences, including one of rape. It was understood at the time that there were many other offences and victims, but these were not taken forward. The CPS wrote to one of these victims indicating that the evidential test for prosecution had been met, but that there were dangers in putting too many charges on an indictment at the trial. For the original 19 offences, Worboys was sentenced to an indeterminate sentence for public protection (IPP), with a minimum time to be served (the tariff) of 8 years. The setting of this tariff meant that the punishment element of these crimes was equivalent to 16 years. We will not dwell on the assessment process involving Worboys (see *R. (DSD and NBV & Ors) v The Parole Board of England* and Wales & Ors and John Radford (2018) EWHC (Admin), for an excellent summary). His proposed release sparked a media and public furore. His tariff had expired on 14 February 2016 by which time he had served 10 years in custody, including a remand period. He was recommended for release in a letter dated 26 December 2017. He was, very exceptionally, to be released directly from a category A prison, with no recommendation to go to open conditions. His licence conditions were not revealed. His crimes, committed whist he was working as a black cab driver, had achieved notoriety. His proposed release sparked a media and public uproar, described by Annison (2020, p. 149) as the 'pressing in' on policy and politics of a range of 'publics', notably those traditionally excluded from the professional sphere. There was not unanimous agreement among the professionals involved in the process in support of release. However, the then Chair of the Parole Board, Nick Hardwick, said that the panel had consisted of three people and had been chaired by a very experienced female member. The panel had considered a dossier with 363 pages of evidence and heard from the four psychologists as well as prison and probation staff. As such, the panel had done everything it was charged to do in law, and having concluded that Worboys' continued detention was no longer necessary for the safety of the public, recommended his release. That decision brought into public focus a number of parole issues, which, in themselves, were indicative of a wider range of justice and penal concerns, and we will briefly discuss these now.

Two victims of Worboys, alongside the Mayor of London, Sadiq Khan and two national newspapers, were granted permission for a judicial review of the release decision. The grounds of the appeal focussed on the view that there were material errors of fact giving rise to unfairness; there was a failure to consider a relevant consideration and the decision to release was *Wednesbury* unfair (in the sense of being irrational, or a decision that no reasonable person would have taken). The court was unconvinced on all three heads but produced another means to quash the Parole Board decision to release and this centred on their view that the Board should have carried out further inquiry into the other matters that were not proceeded with by the CPS, his explanation of events and his lack of honesty and openness over the 80+ outstanding matters. Interestingly, one of the psychologists reporting on Worboys, Dr Jackie Craissati, had said she did not expect offenders to give 'truthful and full' accounts of their behaviour when she was assessing dangerousness. She said that she believed that Worboys posed a low risk of sexual offending. Naturally, this alleged claim was seized upon by the media with a tirade against 'expert' opinion, as compared to the good sense of the public. Three reports of the many which were published give a flavour of the media response, Osborne (2018) in *the Express*, Pollard and Lucas (15 January 2018), *the Sun* and Wells (28 March 2018) in *the Sun*. Interestingly, *the Sun* reports referred to 'shrinks' as responsible for Worboys' release, a term more commonly used for psychiatrists than psychologists.

Following further inquiries and review, Worboys was charged with a further four offences in May 2019, and sentenced to two terms of life imprisonment in December 2019. However, it is very interesting to note that despite the issues raised as part of the Worboys debate, the tariff for these new indeterminate sentences, was only 6 years – shorter than his original IPP. Matters arising from the Worboys case included the transparency of the Parole Board's hearings, the place of victims in the process, the use or not of 'other' information concerning the prisoner and the confusion over the distinction between 'punishment' and the function and purpose of parole. In response to public concern and the raising of a number of issues, the government decided to launch a *Review of the Law, Policy and Practice Relating to Parole Decisions* in January 2018 which was published 4 months later. The findings of the review made suggestions for fundamental changes, with some receiving more favour than others. The government said that there would be immediate action to amend Rule 25 (which forbad the publication of the reasons for decisions taken by the Parole Board). The proposal was for the publication of one-page summaries of deliberations which could be made available, upon request, to victims and other interested parties. In the year 2021–22, over 1,700 such summaries were made available, mostly to victims. The review made two further recommendations, both reflecting concerns that had arisen following the Worboys case. The first was that consultation should be undertaken to consider the feasibility of a review mechanism for Parole Board decisions. The second was that changes should be sought and introduced to improve the communication with victims during the parole process (pre and post any release). It had emerged that not all victims had been notified that Worboys was due to be released.

'You Will Change!' Controlling the Parole Board

As noted, some of these changes required primary legislation and so, included in the Conservative Party manifesto of 2019, was a proposal for a *Root and Branch Review of the Parole System*. This was published in March 2022 (MoJ, 2022) and its contents were quickly seized upon by the then Secretary of State Dominic Raab, to ramp up the criminal justice heat. In his foreword to the report, Raab emphasises his, and the Parole Board's commitment, to protecting the public and improving victims' experience of criminal justice. However, it is not too long into his statement that Raab begins to run together a number of issues to present as one kind of threat. He said, 'in recent years a number of decisions to release offenders who have committed heinous crimes has led to a loss of confidence in the parole system'. This immediately suggests that the nature of the original crime should be an issue in release decisions, when in reality, once 'punishment' has been served, the matter under consideration should be the risk of further offending (although see the proposed changes below). What Raab refers to is actually the punishment initially handed down; either the number of years in a fixed sentence or the length of the tariff in an indeterminate sentence. The Parole Board only comes into play when these points have been reached. We have attempted to argue that it is far too simple to blame the parole board, either for release decisions (they act on evidence provided to them) or for further offending which is of course the offender's responsibility.

The government also felt that the 'statutory test for release' had changed from Parliament's original intention. The test states that the Parole Board must not give direction for release unless the Board is satisfied that it is no longer necessary for the protection of the public that the person be confined. However, in R v Parole Board, *Ex parte* Bradley (1990), the court had described the Parole Board having to balance the risk to the public of releasing the prisoner, with the unfairness of continued detention for the prisoner. Raab believed that this 'balancing act' was not the original intention of parliament (another example of where courts and professionals are conceived as obstructing parliament) and by definition, the people. He went on to say that 'prisoners...should continue to be detained...unless it can be demonstrated that the offender no longer poses a risk of further serious offending'. This point is interesting. We have already discussed the problems of predicting future behaviour with any accuracy. For example, the then chair of the Parole Board Nick Hardwick said (Parole Board, 16 January 2018):

> I would not be honest if I pretended that risk could be eliminated completely. Parole Board members need to be confident a prisoner will not reoffend – but they cannot be certain. If certainty is required that needs to be reflected in the length of the original sentence.

He also stressed that the board could not re-assess guilt or innocence or whether the original sentence was appropriate (even if we would like to do so). It is in this area that it appears to us that the public disquiet with parole in certain cases is very much about the original sentence, but the Board picks up the misplaced flak. As Annison (2020, p. 155) states, 'given its focus on risk and the release of some of the most dangerous prisoners, parole is perhaps *the* point at which penal politics is – or is capable of being – at its most polarised, febrile and anti-political'. If the Government are wanting absolute certainty of no future re-offending, then the natural consequence of this is that no prisoners will be released. This of course would not happen but it is part of the process of politicising the complex issues in these matters and reducing them to quick, populist soundbites. The Parole Board remains the (semi) public face of how the criminal justice process deals with dangerous offenders, but too often anger at it might be better directed at police failings, CPS decisions and Judicial sentencing. The Parole Board cannot escape politics, even, in recent times, from very short serving Ministers of Justice. In his proposals to 'beef up' the parole board membership with police and prison staff, it is clear that Dominic Raab was taking a swipe at what his party saw as the continuing dominance of liberal elites in criminal justice decision-making. This of course belies the actuality of many PB members' professional lives in medicine, law, industry, psychiatry, social work, probation and academia to name but a few. All of these people have experience of considering evidence and making risk decisions. Recent police history in a number of notorious cases suggests that police risk consideration is not, as a default position, better than any others and may particularly be influenced by police culture (HMICFRS, 2022a, 2022b). However, it is not difficult to see how this would play favourably with a public convinced by the media that the Parole Board is soft, and simply releases dangerous offenders back into the community too soon, or at all!

Superdangerous?

The 'way in' for Ministers to have a greater say in parole outcomes was the creation of a 'top tier' of prisoners for whom ministerial oversight of the release process and decision would be automatic. This top tier would consist of those convicted of murder, rape, causing or allowing the death of a child and terrorist-related offences. Interestingly, and as a continuation of we can do more than you, the Labour Party proposed extending the top tier of four to six, to include manslaughter and sexual offences of children (Inside Time, 17 July 2023). However, by using the usual verbal gymnastics, ministers looking to block release would not veto but refer decisions – effectively pass the buck to the Court of Appeal. The clear implication of the government's intent was that the parole board was not acting as it should; it was not exercising sufficient caution with release decisions. We mentioned earlier that it was the government's intention to recruit more parole board members from law enforcement backgrounds. Subsequently, on 15th February 2023, the government launched its recruitment campaign (Gov.UK press release February 16, 2023). The aim was to 'toughen' parole scrutiny, with more ex-police officers and detectives. The plan was to at least double the number of members with policing experience, saying that they will bring first-hand experience of the risk of dangerous offenders. In the case of the top tier prisoners, the attendance of members with policing experience would be mandatory. Overall, the government stated that these developments would place a greater focus on public protection in parole hearings. It is difficult to strip out the party politics from Dominic Raab's statements on the parole changes. His language was, we think, carefully chosen to make the parole board something of a 'wedge issue' with the Labour Party. It is clear that Raab had little faith in the parole board membership, saying that 'the public want to know that parole decisions are being made by those with good insight into offenders' behaviour...their first-hand experience of risk will give parole boards and *even greater focus* (our emphasis) on public protection and make our streets safer'. As mentioned above, the government not only wanted to shape the make-up of the parole board membership, but also wanted powers to intervene and overturn decisions. Speaking to the House of Commons 2 weeks after the press announcement, the Minister of Justice made clear his intentions:

> I want to see the parole process take a more precautionary approach in cases which involve those who have committed the most serious cases, it is right that Ministers should provide a measure of oversight and be able to intervene directly in decisions on release. HC Deb (2023, p. 711).

These measures were brought forward in the Victims and Prisoners Bill (29.03.23). In short, the Bill proposed that Ministers be allowed to overturn Parole Board decisions in top tier cases; allow the Secretary of State to remove the Chair and Vice-Chair of the Parole Board in the name of maintaining public confidence; will allow the Secretary of State to make rules prescribing the composition of Panels and to disapply section 3 of the Human Rights Act, 1998 in relation to legislation relating to the release of prisoners. These proposals have met with widespread opposition, PRT (2023a, 2023b), National Association of Probation Officers (NAPO) over proposals to stop probation officers making professional recommendations in parole reports (see Doughty Street Chambers, 2 March 2023).

In what might be taken as a sideways snipe at the Parole Board, the government decided to extend and mandate the use of whole life tariffs in certain cases, again, the John Worboys release decision was very influential in this development. This takes us back to that confusion in life sentences over the tariff and subsequent release decisions. The Parole Board, in doing its job, is castigated for releasing a prisoner that the public, or media and politicians, consider has served too little time in prison. This in fact is nothing to do with parole but rather is about what people think the *original sentence should have been*. The extension of whole life tariffs – meaning no release is possible unless, in the government's words, there are *exceptional* circumstances (undefined as yet), reduces the role of the Parole Board and in fact eliminates it in a number of cases. The language used by the government to announce the whole life tariff changes was reminiscent of that used in the 1990s during the 'law and order' war between Tory and Labour politicians. A press release from the Prime Minister's office (26 August 2023) said that 'society's most depraved killers would face life behind bars with no chance of release'. Legislation would *require* Judges to hand down mandatory life orders to 'the monsters' who commit the most horrific types of murder. These offenders were described as 'heinous' and those who commit the most horrific types of murder. Sexually motivated murders would qualify for the automatic whole life tariff to sit alongside the premeditated murder of children. The Prime Minister commented that he shared the public's horror of the crimes committed recently and the public rightly, he said, expected life to mean life in the most serious cases. An example of the political 'bidding war' from the 1990s on law and order issues can be seen in the response of the Labour Party to the whole life tariff proposals. Steve Reed, the Shadow Secretary of State for Justice said, no-one will take any lessons from the soft-on-crime Tory Government. Labour is now the party of law and order. In government, we will implement tougher sentences for dangerous criminals and build the prison places to put them behind bars' (Sky News, 27th August, 2023). It is difficult to imagine much tougher policies than whole life tariffs and it is exactly this type of rhetoric than can run away from reality when politicians are determined to prove their tough credentials to the electorate.

Section Summary

In many ways, debates about the Parole Board epitomise those of wider criminal justice issues, a microcosm of broader political and punitive trends (Annison and Guiney, 2022). One of these significant trends has been a growing distrust of professionals and their knowledge base. The Parole Board sits as both a collection of professionals and as a group whose decisions are based upon the work of other professionals. Yet when decisions seemingly 'go wrong', these professionals are attacked for a lack of judgement and expertise. They are 'amateurish' (the whole board), too 'soft' (probation officers, so remove their power to make recommendations) and let's have more police as risk experts, or make wrong risk assessments (psychologists who drift in and out of favour). The end result of these supposed failings is invariably a serious further offence, yet it is too simple to lay the blame at the door of the release decision. As with everything in criminal justice, multiple layers of decision-making by a wide range of professionals feed into the final decision. In the world of blame however, this is rarely acknowledged. Politicians, of whatever political hue, want to *control punishment.* They want to ensure that their tough policies and sentences are not mitigated by liberal-minded professionals, even though, in private, many politicians display these liberal credentials proudly.

The parole process serves useful purposes in allowing the prison population to be adjusted and as an incentive to the good behaviour of prisoners. These functions tend however to be ignored within arguments concerning the mitigation of punishment and the softness of decision-making. This decision-making is though, very difficult and complex. It mostly relies on assessments of behaviour of those in prison, never a good place to show one's true character. It should also, as indicated in reviews of the Worboys' case, include assessments of 'other' behaviour and convictions – a key aspect of all risk assessment in our view. Prisoners themselves may develop skills in showing a side of their character that they feel will help their case. In the Worboys case, the Judge suggested that he had an apparent deftness in impression management. However, by removing the powers of the Parole Board in certain cases and taking them back for a secretary of state to decide, the whole process becomes political. Release can then be decided by poll ratings, media commentary of the incidence of other cases entirely unrelated to that under consideration. This does not fit many models of justice – but does very much sound like retribution. We finish with a few figures to emphasis the power of political influence in parole board decisions and indeed, of removing those decisions completely. Figures released by the PRT (2023a, 2023b) indicate that, during 2021-22, of 549 recommendations for open conditions made by the Board to the Secretary of State, 515 were accepted (nearly 94%). In the year, 2022–23, of 263 recommendations, only 33 were accepted (12.5%). Of the refusals, 38% were rejected on the grounds of public confidence, a criterion not in any official guidance and one over which the prisoner has no control or influence. It might be said, welcome to the new (political) parole process.

The Police and Public Protection

There is little doubt that when thinking about public protection agencies, the minds of many will turn first to the police service. The organisation is synonymous with tackling crime and criminals, and by default, protecting members of the public who may fall victim. However, as we shall explore in this next section, tackling crime, or crime fighting as it may be more popularly known, appears to be forming an increasingly small part of the police's role. Furthermore, public protection as understood by the police service may be quite different from that envisaged by the public. By this we mean that the police-defined role may be a lot less proactive than that imagined by the public, less blue light and more arm around the shoulder, being more concerned with the management of known offenders rather than the prevention of new crimes. This is of course, the complete paradox contained within public protection, but may not sit easily with a public expecting police services to *prevent* murder and serious sexual offences committed by strangers. In general terms however, the prevention of these rare and unexpected events is almost an impossibility. The role of the police, like other public protection agencies, is to try and prevent the *repetition* of seriously harmful behaviour by known offenders, or to try to halt an escalation of less serious behaviour into something far more harmful. Of course, they do have the primary role in trying to detect and apprehend these serious offenders and bring them to justice. This is a clear expectation from the public and is one of the reasons why murder investigations teams (MITs – see below) are relatively well resourced. In this section, we will be exploring how certain aspects of policing have emerged and developed into what we now know as public protection and how this has shaped the working structures and practices of police officers, but also the culture of the police service itself. We will also consider how political discourse and austerity politics in particular has impacted police effectiveness.

The 'modern police' of England and Wales is generally viewed as the creation of Home Secretary Sir Robert Peel in 1829, although Brown (2021) believes the role of his assistants, Rowan and Mayne, was far more influential. What did emerge and indeed endure since this time, was the core principles of policing which bear Peel's name and still manifest themselves in modern core statements of what it is the police strive to do. The principles very much reflect the mood of the times, when suspicion of anything French aroused great fears, notably a 'military style' force or indeed an army of spies, infringing upon an English man's (sic) freedom. Preventing crime and disorder, without using military force, features first on the list of the nine principles, closely followed by the approval and cooperation of the public. The principles also included, absolute impartiality and an equal response to all members of the public; the bond between the public and the police was to be paramount and there should be non-interference with the powers of the judiciary. Finally, the test of efficiency, so beloved of modern forces, was to be the absence of crime and disorder, rather than a large, visible police presence. We do not intend to develop police history further at this point and would refer the reader to Bowling et al. (2019) for an excellent collection discussing historical issues in policing and police development. We will instead leap forward to more recent times when a public protection ethos has developed into a significant component of everyday policing, although possibly not in the sense that the public might understand it. Popular images of policing, associated with crime fighting, catching criminals, visibly deterring criminals from acting and as a result, reassuring the public, continue in the minds of many. Somewhere buried deep in these public images, is the idea that the police could actually prevent murder and other serious crime, if there were more of them, or, if they acted more quickly or, a more modern twist, acted without discrimination. This thinking, idealistically, supposes that a police officer on the street would be able to stop street murders or a heavy police presence would be able to reduce sexual assaults at night. It is of course entirely impossible to be in all the places where crimes may occur, particularly if those crimes are between people unknown to each other. Where the victims do have some form of relationship, then the police do have a few more odds in their favour, but acting on this information requires good intelligence, excellent risk assessment and a determined action to regard so-called domestic crimes as importantly as any other so-called stranger crime. It is virtually impossible to stop what is not known or is not predictable but it could be regarded as a crime not to intervene in what *is* known.

Murder Leads the Way

Just as in sentencing, for the police, the crime of murder is at the top of the order of priority. The investigation of murder cases is undertaken by (usually) well-resourced murder investigation teams (MITs) consisting of, in the Metropolitan police area for example, teams having one DCI, two DIs, four DSs, 18 DCs and one PC (ONS, 2023a, 2023b). Murders undoubtedly have a very public profile and the more 'innocent' and 'normal' the victim, the higher the interest of the press and social media. The public, of course, like to see as much police activity as possible at these times in the hope that such things 'will not happen again'. In reality, the police are responding to an act already committed and their task is concerned with catching the criminal to face justice and reduce that person's opportunity to offend in the future. It does though, have relatively little impact on future such instances committed by other unknown people. The activities surrounding murder investigation are however undoubtedly what the public want to see; they contain considerable symbolic value. Television police dramas have framed their thinking around large teams, busy incident rooms, trawling through CCTV images, extensive forensic searches, testing DNA, conducting intense interviews with suspects and so forth. This is undoubtedly true in many cases, at least for a short period of time, but this level of activity does not, in a sense, reflect the *amount* of different forms of serious offending. For example, in the year ending June 2023, there were 602 homicides recorded in England and Wales, but 68,109 rapes out of a total of 885,393 sexual offences. In many publications on crime statistics, homicides have their own discrete category, whereas domestic abuse *and* sexual offences are bracketed together. Interestingly, the latter are investigated by *public protection* teams, whereas homicide, as we have seen, often has its own discrete unit. It is almost as if homicide is above public protection, meaning that the vast majority of seriously harmful crimes are investigated by teams with fewer members and who are less experienced that their homicide colleagues. As strongly expressed by Baroness Casey (2023) in her review of the Metropolitan Police Service, 'criminals involved in these crimes (public protection) pose some of the greatest risks to society. Their crimes often occur in private spaces where others cannot see or intervene'. She argues that these offenders often repeat their crimes and that the police have struggled to tackle them: 'instead public protection has been actively de-prioritised'.

We have commented on the impact of austerity measures elsewhere in this book, but it is fair to say that this policy has undoubtedly impacted on policing decisions in respect of serious crimes. Casey comments (p. 137) that a decision was taken that public protection should be made into a job that 'anyone can do'. A significant increase in the recruitment of direct-entry detectives has seen them allocated to public protection teams, which will include the investigation of rape offences. As one officer involved in the Casey review commented, 'murder may be dealt with by a whole team of experienced and specialist trained detectives, whereas a woman raped and left in a coma would likely be dealt with by one trainee detective constable. What message does this send to the living victim?' (p. 149). It could be argued that the police rightly prioritise murder investigation, a crime that holds considerable symbolic significance for the public. Yet, it could equally be argued that crimes with truly devastating personal consequences, and crimes which are far more numerous, receive what can only be termed a second-rate service compared with that for homicide. What we are suggesting is that there appears to be confusion in police circles over what exactly protecting the public actually means. The pulling together of a whole range of very serious crimes (and non-crimes) into one category which does not include homicide appears to us as confused, although once again the almost mythical status given to this crime might explain much. For example, in a Performance Tracker on Police, Richards et al. (2022) suggested that non-crime demand took up a lot of police time, and look where public protection was listed... 'in addition to responding to *crimes,* the police also undertake a large amount of *non-crime* work. This includes demands from mental health, *public protection*, safeguarding and missing persons activity'. So, the question must be, how can the investigation of rape be non-crime? Even if this is not the reality of officers' expectations, it is the case that sexual offences investigations appear to be significantly less important than homicide. We already know from many sources that domestic abuse has received an extremely patchy response from the police (see McPhee et al., 2022), for an excellent summary of key issues. Therefore, putting it together with sexual offences is unlikely to help improve the response to these crimes, even though there are a considerable number of sexual and physical assaults bound up in domestic abuse. For example, the police recorded 885,393 offences as domestic abuse in the year ending June 2023, with 699,277 of these recorded as violent and 32,946 as sexual (ONS, 2023a, 2023b). However, the domestic abuse commissioner (2024) argued that actual numbers of domestic abuse crimes may go *down*, due to new counting rules imposed on the police by the Home Office, rather than an actual reduction in the incidence of these crimes.

Police-Defined Public Protection

There may be a lack of fit between what the public understand the role of the police in public protection to be, and what the police themselves understand.

As we have suggested, public protection for the police encompasses a number of roles, a number of which are not regarded overtly as 'crime fighting', although we shall discuss later how we disagree with this idea. The putting together of issues such as mental health, with the monitoring of registered sex offenders, may bring the 'status' of these roles 'down' to a service intervention than a more overtly crime fighting one. An interesting piece of research by Charman (2018) shows that over time, police officers' own perception and understanding of their role changes influenced no doubt not only by the reality of daily policing but also by police culture. In a longitudinal piece of research spanning 4 years, Charman asked a sample of recruits at 5 weeks into service, 6 months, 12 months and 4 years, to express their level of agreement to a read out set of statements. In response to what might be termed a fundamental aspect of policing, *Upholding the Law*, 79.2% of the sample agreed/strongly agreed that it was a core function at 5 weeks, but this fell to 52.9% at 4 years. There was almost unanimous agreement with the statement that a core task was *Protecting Citizens* and over time the positive reaction to this statement hardly varied. The third statement concerned *Protecting Society from Criminals and Deviants*, and one might wonder how this differs from statement two. Yet, the response to this statement was much more differentiated, suggesting that police themselves have a nuanced view of public protection. Although, again, there was a broad positive response to this statement, the numbers strongly agreeing fell from 41.7% at 5 weeks to 29.4% at 4 years, with disagreement with the statement rising from 8.3% to 17.6% over the time frame. The police role as *Crime Fighters* fell from 86.4% agreement/strong agreement at 5 weeks to 53% after 4 years. However, perhaps the most interesting responses in this research were in response to the question *What is the role of the Police?* Given three options, crime related, public service related and safeguarding, the figures did vary considerably. At 5 weeks, 35% of respondents said that crime related was the main role of the police but this fell to 9% after 4 years. Safeguarding, on the other hand, started with a score of approximately 17% at 5 weeks but this increased dramatically to 85% after 4 years. What does this research tell us for public protection? It suggests that police officers believe their role is different from early expectations, whether this is a result of the reality of police work or of actual changes brought on by changes such as austerity. A mish-mash of activities has developed under the general heading of safeguarding, even though protection of citizens is still seen as a primary function. It is undoubtedly the case, that the combined effects of Covid and austerity has reduced the capacity of many public services, leaving the police as the service of last resort. The question for us, is whether what the police regard as safeguarding is the same as what the public understand by public protection.

The police have a clear, legal responsibility to manage sex offenders on the Sex Offender Register (SOR) via the MAPPA. The register had been established under the Sex Offenders Act, 1997. It provided that all convicted sex offenders register, with the police, for varying periods depending on their sentence. We describe the nature and amount of work involved in this task for the police below, but suffice to say that it was and is, considerable and indeed transformative (see Kemshall and McIvor, 2004; Nash, 2006, 2014). This work largely comes under the remit of public protection teams (as defined by the police) and, as we have seen, these teams are not resourced to anything like the level of murder investigation teams. As O'Sullivan et al. (2016) make clear, the SOR 'was not intended as a punishment; rather by keeping police records accurate and up to date, its primary aim was public protection'. Protection was therefore based on gathering and verifying information, or intelligence as the police might term it. This role was essentially to be carried out by police officers who would conduct visits to the offender's home, with frequency based on the assessed level of risk. For the vast majority of offenders this constituted an annual visit. Police officers were not however simply gathering information; they were assessing risk of further sexual offending, a crucial task. However, the Casey review (2023, p. 144) noted that 'roles in public protection are not valued for their high levels of risk management'. Indeed, a number of public protection roles have been civilianised, for example, an advert for a Public Protection Review Officer in West Yorkshire suggested that applicants should have the ability to manage a workload of RSOs and carry out thorough risk assessments to inform risk management plans. Further, the advertisement suggested that *no* previous experience was necessary, although a more detailed role specification suggested that proven experience in the management or investigation of sex/dangerous offenders and/or child safeguarding investigations was 'essential' – difficult to see how these two requirements sit together.

Clearly the introduction of civilian staff into public protection roles has not been without resistance. Regarded as a cost-saving measure in the face of austerity cuts, in a piece of research with police monitoring officers, Mann et al. (2018, p. 632) drew out some of the tensions in the role. They suggested that financial cuts had affected this increasingly important and highly specialised area of policing...resulting in the dilution of good practice that had previously ensured public protection. The result (respondents felt) had led to an increased and unmanageable workload and workforce de-professionalisation. The MOSOVO role (management of sexual offenders and violent offenders) was felt to be weakened by the introduction of civilians. One respondent told the researchers that 'whilst some (civilians) were retired DSs and DCs, the majority had no background in, or experience of, policing'. The lack of necessary training and experience was felt to be compromising investigations and safeguarding. The authors concluded that austerity may have led to a disregard for the importance of specialist knowledge and skills (a common theme throughout the professional public sector in recent years) and a shift away from the development of professional roles in the implementation of the public protection agenda (2018, p. 639). Indeed, in a review of police service strength, Allen and Mansfield (2022) found that of the full-time equivalent workforce, 62% were police officers, 34% support staff or designated officers and 4% were police community support officers. The role of a MOSOVO officer is in contrast to what many police officers believe they signed up for and represents a considerable cultural and professional challenge (Nash, 2014). At the heart of much of this professional tension is the ways in which public protection has developed for the police; they are not investigating crimes and arresting offenders but instead, visiting them at their home, a much more passive role. With RSOs, the role of the police is to assess and monitor. The RSO is not a *suspect* and as such, the interaction changes from what, for many police officers, might be considered the norm. In a recent piece of research, Mydlowski and Turner-Moore (2023) argued that a clear tension existed between police roles and newer roles such as MOSOVO officers, and that this was manifest in the training given for the MOSOVO role. Their research involved observing training sessions in three different police areas and listening to recordings of the home visits. A number of issues emerged, which offers us insight into pubic protection processes in action.

As we noted earlier, the level of management of RSOs is determined by their assessed level of risk. The higher the risk the more frequent the contact. The vast majority of RSOs, over 98%, are assessed to be at the lowest level of risk and therefore receive only an annual visit. On average, those considered to be very high risk are visited monthly, every 3 months for high risk and approximately six-monthly for medium risk offenders. However, it is perhaps less about the number of visits and more the nature and purpose of them which is important. The research identified three types of visit; the *initial* visit, intended to establish rapport and clarify notification requirements, the *ARMS* visit (Active Risk Management System), designed to be a full risk assessment interview and lastly, what were termed *subsequent* visits. All three were felt to have different purposes but the researchers found that training only related to the ARMS type of visit and this therefore clouded or influenced the nature of *all* visits. This somewhat uniform approach carried across to the type of interview methodology used and this was based on the standard PEACE model (Planning & Preparation, Engage and Explain, Account, Closure and Evaluation). This method applies to the police investigation of suspects and, as we have noted, RSOs are not suspected of having committed a new offence (at least not in the majority of cases). PEACE interviewing may therefore preclude the 'chattier' style of interview needed for the first interview and probably the subsequent interviews following the ARMS assessment. By training MOSOVOs in risk assessment, this becomes the defining feature of all home visit interviews. Researchers in the study found that officers focussed on the six risk factors in the ARMS assessment and paid much less attention to the five protective factors. This was most pronounced for the group trained by those without any experience of the MOSOVO role. Police students it was felt disengaged and disregarded a lot of what these non-specialist staff said, especially when it related to protective factors. Citing another study (Kewley, 2017), Mydlowski and Turner-Moore (2023, p. 11) noted that MOSOVOs in general regarded RSOs with suspicion, believing them all to be liars who posed a permanent risk of reoffending. The researchers concluded that specialist training staff, with experience of the MOSOVO role, were best suited to train new staff, but the reality was that in the face of a national shortage, this was unlikely to happen. Furthermore, it was felt that wider police influences were more important, as summarised in a somewhat pessimistic conclusion to the research, 'The MOSOVO role represents a cultural shift from the traditional role of policing and although strengthening MOSOVO training may help, the MOSOVO training and role will still be working against the much stronger tide of wider police policies, practices and culture' (2023, p. 14). It appears as if a role not involved in trying to catch new criminals, but instead monitor those who have already been punished, is less attractive to many police officers. It is this somewhat hybrid role that led Nash (1999a, 1999b) to develop the idea of a 'polibation' officer.

At present there is little sign that the demand for the MOSOVO role is going to reduce. The present (2023) MAPPA population is in excess of 91,000, up 57% since 2013 (MoJ, 2023). There are nearly 90,000 offenders managed at MAPPA level one and of these 76% are category one – registered sex offenders. Responsibility for these falls to the police and thus over 68,000 offenders should receive a minimum of one home visit per year. Indeed, Greater Manchester Police alone reported (GMP, 2022) that they had made over 3,500 visits in the previous year. It would seem that, as presently constructed, the RSO population on MAPPA will continue to grow, eventually producing an unmeetable demand on police time – bearing in mind that police policy is for two officers to attend each home visit. This mounting workload was undoubtedly a factor in the government establishing an independent review into Police-led management of sex offenders in the community, led by former chief constable Mick Creedon. His final report (Home Office, 2023a, 2023b) makes a number of recommendations to Government and partner agencies, all with a broad thrust of reducing numbers. Perhaps among the most eye-catching of these was that, with immediate effect, no further cohorts of offenders be made subject to sex offender style registration and notification. Instead, the Review proposed making full use of existing options such as sexual harm prevention orders and to make greater use of MAPPA category 3, especially for high-risk domestic abuse offenders. It seems unlikely, however, that any government would agree to undoing what has been a flagship sex offender measure for approaching three decades. The Register rode the back of populist sentiment and there is little to suggest public opinion has shifted in respect of dealing with sex offenders. Interestingly, Creedon recommended that MOSOVO training should have a clear focus on desistance, perhaps emphasising the lack of focus highlighted in the work of Mydlowski and Turner Moore (2003) noted above. Creedon did recommend to the College of Policing that MOSOVO should become an accredited professional specialism and that the 1–50 staff-offender ratio be reviewed. In an effort to reduce the demands on the police for sex-offender management, Creedon is clearly going to come up against vested political interest as well as, to be fair, public opinion. For example, he suggested that registration periods be reviewed. These are fixed in law and determined by sentence length. They are therefore unrelated to risk. A sentence of 30 months or more in custody automatically triggers indefinite registration. With average sentence for sexual crimes running at 64.3 months in 2022, up 10 months from the previous year (ONS, December 22, 2022), it is not surprising that registration numbers relentlessly grow year on year. In a book with a focus on politics, it is interesting to read former Chief Constable Creedon's opinion on this subject, 'Once again, the impact of political decisions designed to punish and protect will continue to have an impact on the police service charged with the long-term, post-sentence supervision of the convicted offender' (2023, p. 16).

The police therefore find themselves in the middle of something like a pincher movement, squeezed between a seemingly endlessly increasing workload and the combined effects of austerity cuts and the Covid pandemic collapse of a range of supportive services in the community. The result was that the police became the emergency service of first and last resort. Perhaps this was marked no more than in the field of mental health where throughout and following the pandemic, demands on police time grew exponentially. In London, the Commissioner of the Metropolitan Police, Sir Mark Rowley, hammered out an agreement with the NHS (albeit a seemingly reluctant agreement on the part of the NHS), to reduce the number of police officer call outs to mental health incidents. Part of the rationale was that approximately 78% of incidents under S.136 resulted in the person being sent home after assessment, and thus a view that mental health was over-policed in London. Following on from a pilot scheme in Humberside, known as Right Care, Right Person (RCRP) where it was felt that 7% of officer time had been freed up by the scheme, the Met introduced it into London. It was believed that nationally, one million hours of police time could be saved annually (NPCC, 2023a, 2023b). In describing this development, the Guardian (17 August 2023) said that agreement followed 'a tense behind the scenes row' but that as a result, police would stop being diverted from 'crime fighting'. The NHS on the other hand were reported as saying that they did not know how they would cope.

It is evident that austerity measures and public sector cuts have placed a huge strain on the delivery of public services. The police service has found itself in pole position to fill the gaps even though it has suffered a considerable reduction in funding and staffing in recent years. Overall, police full-time equivalent numbers (included police officers, support staff and designated officers and police community support officers) have fallen from a peak in 2010 of 244,000 down to an average of 200,000 from 2016–19 and have recently risen to 225,000 in 2022. The recent increase has been a result of the Government's pledge to increase numbers by 20,000 in its 2019 election manifesto, a target which has more or less been met. As with the probation service, recent, sudden and significant recruitment has led to an inexperienced workforce, with figures released in 2022 suggesting that 34% of the total had less than 5 years' experience and 60% under 10 years (Allen and Carthew, 2024). The surge in recruitment was also felt to be a concern over the vetting procedures used by the police, with public confidence already low following several high-profile revelations of serious, criminal and misogynistic conduct, notably in the Metropolitan Police (HMICFRS, 2022a, 2022b). Particularly damaging for the reputation of the Met was the case of PC David Carrick of the Parliamentary and Diplomatic Command, who, was convicted for 49 sexual offences which included 24 rapes, over a 17-year period, whilst serving as a police officer. Indeed, his status was a primary weapon in enticing and then coercing women into forced sexual activity. Carrick had been successfully vetted in 2001 and again in 2017, by which time he was well into his destructive pattern of behaviour. He received 36 life sentences and his conduct was summed up by the trial Judge as 'The broad devastation you have caused through sexual violence and exploitation, all the time carrying the unique and defining office of a police constable' (Courts and Tribunals Judiciary, 7th February, 2023). As a result of the omissions and collusions revealed by the Carrick case, the Independent Office for Police Complaints (IOPC) launched multiple investigations into the handling of reports about the case (IOPC, 20th July, 2023). This case, following on closely from the murder of Sarah Everard by serving police officer Wayne Couzens, led, according to numerous surveys, to a collapse of confidence in the police by women in particular (for example, Politics Home, 22 November 2023; End Violence Against Women, 18 November 2021; Brown & Hobbs, 2023). One upshot of both the offences against women and the loss of confidence has been that the National Police Chiefs' Council (NPCC) established a new priority area of bringing consistently high standards to the police response to violence against women and girls. Part of this initiative is to respond unequivocally to allegations of police-perpetrated abuse, as well as addressing sexism and misogyny. In reporting on this new benchmark, the NPCC (14 March 2023) noted 653 conduct cases against 672 individuals were flagged as relating to violence against women and girls, and 524 public complaints against 867 individuals. This amounted 0.7% of the police workforce. This may represent a small percentage of police officers and staff but it is significant nonetheless in terms of public confidence. Sky News reported on 17 January 2023 that the Metropolitan Police were investigating over 1,600 cases of sexual offences and domestic abuse involving its staff. These cases will take many years to unfold nationally and it will be how they are actually dealt with by the police, that will be the future test of public confidence.

We have attempted in this section to explore public protection from the mindset of the police service as compared to the expectations of the public. We believe we have demonstrated that there is a gap between the two in terms of understanding and delivery. It does occur to us that terminology causes problems in terms of understanding. For example, the police have an overriding duty to fight crime but some of the research quoted here suggests that this is becoming less of a dominant task. Public protection is another term which offers the potential for confusion. For the public it might fit better under that crime fighting role, whereas for the police it is often interchanged with safeguarding. This, for many police officers, is not a crime fighting role; it is instead a more passive, monitoring role often with those who are not, at least superficially, active criminals or at least not suspects. Thrown into this mix are serious issues such as sex offender monitoring, domestic abuse and sexual offending, mental health and child protection. In fact, all four of these areas offer the police huge opportunities to reduce offending and thereby protect the public, but too often end up being staffed by inexperienced officers or those occupying civilian roles, in itself reducing the significance of the position. The Casey Review (2023) recognised the importance of these roles and the need for improvement in them. Her report suggested that a 'dedicated protection service' for women be established, alongside a new children's strategy and reinstating sexual and domestic abuse services a specialist functions, rather than the recent attempts to make it a job that 'anyone could do'.

A major report commissioned by the Police Foundation (2022) echoed much of the thinking in Casey again, arguing that many of the roles which had become less important to core policing should be moved mainstream *or* become subject of a new agency. In the face of hugely challenging societal changes, the Report notes that although *traditional* crime has decreased, performance, public confidence and officer confidence are all down, especially over the past decade. These failings include issues such as a perfunctory response to crimes such as burglary the Telegraph (June 5, 2023) reporting that not one burglary had been solved in one half of neighbourhoods). No doubt at least in part influenced by negative publicity, the National Police Chiefs announced that Police would now attend the scene of every home burglary; what for many would be an extraordinary statement. The report also commented on the huge decline in charge/prosecution for rape allegations (1.6% in 2021, down from 8.5% in 2015). Similarly, violent offences saw a fall from 7% charged in 2021, down from 22% in 2015 and robbery charging down from 17% to 8% over the same period. Alongside performance disappointments, the Report also identifies new challenges such as a 194% increase in hate crime reports 2102–2019, worries about an increasing number of volatile public protests, a massive increase in cyber-enabled child sexual abuse, with for example 8.3 million images added to the child abuse image database from 2015 to 2019 (2022, p. 36). Interestingly, the report cites, as one reason for increased demands on the police, that people are wanting a better response to 'previously marginalised forms of violence, abuse and exploitation'. This of course includes domestic abuse, violent and sexual crime, as well as similar perpetrated against children. If indeed this was a marginalised aspect of crime then it is a scandal and one must ask, who was responsible for the marginalisation? This is without doubt a crime-fighting role but one which, for far too long, has been regarded as outside of police *action* stereotypes. The Report recommended the formation of a public safety system, to sit alongside the criminal justice system and which was focused around a new national crime prevention agency. In terms of the focus of this book, the report had a telling conclusion, 'currently police forces are simply unable to proactively focus on the most harmful offenders and the most vulnerable victims' (2022, p. 59).

Section Summary

It is clear to us that for the police service, public protection and public safety are intertwined, but mean different things. These understandings may also not accord with the public, or indeed other, partner agencies. In terms of how the public understand police public protection, it is likely to fit under the umbrella term of crime-fighting where police investigate crimes and arrest serious criminals. This possibly fits an image that many police still strive for, but as research in this section demonstrates, it is an increasingly small part of modern policing. This type of activity involves, in a sense, looking back towards a crime that has been committed, seeking evidence and building a case. The harm is done and there is not too much thought to the future once the suspect is apprehended and punished. The probation service on the other hand looks in a different direction. Public protection for it, is forward looking, with assessments of the risk of *future* serious harm. This monitoring and assessment work is not beloved of the police, with respondents in one piece of research saying they believed that undertaking risk assessments means taking police 'off the streets' (Mann et al., 2018, p. 635) and that form completion stops them actually *talking* with offenders. These two positions appear to represent a different mindset on public protection. Catching criminals as a means to reduce future crime is the crime fighting function that police and public appear to want, but this is singularly not seen in the activities of probation officers or indeed police MOSOVO officers. A change of thinking is required. It maybe that setting up a new Public Safety Agency, as recommended in the Police Foundation Report, will be the answer, but even this still leaves open the issue of the perception of activities such as domestic violence, often subject of repeated offending, as 'crimes' rather than 'safeguarding'. Our understanding of public protection in this book is reducing the amount of seriously harmful behaviour perpetrated on members of the public by offenders. It is important to remember that many of these offenders will be known to one or more public agencies. Therefore, if this knowledge is acted upon there is a chance of avoiding repetition. Violence and sexual assault committed by strangers however, where many members of the public and police officers appear to see the problem, is much more difficult to stop, if at all, by conventional policing methods. We have said before in many previous publications that in all those cases where there is at least some form of relationship or acquaintanceship between offender and victim that they are still members of the *public*. As such they are entirely the correct object for public protection measures, with at least a reasonable chance of preventing future harmful crime.

Chapter 4

The Probation Service: At the Heart of Everything?

The Probation Service

We do not intend to outline a detailed history of the probation service as events from the 1990s are most pertinent to this book, but readers can access the following for greater depth (Jarvis, 1972; Vanstone, 2004; Whitehead and Statham, 2006). The 1990s are significant because, as we have described elsewhere in this volume, criminal justice took a punitive turn (Garland, 2001) during this period and as a result, organisations not used to being 'punitive', such as the probation service, faced stark choices. An issue for probation, along with many public agencies, was that of continued funding at a time when there was a determined attempt to cut back on the cost of the public sector. As Worrall (1997, p. 5) argues, 'the fact is that people are prepared to pay for the punishment of criminals; they are not prepared to pay for their treatment. Community corrections will attract resources if they are dressed up as punishment'. Aside from the financial imperative there was, of course, a huge political one. As we have said elsewhere in this book, the 1990s were something of a political battleground over law and order policies. Traditionally safe ground for the Conservative Party, the emergence of Tony Blair's New Labour Party saw them challenged and indeed outbid in the punitive stakes. Much of the hype (we wouldn't call it debate) centred on sentencing and prisons, with probation having a key stake in both. It was most unlikely that the supporting and befriending ethos would survive into the new century and indeed, by the early 1990s, major incursions had already taken place.

The 1991 Criminal Justice Act was perhaps the last to show signs of significant influence from the old liberal consensus. Its underlying ambition, although not necessarily shouted from the rooftops, was to reduce the use of custody. Indeed, many criminal justice acts since then have sought to achieve the same aim, by greater or lesser means and with varying degrees of public acknowledgement. Central to these ambitions was the position of the probation service, in particular, its relationship to punishment and custody. The main achievement of the Act was the establishment of a sentencing framework based on offence seriousness.

Offences were either to be 'so serious' that only custody would suffice or, were 'serious enough' for a community penalty. This meant that probation orders as a community penalty were to be seen as a sentence in their own right, and no longer in place of a sentence. Significantly the long-established requirement to 'consent' to probation was abolished in the Crime (Sentences) Act, 1997 – another symbolic breaking from the past. In many ways, had the original framework divisions been maintained, there might have been less confusion over whether community penalties were an alternative to custody or not. As an alternative to custody, of course, they had to become much more punitive to gain the confidence of sentencers. That confidence was fragile though, and this is unsurprising if the public believed that the probation service was administering punishment which was meant as an alternative to custody. It is hardly possible to recreate the prison experience in the community; the whole language of alternatives then poses many more questions than it provides answers. As Smith (2005, p. 624) notes, no matter how rigorous the supervision, or tagging and tracking, etc., nothing is so successful as prison at protecting the public. It was public protection as currently envisaged that Smith felt the probation service could not provide. We would argue that there are other ways for the probation service to do this and helping to change a person's thinking and behaviour must be as valuable in the long term as periods of incarceration; although that will of course always be a requirement for some.

Shifting the Service

It will not have escaped readers' attention, that the probation service was being pushed quite rapidly into radical change. Its customer base, for want of a better term, was shifted from 'client' to 'offender'. Rehabilitation, the primary function of the probation service throughout its history, began to be interpreted in a variety of ways, and in a punitive era, became popularly associated with notions of being soft on crime and a let off. The public face of a rehabilitation ethos for the probation service came about through its writing of what had been called social en(In)quiry reports. These gathered and assessed information on the offender family background, education, health, social context, education/work, relationships, and pastimes. A complete social picture in other words. By the 1990s, this information was reconfigured as unnecessary, as it too often avoided a discussion of the crime, its impact and seriousness along with the culpability of the offender. SERs therefore became PSRs (pre-sentence reports) with an explicit offence focus, with offence seriousness guides developed for use by probation officers, alongside Likelihood of Custody scales, so that report recommendations could be correctly targeted. As Worrall (1997, p. 78) commented, 'PSRs represented an uncoupling of the relationship between crime and the "social," locating it firmly in the moral; the main focus was individual intentionality, remorse and capacity to respond to normalising instructions'. It is not difficult to see how a language of advise, assist, and befriend and clients did not sit easily alongside that of punishment, restriction, enforcement, and intentionality. The 1991 CJA therefore aimed to structure sentencing more fairly. Previous convictions for example, if of a random nature, would not escalate the seriousness of the current crime. Similar previous offences however would *aggravate* current offence seriousness as it might indicate a *pattern of behaviour*. Probation officers would fit into this process with their PSRs, helping the court to decide upon seriousness in terms of an appropriate sentence. The underlying principle was based upon proportionality and aimed to avoid discrimination and arbitrariness. Similar offences would in general receive similar sentences. Tonry (1994, p. 136), however, raised three objections to a strict principle of proportionality:

- By celebrating equality in suffering for 'like-situated' offenders, it often requires the imposition of more severe and intrusive punishments.
- It misleadingly objectifies punishment, by allocating punishments in terms of like-situated offenders and generic penalties.
- It ignores the problems of just desserts in an unjust society – a proportional system invokes the question of whether offenders from deeply deprived backgrounds, deserve the same penalties as do other, less deprived offenders.

The last point, we feel, takes us back to the issue of the 'social' and the work of probation in terms of rehabilitation. As Rotman (1994. p. 285) observes, the rehabilitative ideal aims towards a consideration of the offender's whole life, past and future. He suggests that it is a concept of justice which goes beyond the symmetrical reaction of retribution and inquiries into the subjective reality of the offender. Interestingly he suggests that the rehabilitative idea introduces broader social issues into the criminal justice system, creating an area of convergence with the social welfare, public health, and educational systems. This 'joining-up' has been much admired by governments since Tony Blair and New Labour. However, their idea of joining-up appears to have been more about extending the network of control and alleged protection, than bringing the 'social' back into justice.

Rehabilitation has not however been entirely rejected. It remains one of the aims of sentencing, although usually fairly well down the list of priorities. In almost every statement from a minister of justice, inevitably couched in the tough language of punishment and prisons, there will be mention of rehabilitation, although this is increasingly referring to post-prison. Indeed, community penalties themselves are increasingly referred to as 'tough', for instance Justice Secretary Ken Clarke, said that:

> ...community penalties can be a tough, effective way of making offenders turn away from crime and protecting the public...I am aware that for years successive governments have tried to make community penalties more tough and effective. I am also aware that the public are still not convinced that they are as effective as prison. Mills (2011, p. 22)

So, the probation service increasingly found itself being pushed towards becoming a punishment agency (dressed up as rehabilitation), whilst all the time attracting negative responses from politicians and the public. Politicians in particular appeared to enjoy getting their teeth into the organisation. John Major for example described it as 'weak, failing and on the side of the offender' (Deering & Feilzer, 2019). Jack Straw had told the probation service that it was falling into disrepute and that rehabilitation was *not* inconsistent with law enforcement, but in a more threatening tone, that there was no case for having a probation service if it was not effective at reducing offending (King & Wilmott, 2022). Michael Howard as Home Secretary had what was said to be a 'sneering disregard' for probation officers and social workers – who he regarded as representing the left-wing and liberal establishment, were politically correct, soft on crime and on the offenders' side rather than victims (Raynor & Vanstone, 2007). Labour Minister Charles Clarke had said that probation was a 'dagger at the heart of criminal justice, undermining confidence in criminal justice as a whole, this following a particularly violent and horrific serious further offence in London' (Allen & Hough, 2007, p. 56).

Clearly the probation service sat on the horns of a dilemma. On one hand it was being asked to sacrifice much of its entire professional and moral history and on the other, facing the possibility of being disbanded and merged or re-created in a different image. The attacks took two forms essentially, one was criticism for a seemingly minimal impact on reducing offending and the second, a failure to correctly assess and manage risk with high risk of harm offenders, an increasingly significant role for the service. More broadly, there were attacks from the political left for the Service's neglect of the role of social injustice as causes of crime through seeking explanation only in terms of personal shortcomings. Attacks also from the political right focussed the services' erosion of personal responsibility in claiming to find reasons that were too readily seen as excuses (Burke & Collett, 2010, p. 242). David Garland identified the predicament for the probation service when he said, 'probation has had to struggle to maintain its credibility, as the ideals upon which it was based have been discredited and displaced' (Garland, 2001, p. 177). Those ideals had resulted in the adoption of social work as the professional base for probation and this in particular came under sustained attack from politicians from the right and the left. Worrall (1997, p. 73) summarises the position in respect of the establishment of National Standards in 1994:

> (They) limited the discretion of the individual probation officer and focussed on the management of supervision rather than its content. And it followed that the need for probation officers to undertake two years training as social workers, when all procedures they will ever need to follow were now laid out in a glossy ring-bound booklet, must be open to question.

It was more than open to question. The government had decided that the language of social work was not the appropriate way in which to conceptualise the work of a core criminal justice agency. A Law Report in the *Independent*

Newspaper (15 February 1996) indicated that the 1993 Probation Service Act had said that the Secretary of State may make rules regulating the qualifications, manner of appointment, and duties of probation officers. The Home Secretary therefore felt he was able to delete the requirement in the 1984 probation rules requiring newly qualified probation officers to hold a Certificate of Qualification in Social Work (CQSW). The Court agreed and said he was entitled to prescribe no qualifications and delete requirements for a particular academic qualification. The Home Secretary had argued that these rules dissuaded particular types of persons from applying to join the probation service. Elsewhere we heard who these people were, when Howard spoke of a desire to recruit redundant ex-service personnel who 'knew how to handle men' (Home Office, 1995). He was also accused of creating a void by not having an alternative to the CQSW, but this was refuted during the appeal case implying that, because it was up to the Home Secretary to decide what qualifications there should be, *if any*, then no such void existed.

The probation service therefore faced not only the removal of its knowledge base but also the loss of professional status. For many in probation, the anticipated outcome of the 1997 general election could not come soon enough. There was hope that Labour might reduce or reverse the onslaught, although this seems somewhat naïve given the trajectory of law and order rhetoric in the 1990s. In some ways there was positive news for probation with increased budgets. However, although professional status was secured with a new qualification, the Diploma in Probation Studies, the then Home Secretary Jack Straw made it clear that there would be no return to social work. He said in the House of Commons (30 July 1997) that probation was a 'profession in its own right...and should no longer be linked to social work education'. If he applied the logic of Howard, he could have set a social work qualification as mandatory requirement – his choice not to do so, says much about where New Labour would take probation. The hope, at least for some within the probation service, was Labour's great desire to modernise and work from sound evidence bases any new evidence-based approach would however have to evolve against an extremely pessimistic background. David Smith (2005) described the years 1975–92 as the period of 'nothing works'. This view, widely but not fully correctly ascribed to the research works of Martinson (1974) in the United States, held enormous sway for a number of years, and, at the end of a period of pessimism, the search for 'what works' gained ground. Of course, the story of Martinson's alleged conclusion is an interesting example of the power of public messaging when it is what the public want to hear (Belanger, 2021). Having reviewed 231 studies on correctional rehabilitation with two co-collaborators, Martinson went ahead and published the report in his name alone in a neo-conservative journal *The Public Interest*. Although the findings were more nuanced with particular importance to the conditions under which treatment was offered, what the public heard and what they wanted to believe was that 'nothing works'. As a gifted communicator, Martinson across all media became firmly associated with the message. The conclusion drawn by many was that investing in prison reform was a waste of time and instead resources should go into a 'war on crime'. By 1979, Martinson had rowed back on his views, saying that 'contrary to my previous position, some treatment programs do have an appreciable effect on recidivism. Some programs are beneficial' (Belanger, 2021). In 1980 Martinson took his own life.

A mood of penal pessimism followed the publication of Martinson's work which, as we indicated earlier, was filled by politicians of all persuasions to extol the virtues of imprisonment for its own sake. Most famously this resulted in Michael Howard, Conservative Home Secretary, announcing at his party conference in 1993 that 'prison works'. Coming at the end of the period described as nothing works by Smith noted above, this statement represented a new twist in that it indicated that somethings did work, and for Howard, prison worked by taking criminals off the street. Here we see a definite switch in looking for a positive change for the offender, to one where the greater public good was the sign of success, in this case a reduction in offending for all. Interestingly, in the US, the Supreme Court had upheld a decision that removed the goal of rehabilitation from serious consideration when sentencing offenders (Sarre, 2001, p. 2). Defendants could henceforth be sentenced strictly for the crime – deserts-based – with no recognition given to amenability to treatment, personal or family history, etc. The court noted the 'outmoded rehabilitation model' and said that rehabilitation had failed. In contrast, Gendreau and Ross (1987) had published a positive review of over 200 studies, observing a reduction of reoffending of up to 80% in some cases. Perhaps reflecting the position that it was harder to get across positive messages about rehabilitation compared to the benefits of imprisonment, Gendreau and Ross said, 'All too often, in the face of all contrary evidence, we adhere to theories for political or ideological reasons…or cavalierly switch ideologies depending upon transient political developments' (1987, p. 395). Such sentiments may be familiar to students of criminal justice history in the UK from the 1990s onwards.

From Punishment to Protection

It is perhaps easier to view probation service history in three phases – although many more nuanced versions could be identified. These three phases might be thought of as a social work assistance phase, a punishment phase, and now, a protection phase. In simple terms, the ending of one phase ushers in the next, although there are inevitable hangovers, so the 'new' phase becomes something of a mishmash of old and new. We have seen that the old and original social work phase came under continued attack since the 1970s. For those who believed that more punishment and longer prison sentences were the answer to crime, then an ethos of empathy and assistance did not sit easily. There was no real recognition that criminal behaviour might be reduced or changed by social work–based interventions; it was forever cast as soft, and not a proper alternative to custody. So, by the 1970s, the drive was on to toughen up community disposals, with rehabilitation as a poor second in the ambition stakes. Before we move on with the three-stage analysis, we would like to briefly digress to discuss one of the author's professional experiences of community service orders, introduced in the

1972 Criminal Justice Act, to attempt to show the growing tensions between help and punishment. We will present this in the form of a brief narrative account.

My first job in the probation service was to set up the framework for community service orders. We had a six-month lead time to get everything ready. There was very little in the way of central direction outside of the minimum work commitments; 6 hours each week until completion of the 40-240-hours order. We operated under a loose and wide brief that the work should be of benefit to the community - broadly defined – and should not be work that would normally be undertaken by someone paid to do it. There were many negotiations with trade unions. The first task then was to find community agencies and organisations prepared to take offenders for 6 hours each week. Our job, at the beginning, was to 'sell' offenders to the community. We did this by visiting almost every church hall, community centre, children's projects, disabled centres, youth clubs, residential homes for the elderly and so on. Our task was, of course, to assess the risks to residents or service users where offenders were to be placed. We also needed to sell our offenders, and assess what the placement could do for the offender; we wanted them to gain as much as the placement. This was not a view widely shared however. It was however remarkable how many people willingly joined the scheme and felt remarkably relaxed about any potential risks. Therefore, we also assessed the main supervisor, often a matron in a home for elderly people, or the lead worker for children, or a local vicar. Our goal was to match offender and supervisor in an attempt to maximise the potential gains. At the end of six months we were ready for the first orders to be made, having also sold the scheme through magistrates' liaison meetings and sessions with local Judges. The process was that the sentencer would indicate that a custodial sentence was a possibility and that community service could be considered as an alternative. We would then make a specific community service assessment, face to face, all the while working through potential placements. The first order made was for a young man, aged 24, who had been convicted on several counts of violent behaviour. He had a history of violent altercations, usually with other young men but had never shown any aggression towards women. He had not used weapons. He had a short temper and was prone to lose it after drinking alcohol. He was not in a relationship at the time. After discussion in the team we decided to place him in a residential setting, a home for domestically abused mothers and their children. This might surprise readers but, our young man had younger siblings and spoke warmly about his relationship with them. He was very pleasant in normal conversation, was personable and, perhaps like our readers, was surprised at the placement under consideration. In this case the head of the home met him first and agreed to take him into the home. Although this was nearly fifty years ago, I can still remember how well he did; how staff and residents thought so highly of him. He had a natural ability with children and spoke in respectful ways to their mothers who thought he was a great addition – a so-called nice and normal man. He completed his order without any breaches and stayed on at its end to work 'voluntarily' at the home. It could be argued that this placement was not 'punishment', not an 'alternative to custody'. Yet for him it was very hard at first; he could not imagine doing that type of work. Yet he learned something about himself, found he could do well, what he never thought he could do. He was accepted as he was and did exceptionally well. This may not fit the standard definition of punishment and the benefits do appear to be from a social work manual. Yet there was punishment in this order, there was payback, but there was also rehabilitation. The subsequent development of this scheme to become public work groups, with offenders identifiable by their clothing and working on projects outside in the community, shows an evolutionary passage from a mixture of punishment and rehabilitation through to what appears to be pure punishment, with public shaming thrown in. To us, punishment with benefits offers a better prospect than punishment pure and simple.

Probation from this time on was to see a number of changes to the orders it had responsibility for, along with the creation of new ones, all pointing in the direction of more punishment and deprivation of liberty (for a very good summary of developments in community penalties see Solomon and Silvestri, 2008). Probation had of course been thrust into the punishment camp by the 1991 Criminal Justice Act which had made it a part of the sentencing framework, thus a punishment in its own right, rather than a form of alternative. Built on the discredited grounds of social work, a punishment ethos might have offered hope for the probation service's survival, but this clearly came at a cost. The overriding push from the New Labour governments for efficiency, modernisation, and evidence-based working similarly offered hope for continued rehabilitative efforts in the face of the demise of one-to-one casework. New forms of group work offered hope, based on evidence of what works, but as Smith (2005, p. 627) noted, people forgot that group work was originally seen as a way of enhancing or supplementing 'normal' supervision, not replacing it. Having acceded to the prison works agenda, by not actively opposing it, the New Labour government benefited from a coincidental fall in the crime rate during its first term. This enabled it to look again at community penalties, bringing together the twin aims of punishment and modernisation (Burke & Collett, 2010, p. 239). George Mair (2016, p. 8) described the policy making of New Labour as suffering from 'initiativitis', with new policies rolled out before the previous one was established and with little in the way of rigorous evaluation. Naturally any drive for efficiency looked towards saving money and in simple unit costs, rehabilitation works on only one offender at a time, whereas deterrence is aimed at the many. Probation was therefore competing in a market for funding which increasingly followed the punishment trail. As a result, it had to prove it was a punishment in its own right, although in the minds of the public, it was always going to be compared unfavourably to imprisonment. As part of the punitive agenda, probation was charged with reducing offending by utilising increasingly tough measures, and enforcing those measures more rigorously. This laid the ground for a more specific form of public protection, based on high risk of harm offenders. The enormity and significance of this task was perhaps underestimated in the first instance.

Protecting the Public

Since the 1991 Criminal Justice Act and the Criminal Justice and Court Services Act, 2000, the probation service had been mandated to protect the public. In fact, it was given first priority, followed by reducing reoffending, punishing offenders, ensuring offenders are aware of the effect of their crime on victims and lastly, rehabilitating the offender. Burke and Collett (2010, p. 240) suggested that public protection had displaced or qualified the priority of rehabilitation and assessment and management of risk was now the single most important task for probation officers. Robinson (2002) as noted in Burke and Collett (2010) said that probation officers had emerged from this process as 'pivotal (risk) knowledge brokers', moving closer in alignment to the police service. Locating these developments within a wider context, Kemshall (2010, p. 201) suggested that 'community protection is characterised by compulsory conditions, surveillance and monitoring, enforcement, compulsory treatment and the prioritisation of victim and community rights over offenders'. In many respects, probation was being moved much closer to the ethos and practice of other criminal justice organisations, notably the police and prison officers. At an organisational level, the creation of the National Offender Management Service (NOMS) in 2004 had sought to develop end-to-end offender management following the Carter Review (2007) concerning the management of offenders. Needless to say, this situation did not remain the same for long as in 2007, the correctional services element was moved to the new Ministry of Justice. Within a year though, prisons and probation were moved closer with the appointment of Phil Wheatley assuming responsibility for prison and probation services. By 2017, NOMS disappeared to become Her Majesty's Prison and Probation Service (HMPPS). This is 'initiativitis' in the extreme! At practitioner level collaboration perhaps worked a little more smoothly for probation, prisons, and police services (see Mawby & Worrall, 2004; Mawby et al., 2007; Nash, 1999a, 1999b, 2008 for descriptions of joint working examples).

In terms of public protection, we would argue that it is fair to say that the probation service holds centre stage. It not only has a key role in attempts to reduce offending but plays a major part in trying to prevent future harm from known serious offenders. This role is in large part concerned with the assessment and management of risk. This happens at key decision-making stages, such as in reports for courts and parole boards, but also in respect of breach proceedings. Their risk decisions might therefore influence the choice of sentence in court; the decision to release or not from custody and the decision to recommend a recall to custody in breach proceedings. More than that though, it may be the ongoing working with risk which is the most important. Working with offenders who *pose a risk of harm* means that risk assessment and management requires an awareness of risk factors (warning signs), and how to manage those is crucial in attempting to prevent further harm. We would argue that no other agency contributes so much to this process as the probation service. It has come an enormous distance from its roots, but we would argue that the early skills honed from its social work origins remain vital to modern public protection methods. The next section will explore how risk decisions which are allied to, or used as an excuse for, financial and commercial decisions, has had a huge, and in our view, damaging impact on not only probation officers but the public they are meant to protect.

Bring on the Revolution – A Shaky Ideological House of Cards

Readers will hardly be surprised that a book on the politics of public protection which includes a chapter on probation should also include a review of what we regard as one the biggest political mistakes in criminal justice history – the Coalition government's transforming rehabilitation revolution. In this section, we only focus on some of the key political arguments and rationales in the run-up to its implementation in 2014. For readers wishing for a more in-depth overview of the issues, problems, and processes within TR, please consult the various articles in the three TR special editions – 2013s *British Journal of Community Justice (Volume 11)*; 2016s and 2019s *Probation Journal (Volume 63 and 66)*; as well as Burke and Collett's *Delivering Rehabilitation* (2015) and Deering and Feilzer's *Privatising Probation* (2015). This central piece of criminal justice policy was first set out in their programme for government:

> We will introduce a 'rehabilitation revolution' that will pay independent providers to reduce reoffending, paid for by the savings this new approach will generate within the criminal justice system. HM Government (2010, p. 23)

The revolution included the complete transformation of probation and how offenders were managed in the community; by part-privatising probation and allowing the management and rehabilitation of offenders to be undertaken by non-criminal justice experts and based on their assigned level of risk. This section explores this transformation and, alongside many other commentators (see Burke & Collet, 2016; Evans, 2016; Fitzgibbon, 2013; Gosling, 2016; Senior, 2013) argues that it included rushed planning; a lack of evidence to support the proposals; and was based on a poor understanding of reoffending behaviour, risk assessment and risk management planning. Even more, it explains how the government's framing of the issue was actually an attempt to devalue the probation service, stripping it of its cultural, social, and symbolic capital and weakening its strength within the heteronomous pole in the sub-field of community sanctions (Phillips, 2020). It achieved this so as to implement its intended plans, which were outlined across the following documents:

- *Breaking the Cycle* (Dec 2010).
- *Competition Strategy for Offender Services* (July 2011).
- *Punishment and Reform: Effective Probation Services* (Mar 2012).
- *Transforming Rehabilitation: A Revolution in the Way we Manage Offenders* (Jan 2013).

The first was the 2010 Green Paper, which effectively framed the problem as being because of the cycle-of-crime (i.e. the revolving door of most reoffending) and disingenuously linked these groups of offenders to probation. This set forth evidence that this was the fundamental problem within the criminal justice and public protection approaches to crime. The next paper in 2011 made it clear where the government was heading – competitive private sector tendering for offender management or, as the then Secretary of State Kenneth Clarke put it, 'the guiding principle for offender services will be that competition will apply to all services not bound to the public sector by statute, rather than as a means to select providers for new services or to address poor performance' (MoJ, 2010, p. 2). The third report listed above, moved the first two reports further along and was a consultation of the government's proposals to improve the probation services in England and Wales and make them value for money (MoJ, 2011, p, 5). Finally, the 2013 Transforming Rehabilitation consultation (MoJ, 2013a) set out the precise nature of these proposals. Whilst there is no need to regurgitate everything within these documents here, we do feel a review of some of the more pertinent elements linking politics to public protection would be useful. Kenneth Clarke's Green Paper *Breaking the Cycle* (2010) set the framework for this issue, stating that there were numerous problems caused by the previous Labour government's approach to punishment and rehabilitation. These problems were (2010, pp. 5–6): (i) the increasing use of imprisonment rather than tackling reoffending; (ii) the over-use of short-term sentences with no rehabilitation; (iii) the lack of innovation in the punishment system leading to reoffending rates for short prison sentences increasing to 61% in 2008; and (iv) the cost of this reoffending committed by those on short-term sentences estimated at being between £7–10 billion a year (2010, p. 6). The Green Paper set out a number of proposals to solve these problems, and these proposals were to be achieved using the following four principles:

(1) protecting the public
(2) punishing and rehabilitating offenders
(3) transparency and accountability and
(4) decentralisation

These are pretty much the same problems and issues raised by Tony Blair's government when they first came to power in 1997. Historical amnesia (Pearson, 1983), it seems, is a perfect tool for politicians to repeat the same problems whilst persuading the public they are the ones who have *the* solution. For the Coalition, this solution was part-privatisation based on the principle 'to bring in a wider range of organisations from the private, voluntary and community sector, alongside the public sector, to compete to provide services for offenders, with providers increasingly paid for the results they achieve' (MoJ, 2012, p. 6). This was to be the start of plans for the commodification of public protection and rehabilitation, with offenders reframed as customers and an attempt to make the hundred-plus years of probation professional development and practice minimised to the role of service provider. Both the *Breaking the Cycle* (MoJ, 2010) and *Competition Strategy for Offender Services* (MoJ, 2011) documents used the short-term sentence cycle-of-crime thesis and a manipulation of the intentions within the Offender Management Act 2007 (see Burke & Collett, 2016) to great effect, forever linking politics and public protection. The pathway to privatisation was laid by the Labour government, especially their implementation of the Offender Management Act 2007. S3 of the Act allowed for the outsourcing of probation services, paving the way for privatisation and the complex mix of public and private service providers. This was the first way Clarke and the government framed the issue - it was simply a continuation of the on-going implementation of OMA 2007 (MoJ, 2012, p. 2). But why was it necessary for a revolutionary solution in the first place? The rationale behind privatising probation was the problem of the revolving door or cycle of crime, highlighting that short-sentences of under a year meant little to no rehabilitation and this was feeding persistent reoffending. Most governments over the last 40 years have tried to solve the issue of persistent and prolific offending (PPO), as many of these offences are committed by repeat offenders who, if caught, receive small custodial sentences of usually less than a year, are released early without any rehabilitation, only to reoffend. Much of this is true. That's why in the ratcheting up of criminal justice over the last 40 years or so, different governments have introduced numerous PPO schemes (HMIP et al., 2009) – they have to be seen to deal with the large number of offences and re-offences committed and there is nothing wrong with this. What the likes of Clarke and his disastrous successor Chris Grayling failed to mention was that before the introduction of the Offender Rehabilitation Act 2014 (see below), these individuals weren't even managed by probation. The Coalition government made a great deal of noise about this group and then, in a disingenuous ideological sleight-of-hand, used this argument as the rationale for their probation privatisation plans (we explain this further below). Clarke's vision was to bring innovation into public protection by opening up risk management and rehabilitative provision to competitive market-driven forces (MoJ, 2010, 2011, 2012). As usual, this type of vision rests on the belief that neo-liberalism is not only the best structure but a free-market economy lacking in regulation is cost efficient and innovative. This is blatantly untrue (see Albertson et al., 2020). Free-markets tend to move towards monopolies and monopolistic price-fixing (just look at the food, water, energy and social media sectors), so competition and innovation is actually stifled (see Dunn, 2017). Neo-liberalism is just code for monopolistic conglomerates doing more with less; and the 'with less' part often involves reducing labour costs. Moreover, there is very little evidence to suggest that private sector operations can be easily and successfully translated to the public sector arena, such as criminal justice and public protection (see Albertson et al., 2020).

Despite all this, the Coalition government was determined on their pathway to rehabilitative enlightenment. *Punishment and Reform: Effective Probation Services* (2012) was a 'consultation' on the government's plans and included proposals which would: 'further extend the principles of competition...(which)...the Offender Management Act 2007 set the basis of this policy and its implementation' (p. 2); and explores how 'best to ensure that probation can lever in the expertise of the voluntary and private sectors' (p. 2); and take 'a stronger role as commissioners of competed (sic) probation services, contracted to be responsible for driving better outcomes' (pp. 2–3); with 'the potential involvement of Police and Crime Commissioners and local authorities at a later stage' (p. 3). This final aspect was yet another indication of a move-towards punitiveness in offender management, suggesting a somewhat mixed-message in the proposals. This consultation was open on 27 March 2012 and ran until 22 June 2012, and one of the central and more controversial proposals was to split offender management between public sector (probation) and private companies. This new structure of offender management was to be based on the level of risk assigned to offenders, with high and very high-risk offenders being managed under probation and low and medium risk offenders managed under newly created private community and rehabilitation companies (CRCs). The strategy of opening up offender management to a supposedly more efficient and competitive market was clearly set out in the MoJ 2010, 2011, 2012 reports and consultations. For example, before there were any consultations, Kenneth Clarke had already made up his mind and committed the MoJ:

> The Ministry of Justice Business Plan commits the Department to creating a functioning market in the provision of legal aid, offender management and rehabilitation, with the aim being to ensure that justice services are provided by whoever can most effectively and efficiently meet public demand. MoJ (2011, p. 3)

In September 2012, Chris Grayling replaced Clarke as Secretary of State for Justice and ramped up the time-table for completion. Again, the central proposal was clear: the push towards part-privatisation of probation, with the offender allocation based on level of risk, with private companies engaging with offenders on a payment-by-results (PBR) basis. Let's be clear, the TR proposals were another move to 'policy-based evidence not evidence-based policy' (Senior, 2013, p. 1), and, unsurprisingly, were met with different responses, depending on whether the respondent was from the public or private sector. For example, probation trust responses raised concerns that splitting offender management on the basis of risk 'failed to recognise the dynamic nature of risk' (MoJ, 2013b, p. 5), whilst the private sector responses gave 'general support for competing offender management' services (p. 6). Across the public and private sector responses, concerns were raised about the proposals in terms of creating a segmented offender management process, with additional bureaucracy adding complexity to an already overburdened bureaucratic process (p. 5). Despite the concerns raised, it turns out that the consultation wasn't really a consultation. It was merely a tick-box exercise so that if the government were ever challenged, they could say the relevant sectors were consulted. The fact that this was being forced through so quickly also raised a number of concerns, all to no avail. In January 2013 the *Transforming Rehabilitation* consultation was opened, the basis of which was the following proposed allocation of functions for different offender groups shown in Table 1 (2013, p. 15):

Unfortunately, this wasn't a consultation in the usual sense of the word, where anyone who wishes to respond can critically review and openly express opinions about a proposal. This was a consultation on something that had already been decided, and Grayling was all too willing to see it through. What is telling is when one looks at the content of the response summary document to the TR proposals (MoJ, 2013b), it glosses over (or ignores) any critical responses about the splitting of the service based on the level of risk proposal itself. This document only reports responses to specific questions and ignores any criticisms of the proposals but goes out of its way to focus on what should be implemented to make privatisation work. For example, effective integration and working practices, transparency, and the avoidance of fragmentation in service delivery were all identified as possible issues by the respondents (MoJ, 2013b, p. 4). Absolutely nothing was included about whether the government had received negative or critical responses about the proposal's themselves – which is highly likely. Furthermore, in what has become a typical government strategy of politics before evidence, Grayling also cancelled the PBR pilots which were designed to test the key proposals on a small scale. As Burke and Collett (2016, p. 125) note, the reasons behind this were obvious and not what Grayling claimed:

Table 1. TR Proposed Allocation for Different Offender Groups.

	Market	Public Sector
Low/medium risk offenders	Paid-by results to rehabilitate offenders (private sector CRCs)	Accountable for public protection (remaining public sector – probation)
High/very high risk offenders		Accountable for public protection (remaining public sector – probation)

The pilots to test **PBR** in the community were cancelled by Grayling and in his evidence to the Justice Committee, he claimed that this was because it was a common-sense approach that wasn't 'rocket science'. In truth, the more likely motivation for cancelling the pilots was the Justice Secretary's rush to ensure that his reforms were introduced before the general election. He did not want to be inconvenienced by having to wait for the outcomes of evaluations which might not support his political ambitions.

In short, the TR proposals were not based on any evidence at all, they were simply a drive towards the neo-liberal ideology of the marketisation and commodification of public protection (see Albertson et al., 2020), which trumped evidence-based policy. Of course, at the time the government was forcing through TR, there were many who were very vocal in their opposition. Academics and members of the probation service tried in vain to raise some key concerns, many of which were published in a 2013 special edition of the *British Journal of Criminology* (see Bowen, 2013; Calder, 2013; Dominey, 2016; Fitzgibbon, 2013; Senior, 2013). All of these fears – most of which have since been proven to correct – were ignored by the government. Phillips (2020), using Bourdieu's work on field theory (see Bourdieu, 1986, 2000), links this failure to influence government policy, not because of a lack of effort from probation but because the government had delegitimised and weakened their social capital in the sub-field of community public protection. Furthermore, many members of parliament raise important points in criticising the TR proposals and whilst it is not possible to discuss all of these in detail here, an example will illustrate the political debate that was taking place. Lord Ramsbottom (HL Law, 2013 col 661 and col 662) raised some important questions when the proposals were debated in the House of Lords.

> Until last summer, the criminal justice system was embarked on a rehabilitation revolution led by a Secretary of State whose method included careful examination of practicalities and attention to the all-important role of people in the rehabilitation process. In the new rehabilitation revolution on which we are now embarked, people appear to be made to play second fiddle to the market, while the timing appears to be determined by the need to present tough achievements to the electorate in the 2015 election manifesto. The problem with it is that in addition to punishing offenders it also punishes those who work with them, particularly the probation service, for all the wrong reasons. My unease stems from the inconsistency in two statements by the Justice Secretary. First, in launching the consultation associated with Transforming Rehabilitation on 9 January, he said:

Despite significant increases in spending on probation under the previous government, almost half of those released from prison still go on to reoffend within 12 months.

This confirmed my fear that – for entirely illogical reasons, because this is the one group of offenders for whom the probation service currently has no responsibility – he blamed probation for the fact that three-quarters of the annual cost of reoffending could be attributed to this group and was bent on total reorganisation, despite all the various changes that had been imposed on the service over the past 15 years and the fact that it was hitting all its targets. Secondly, in his foreword to Transforming Rehabilitation: A Strategy for Reform, published on 9 May, the same day as the Bill, he says:

Through the savings we make, we will extend rehabilitation support to those on short-term sentences, who currently have the highest reoffending rates but who are typically left to their own devices on release. This support will be guaranteed through legislation, which is the only way to ensure we target the hardest to reach and most prolific offenders.

When has legislation ever been able to guarantee the consistent availability, provision, and affordability of the money and people required to produce that support?

Despite all of the opposition to the proposals, TR was introduced and the part-privatisation of probation went through. As we previously mentioned above, the key political framing for TR was the cycle-of-crime and the need to reduce reoffending committed by those who had previously received short-term sentences. These individuals were never within scope for probation so the government decided to change that. Through the Offender Rehabilitation Act 2014 these offenders were brought under the scope of Probation: 'the introduction of supervision on release for offenders serving custodial sentences of less than 12 months and changes to the requirements available to the court as part of community orders and suspended sentence orders' (https://legislation.gov.uk). Bringing these under the scope of probation who were then split, bringing CRCs to manage these offenders. In June 2014 probation was part-privatised and 21 CRCs were created.[1] These CRCs were mainly owned by larger corporations, most of whom had previously links with procuring criminal justice contracts (e.g. Sodexo). Unsurprisingly, once implemented, most of the objections and claims about the issues privatisation would cause, came to fruition and probation services were reunified in June 2021 (HoC, 2021). The CRC contracts were cancelled but not without significant cost to the public purse. The National

---

[1] For a full list of the original 2014 CRCs, please refer to https://assets.publishing.service.gov.uk/media/5a7e39a3e5274a2e8ab46a65/table-of-new-owners-of-crcs.pdf.

Audit Office (NAO, 2019, p. 9) estimated this cost to be £467 million, which includes 'additional projected payments to CRCs above the original terms of the contracts between 2016–17 and December 2020 (£296 million) and minimum contract termination costs (£171 million)'. Once again, private companies have benefited from the public purse.

Summary

This chapter provides a comprehensive overview of the evolution of the probation service, particularly focussing on the pivotal changes it underwent during the 1990s. This period marked a significant shift in criminal justice policies towards a punitive approach, leading to profound transformations within the probation service. Initially rooted in a social work assistance phase, the probation service gradually transitioned into a punishment phase in response to political and societal pressures. The 1991 Criminal Justice Act played a crucial role in reshaping sentencing frameworks, positioning probation as a punishment in its own right rather than an alternative to custody. This shift towards punishment was accompanied by the erosion of the rehabilitation ethos, which came under scrutiny for being perceived as lenient. The narrative offers a personal account of the implementation of community service orders, highlighting the tension between punitive measures and rehabilitative efforts within the probation service. Despite efforts to balance punishment with rehabilitation, the prevailing rhetoric favoured punitive measures, leading to a decline in the prioritisation of rehabilitation. Furthermore, we explored how the probation service's evolving role in public protection, emphasising the increasing focus on risk assessment and management. With mandates prioritising public safety, probation officers assumed pivotal roles as knowledge brokers, aligning closer to law enforcement agencies. The formation of the National Offender Management Service and subsequent reorganisations underscored the probation service's integration into broader criminal justice frameworks. However, this institutional restructuring often led to bureaucratic challenges and shifting priorities, impacting frontline practitioners. Despite these challenges, the probation service remains central to efforts aimed at reducing reoffending and preventing harm from known offenders – two of the key aspects of public protection. Drawing on its historical roots in social work, the probation service continues to navigate complex terrain, balancing punitive measures with rehabilitative interventions in pursuit of public protection.

The exploration of the TR revolution unveils a narrative of political ambition overshadowing evidence-based policy, leading to the shaky foundation of a significant criminal justice reform. Initiated under the Coalition Government, TR aimed to revolutionise offender management by partially privatising probation services. However, a closer examination reveals rushed planning, lack of evidence, and a fundamental misunderstanding of reoffending behaviour in terms of risk level. The ideological underpinning of TR rested on the premise of a rehabilitation revolution, promising reduced reoffending rates through private sector involvement, funded by savings within the criminal justice system. This ambitious agenda, outlined in various government documents, aimed to address perceived failures in the existing probation system, emphasising a shift towards a competitive market-driven approach. Central to TR's justification was the portrayal of a revolving door of reoffending, attributed to the shortcomings of the probation system. However, numerous evidence suggests that this narrative conveniently ignored the complexities of reoffending dynamics and misrepresented the role of probation in managing offenders. Moreover, TR's implementation lacked genuine consultation, with predetermined decisions and disregard for critical feedback, exemplifying a politics-first approach. Despite opposition from academics, probation professionals, and some members of parliament, TR proceeded, resulting in the creation of the CRCs tasked with managing low- and medium-risk offenders. However, the aftermath exposed the flaws of privatisation, with CRCs failing to deliver on promises while draining public funds. The eventual reunification of probation services in 2021 marked the acknowledgement of the failed experiment, underscoring the inherent instability of TR's ideological framework.

The TR saga highlights the dangers of prioritising political agendas over empirical evidence and expert advice in shaping criminal justice policies. It serves as a cautionary tale, emphasising the need for robust evaluation and stakeholder engagement in policy formulation. Ultimately, TR's legacy underscores the resilience of evidence-based approaches in navigating the complexities of public protection, while exposing the fragility of ideological constructs built on shaky foundations. While grappling with shifting political landscapes and organisational changes, the probation service remains committed to its core mission of promoting public safety and reducing reoffending, albeit within an increasingly complex and challenging criminal justice landscape.

Part Three

Other Dangerous Groups

Chapter 5

Mentally Ill and Personality Disordered Offenders

Perhaps nothing more embodies dangerousness than the image of a 'mad' person, running amok and out of control, randomly attacking 'innocent' people. Due to the not so careful construction of a dangerous person as 'the other', 'the abnormal', and the 'not one of us', it is no surprise that those suffering from mental illness and engaged in some form of criminality (or even suspected of it) find themselves cast readily into one of these three groups. Many people rush to exclude rather than include and, if the presenting behaviour is one of violence or similar, the wish may be to exclude for a very long time. This chapter will explore the interplay between mental illness and seriously harmful criminal behaviour, with a particular focus on homicide, and the relationships between mental health and criminal justice systems. It will use a case study which, at the time of writing (February 2024), was very much prominent across all media outlets, a significant matter for politicians and of course, of huge importance to the families of the victims. We will use this case as a means of setting the scene for the discussion that follows.

In June 2023, Valdo Calocane murdered three people and attempted to murder three others in Nottingham (HMCPSI, 2024). In the early hours of the morning, Calocane, who had been hiding in shadow, confronted 19-year olds Grace O'Malley Kumar and Barnaby Webber, both students of Nottingham University. He began attacking Barnaby whilst Grace bravely tried to fend him off. Both were brutally murdered. Shortly after, Ian Coates, 65, a school caretaker on his way to work, was attacked and killed by Calocane, who then used Coates' car and drove directly at three other people with an intention to kill them, fortunately failing to do so. The sentencing Judge described the crimes as 'sickening' which 'both shocked the nation and wrecked the lives of your surviving victims and the families of them all'. Whilst not belittling the awfulness of these events, we feel that this case serves as a very good example of a number of the issues we have raised in this book, which make the task of protecting the public so difficult and complex. It will show how individual cases can shape and challenge legislation, policy, and practice. This case is an example of the crossover between criminal justice and mental health services. On the evidence of no less than five psychiatrists, Calocane had been found to be suffering from paranoid schizophrenia, and therefore, not responsible for his actions. As a result of these diagnoses, the prosecution accepted a plea of guilty to manslaughter on the grounds of diminished responsibility. The outcome of this (of which more detail below) was that the defendant was sentenced to a Hospital Order under section 37 of the Mental Health Act, 1983, with Restrictions under section 41, with the Judge expecting him to be detained probably for life. However, he declined to use the power under section 45a of the act, to impose a parallel prison sentence which would become active if the patient were ever deemed to have recovered. It is the decisions leading to the final outcome which has so distressed the families in this case, and which we will now discuss as examples of the potential difficulties in many public protection cases.

Police (in)action

As we have seen in the parole section, in cases of murder by released prisoners, the feelings of many victims are that the prisoner should not have been released, early or otherwise, and therefore should not have been free to commit the crime. In the Calocane case, the victims pointed to an arrest warrant which if executed (it was not in the nine months it was active prior to the murders) might have meant the offender would have been in custody or mental health detention (this is, of course, by no means certain). He had a history with mental health services in Nottingham, having been sectioned on several occasions, with police assisting NHS colleagues. In September 2021, the police had been called in to help serve a S.135 warrant to section the suspect. He was taken to hospital during which time he assaulted a police officer. Police were further involved in January 2022, when called to an incident in which he was alleged to have assaulted his flatmate. Nottinghamshire police said that police action was 'not supported' so no arrest was made, though he was again briefly detained in hospital. In August 2022, he was reported for summons on the assaulting a police officer charge, but he failed to appear. An arrest warrant was issued in September 2022, a warrant that was still outstanding at the time of the murders. It was this lack of police action that was to lead Barnaby Webber's mother to claim, that the police had 'blood on their hands' for failing to arrest Caloclane. Assistant Chief Constable Rob Griffin had said that 'we should have done more to arrest him' although with a caveat that he felt it unlikely the offender would have been imprisoned or that he would have engaged in the mental health process if that had been the alternative route (Nottinghamshire Police, 25.1.24). There may be a number of reasons why the police may not act in a particular case, but in this instance, there appears to have been a certain amount of second guessing to justify the non-action. In the event, Nottinghamshire Police referred themselves to the Independent Office for Police Complaints (IOPC), because shortly before Calocane ploughed his stolen car into three people, he was being followed by a police vehicle. The Daily Mail (2.2.24) commented on what might be considered the final insult for the victims. They reported that the police, allegedly, failed to take toxicology samples from Calocane, as he refused to give urine or blood samples. They did not take a sample of his hair. The significance of the alleged omission is that if there were drugs in his system, voluntarily taken, these could exacerbate the signs of mental illness. Sentencing guidelines suggest that this action can *increase* responsibility on the part of the offender, rather than diminishing it. This failure to take samples caused distress to the families of the victims. Grace's father, Dr Sanjoy Kumar told the Daily Mail (2.2.24) that... 'Whilst we have never questioned this man's diagnosis, the lack of toxicology, contemporaneous mental health assessment as well as missed opportunities to divert his legal path, will forever play on our minds'.

The Crown Prosecution Service

The Attorney General, Victoria Prentis, ordered an investigation into the CPS role in the Calocane case following statements from the victims' families that 'justice had not been done' and that they had been 'railroaded' into accepting the manslaughter charges brought forward by prosecutors. We will briefly examine the role of the CPS before considering their specific decisions in this case. The first rule of thumb for prosecutors entails two tests, that of evidential sufficiency – is it enough to provide a 'realistic prospect of conviction' and whether or not prosecution is in the public interest. For our purposes, further aspects of the CPS role, that of selecting the charges and the acceptance of guilty pleas, is most relevant to discussions in this case. In the Calocane case, the CPS authorised the police to charge him with three counts of murder and three counts of attempted murder within 3 days of the crime. According to the official CPS account, over the following months he was assessed by three psychiatric experts, instructed by prosecution and defence, who all agreed that he was suffering from mental illness, namely paranoid schizophrenia, which led to an abnormality of mental functioning and impaired his ability to exercise self-control. He believed that voices in his head were telling him to act as he did and that his family would be hurt if he did not obey. The CPS then took the unusual step of commissioning a fourth independent review which came to the same conclusions as the other three. As a result of these assessments, the CPS decided that there was 'no realistic prospect' of a conviction for murder and accepted the guilty pleas to charges of manslaughter. Clearly there was a good deal of consideration of the medical evidence in light of the seriousness of the charges and the public interest in the case, even before sentencing. The Sentencing Council (1 October 2020) acknowledge that defendants may wish to plead guilty to lesser charges but the prosecution should only accept this if the court is still able to pass a sentence which matches the seriousness of the offending, whilst also saying, 'particular care must be taken when considering pleas which would enable the defendant to avoid the imposition of mandatory minimum sentences'. The Guidelines also pick up on a point made by the victims and families in the Calocane case, namely the degree to which they were consulted and their views taken into account. The Guidelines state that where possible, the views of victims and victims' families should be considered, 'however the decision rests with the prosecutor'. Emma Webber, mother of Barnaby, said after sentencing, that in November 2023, the families had been presented with a *fait accompli*, that the decision to proceed with manslaughter charges had already been taken. She continued, 'at no point during the preceding two and a half months, were we given any indication that this could conclude in anything other than murder...we trusted our system – foolishly as it turned out' (BBC News, 25.1.24). As the Code for Crown Prosecutors (26 October 2018) explains, 'the CPS does not act for victims or their families in the same way as solicitors for their clients, and prosecutors must form an overall view of the public interest'.

It is perhaps not difficult to see why the family might have felt aggrieved or at least confused by the outcome. Perhaps the notion of diminished responsibility does not sit easily with what the CPS described as a pre-planned attack. In responding to the sentence, the Chief Crown Prosecutor for the East Midlands stated that:

> ...although his actions and self-control were impaired, the defendant knew that what he was doing was wrong. We presented evidence during sentencing of pre-planning, evidence that he had lain in wait for his victims and that he only stopped his attacks when detained and subdued by the police. CPS (25.1.2024)

Although pre-planning and diminished responsibility are not mutually exclusive, it is not difficult to understand the families' confusion over some of the statements released in the wake of sentencing, and indeed during it. In part responding to this distress, the Attorney general ordered a rapid inquiry into the CPS actions in the Calocane case, which reported in March 2024. In a long and detailed report, HMCPSI (2024) addressed two of the key points raised by the families in their meeting with the Prime Minister, and these concerned the decision not to charge Calocane with murder and also the way in which they had been included in decision-making. On both of these matters, the CPSI felt that the decisions taken in the case were correct as the law stood and that the CPS had acted correctly with the families but could have been better. The report did however refer back to a Law Commission suggestion dating from 2006, that murder be classified into three tiers. Tier one would be first-degree murder, Tier two would be second-degree murder to include the defence of diminished responsibly and manslaughter. The report concluded that, had Calocane been found guilty of second-degree murder, the decision may have reflected the reality felt by the families more accurately. We believe that a law change in line with the Law Commission's 2006 recommendations may become government policy in the near future. If so, this will be another instance when legislative changes arise from particular cases and strong campaigns by informed and 'worthy' victims. We will now move on to a brief examination of the trial of Valdo Calocane.

The Trial and Judge's Comments

The Judge's opening comments summed up the horror of the case:

...you committed a series of atrocities in this city which ended the lives of three innocent people. You went on to attack three more; fully intending, but failing, to kill them too. Your sickening crimes both shocked the nation and wrecked the lives of your surviving victims and the families of them all.

The Judge stated that there was never any doubt that Calocane had committed the crimes, 'the central issue in this case would relate to whether...you were suffering from severe symptoms of mental disorder and, if so, what part they played in what you did'. The court was reminded that for a period of 3 years following his first signs of mental illness in 2019, he continued to hear voices which he believed were threatening him and controlling him. It was also pointed out that he had stopped taking his medication because he did not believe that he was ill. As we have seen above, there were incidents of aggressive behaviour and attempted breaking into other properties. There had been four hospital admissions. The Judge referred to an almost exceptional number of five expert reports commenting on Calocane's health. All agreed that he was suffering from paranoid schizophrenia. The Judge remarked that he had to factor these opinions into the process of sentencing but he was not bound by them. He said that he was entirely satisfied that the prosecution was right to acknowledge that Calocane's mental condition satisfied the criteria giving rise to the partial defence of diminished responsibility. He pointed out that this defence did not apply to the three counts of attempted murder to which Calocane had pleaded guilty.

Judges undoubtedly face a difficult task in deciding on the final disposal, in particular the balance between treatment and punishment, where there is room for families to feel that their wish for punishment is not being met. The Judge was persuaded by the psychiatric evidence that the defendant needed treatment and was suitable for it. He was persuaded that the offending would not have occurred were it not for his mental illness. However, and it is here that the possibility for confusion and misunderstanding can arise, when the Judge said that, aside from the need for treatment, he also had to consider the extent to which 'punishment is required'. He eventually decided in favour of not including a punitive element in the hospital order he was to impose, on the grounds that the diagnosis of treatment resistant schizophrenia means it very likely he will never be released. In other words, put crudely, punishment was not imposed because the defendant would never be cured and therefore never released. There are of course unknowns here. Who is to say that new treatments might not be found in the future? Indeed, Dr Blackwood in his evidence outlined just how a restricted patient could be returned to the community if satisfactory progress could be shown, a fact that would not have been lost on the family members watching on in court. What the Judge rejected was the making of a section 45A Hospital and Limitation direction (a hybrid order), which offers up the opportunity for some part of the sentence to be served in prison (if the patient was later to be assessed as no longer suffering from a mental illness). Although unlikely, the scenario being outlined in court was that a punitive element was not required because the defendant was incurable and would never be released – even though theoretical release plans were outlined.

The Judge concluded his justification for the hospital order, by saying that it offered greater protection in the very unlikely event of release. A health disposal allows for release supervision by a team of mental health experts he said, rather than a probation officer lacking the training to spot the subtle signs of mental health deterioration and lacking the powers to intervene if things did deteriorate. The Judge appears to have overlooked the high degree of multi-agency working for serious offenders, described on many occasions in this book. Interestingly Judge Turner quoted the sentencing guidelines for such cases… 'there will be cases where the protection of the public via a restriction order will outweigh the importance of a penal element and *other cases where a greater public protection is provided by a hybrid order*' (emphasis added). He appears to have accepted the first part of this statement but disregarded the second in determining his Judgement. We will now move on to consider the possibilities for the criminal justice system when it has to deal with serious offenders who display signs of mental illness, and how this plays out in custody and the community. We will also explore the issues with personality disordered offenders and the problems this poses for both mental health and criminal justice professionals.

The Scale of the Problem

Establishing the numbers of people who pose a risk of serious harm is a very difficult task, not least because it rests upon a number of assumptions and prejudices. Many people might readily link mental illness and homicidal violence, without really examining the evidence. Fear of the thought of people unable to control their urges and attacking strangers is a powerful driver. For example, Angermeyer and Matschinger (2003) found that in a study of public attitudes to schizophrenia, it was considered to be more dangerous and unpredictable than other diagnoses. Stark, Paterson, and Devlin (2004) reviewed a range of studies that revealed a public association between mental illness and violence ranging from 33–49%. Halle et al. (2020) argued that there was not a clear, established link between mental ill-health and violent criminal behaviour. However, they identified persistent stereotypes, with the media creating, shaping and propagating negative public attitudes and beliefs and misconceptions surrounding mental disorder and its relation to crime and violence. One way of measuring the association between mental illness and serious crime has been to explore the ratio between homicides committed with and without the presence of mental illness, with assumptions that the more homicides there are, the more will be committed by those with serious mental illness. For a while this did appear to be the case. Large et al. (2008) argued that the relationship remained fairly stable as the number of homicides in England and Wales rose steadily until the 1970s, with the ratio fairly constant. However, from the 1970s, the number of homicides continued to increase whilst those committed by those *diagnosed* with a mental disorder, fell. This might suggest improvements in the treatments for mental illness *or* changes to the way is which assessments are made and the criteria used. In total numbers terms, Large et al. (2008, p. 10) say that homicides rose from 0.3

per 100,00 of population in England and Wales from 1900–1959 to 1.5 per 100,000 in 2000. Homicides committed as a result of mental illness peaked in 1973 and has since fallen to historically low levels. In other countries though the data may show something different; for example, Kim (2019) in South Korea, found that although crime rates among those with schizophrenia were generally lower in almost all crimes than the general population, for murder it was 5x higher and for arson 6 higher. Antar (2023) quotes Shaw et al. (2001), who found that 5% of convicted murderers were diagnosed with schizophrenia. In referring to psychopathy, Stone (2007) cites Hare's (1993) study which estimated psychopaths to be 1% of the general population but between 10–30% of the prison population and responsible for more than 50% of serious crimes.

Figures are of course difficult to pin down, with patients/prisoners spanning and having contact with a number of agencies. However, what does emerge is that many of those with mental health difficulties present a considerable threat to their own well-being. The NHS Confidential Inquiry into Suicide and Homicide (2017) for example, found 17,823 patient suicides over the period 2005–2015. Over the same period, 11% of 7,404 homicide convictions were in mental health patients (835 or 76 per annum) on average, although this was estimated to have dropped to 45 p.a. by 2015. It was also reported that 11 stranger homicides per annum were committed by mental health patients. Of all homicides in the period 2005–15, patients with schizophrenia committed 6% of the total (417), with 392 alcohol related and 337 drugs related. Overall then, mental health patients represent a threat to themselves which is over 21 times greater than it is for others. These figures belie the public perceptions referred to above but actually graphically confirm the misconceptions in this area and explains, at least in part, why governments rarely present evidence (at least in public), to debunk some of these persistent myths. It is of course the area of personality disorder, and its relationship with or to mental illness, that causes a number of difficulties for all professionals. As Kendell (2002, p. 110) notes, there has been a tradition among British psychiatrists not to regard personality disorder as a mental illness and often used this as a reason not to admit to hospital for treatment. He cites a prevailing view in Germany where personality disorder is regarded as, abnormal variations 'of sane psychic life'. Kendell (2002, p. 110) makes the point that whether or not personality disorder was a mental illness was an unresolved issue in Britain (and still is in many ways), but proposals put forward by the Labour government in 1999, began to force thinking on this matter. Personality disordered offenders had been propelled into the public consciousness during the late 1990s following three high-profile murders in particular. These were those of Jonathan Zito, killed by Christopher Clunis in 1992, and Lin and Megan Russell, killed in 1996 by Michael Stone. These awful murders were committed by those who had had extensive contact with a range of health, criminal justice, and social services, and we will briefly summarise both cases to pull out the issues common to them both and of concern more broadly.

Making Disorder an Illness

Jonathan Zito had been standing on Finsbury Park tube station with his brother Christopher, in December 1992. Christopher Clunis was on the platform and his general behaviour and presentation, allied to his size (over 6 feet and 18 stone), caused some disquiet among waiting passengers, including Jonathan's brother. Clunis then attacked Jonathan with a knife, stabbing him three times in the face, with one blow penetrating his brain, proving fatal less than two hours later. Subsequent police searches of Clunis' flat revealed large amounts of untaken prescribed medication. Clunis had a long history of paranoid schizophrenia, of institutional care, violence and non-compliance with treatment (Butcher, 2007, p. 116). Days before the murder, Clunis had punched a stranger in the face and chased schoolboys brandishing a screwdriver. In analysing the enquiry into the case, Coid (1994) noted that Clunis had been seen by 30 named psychiatrists including 10 Consultants, there were other unnamed professionals and in total, Butcher (2007) suggested that the number might have been 43 over a 5-year period. Clunis's history included both a fascination with knives and with stabbing people in the head, particularly the eyes. He had attacked people in almost all locations where he lived. The inquiry (Ritchie et al., 1994) had argued that there had been a prolonged tendency to overlook or minimise these violent incidents with a consequent failure to assess the propensity for future violence. As we shall see from the Wooton case (below), there was a tendency to see each incident in isolation, a failure to build the bigger picture over time. It is clear that a picture was emerging of (community) psychiatric services struggling to deal with seriously mentally ill patients. Furthermore, there remained disagreement over 'treatability' and the role of in-patient care. As Coid (1994, p. 452) concluded in his article, 'Jonathan Zito died because the ideology and organisation of mental health services, the training of health care professionals and the facilities available are simply inadequate for patients whose conditions remain intractable and render them uncooperative with care in the community'. He then summarised his view on an enduring issue, 'the type of in-patient facility that he truly needed has been closed in much of the UK. If ever a patient required prolonged institutional care it was Clunis'.

A phrase heard all too often following tragedies is that lessons will be learnt, but sadly this simply does not appear to be the reality. The Clunis case, for example, was preceded 10 years earlier by that of Sharon Campbell, a mental health patient suffering from schizophrenia, who killed her 23-year-old social worker, Isabel Schwarz. In similar vein to Clunis, Campbell had a history of brandishing knives and she had previously attacked her victim in her car. She had received in-patient treatment for her schizophrenia. It was evident that she was dependent on her social worker and did not want the relationship to end when Ms. Schwarz moved jobs. She made numerous phone calls to Isabel before eventually carrying out her threat to kill in July 1984, when she stabbed her in her office. We will not examine the inquiry into the Campbell case in detail (Spokes, 1988), but will pick out two points about it raised in a House of Lords debate (Hansard, 1988) introduced by Lord Winstanley. He referred to an article written by Isabel's father, a doctor, in which he bemoaned the over-use of the phrase 'with the benefit of hindsight'. Dr Schwarz's view was that it was the business of professionals to exercise foresight, not hindsight, based on a thorough acquaintance with the established facts and with the detailed history of the patient. In other words, his daughter's murder might have been prevented if more attention was paid to both history and current threats. Dr Schwarz had quoted Gibbens (1983) in discussing homicide by schizophrenics:

> Homicide often occurs in schizophrenics who have been ill for over a year. Strangers rather than members of the family were victims mostly, when paranoid delusions suggested that they were responsible for persecution. Homicide by schizophrenics is more often a feature of those who have lost contact with the hospital, having received no after-care or follow-up treatment. Many homicidal patients have given prodromal evidence of impulsive physical violence...in the majority of schizophrenic homicides the motivations are clear; anger, resentment or fear.

Isabel's father had concluded in his article that there 'could be no clearer textbook description of Campbell's case'. Echoing the tailing-off of care in the Campbell case, the Clunis inquiry had said that the more difficult he became, the less effective was the care he received.

Almost as an aside, but a relevant one, is the way in which different incidents involving mentally ill patients are reported. In a detailed article concerning the nature of public inquiries, Sulitzeanu-Kenan (2008) noted that within a few days of Jonathan Zito's death being reported, there was scarcely any mention of the case in national reporting; certainly, no mention of the role schizophrenia might have played. Contrast this with the reporting of the case of Ben Silcock, a young man who had climbed into the lions' enclosure at London Zoo on New Year's Eve, 1992. The British public were transfixed by video footage of him being mauled by three lions before being rescued by staff. It was later reported that he was an untreated schizophrenic. The Daily Mail ran a headline, 'can no-one help tragic young men like Ben?' (Sulitzeanu-Kenan, 2008, p. 10). According to Rumgay and Munro (2001, p. 358), Ben Silcock became an instant symbol of the apparent failure of community care policy. Interestingly there were no calls for a public inquiry and, despite the extensive media coverage, no reference was made to the Clunis case. Yet, the day following the conclusion of the Clunis trial in June 1993, a series of long articles in the press referred to a knife-crazy paranoid schizophrenic who had been released into the community with no supervised treatment. Two statements, 30 years apart, perhaps reflect very well the changing environment in terms of health, crime, and violence. In the immediate aftermath of the Clunis trial, Jonathan Zito's wife Jane said, 'the man who stabbed Jon was so disturbed and vulnerable and distressed and frightened and scared, that he murdered my husband without needing to see his face' (Daily Mail, 29/6/1993). Following a decision to refer the Valdo Calocane sentence (above) to the Court of Appeal as unduly lenient, Barnaby Webber's mother said she had 'utter rage and pure hatred' for her son's killer, whilst Ian Coates' son said that Calocane was a selfish monster who decided to go on a spree killing. A joint victim's statement referred to Caloclane as 'so viciously and calculatedly killed our loved ones' (The Guardian, 26 January 2024). It represents a different take on the role played by schizophrenia in homicides and almost as a determined attempt by the families to 'take out' the mental illness element from sentencing.

We will briefly discuss two more cases, not in great detail, but to consider broader issues raised in subsequent inquiries, before asking if more recent government developments, particularly in relation to personality disordered offenders, have helped address some of the clear shortcomings of earlier cases. The first Case we will mention is that of Michael Stone. On 9 July 1996, Dr Lin Russell, aged 45 and her two daughters, aged 6 and 9 years, were brutally attacked whilst walking down a country lane in Chillenden, Kent. Both Lin and Megan, the 6-year-old, died from massive head and brain injuries following a blunt force attack with a hammer. Nine-year-old Josie was left for dead at the scene, but, in subsequent years has made a miraculous recovery. Police arrested Stone exactly 1 year after the attacks took place and following a BBC *Crimewatch* reconstruction. Josie had also sufficiently recovered to be able to talk to the police in May 1997. For our purposes, it is the interplay of mental illness, personality disorder, and violent criminality which has caused so many difficulties in this case. Stone had a very long history of mental ill-health overlaid with a deprived and abusive childhood. The *Report of the Independent Inquiry into the Care and Treatment of Michael Stone* (September 2006) was commissioned by South East Coast Strategic Health Authority, Kent County Council, and Kent Probation Area. It was chaired by Robert Francis QC. Running to well over 300 pages, this report describes in considerable detail, Stone's contacts with GPs and Psychiatric Services, police and probation staff over a number of years. For readers with an interest in how a person might pass through so many agencies and professionals without really seeing an improvement to the situation, the Report offers salutary lessons. We have already discussed in this book the problems caused by disagreements within the medical professions of the differences between mental illness and personality disorder and between what is treatable and what is not. For example, the report noted (2006: 10.3, p. 53) that in 1983, whilst in Canterbury Prison, Stone was found to be a:

> ...volatile and emotional man who found it difficult to co-operate in interview...he is very unstable, but there is no evidence that he has a mental illness for which treatment in a psychiatric hospital would be advisable...his very deprived and unsatisfactory childhood has led to a very severe personality disorder.

A form used to classify prisoners for suitable prison accommodation found him to be extremely aggressive, short-tampered, and almost certain to use weapons (2006, p. 53). He was transferred to HMP Albany where he wrote to the Home Secretary saying that he was not insane and saw no need to see doctors or psychiatrists. His history is made up of repeated attempts to secure for him the right treatment, although there was disagreement about this including from Stone himself. He was variously described as a paranoid schizophrenic and as having a personality disorder, with a history of chronic schizophrenic illness. Various reports described him as a determined and dangerous man. He continued to alternate between not taking his prescribed medication and demanding higher doses, supplemented by drugs he bought on the streets. In 1994, two consultant psychiatrists said 'he was suffering from paranoid schizophrenia, was psychotic and dangerous. He needs to be admitted to a psychiatric hospital but not on an ordinary ward, where it was felt he could not be contained' (2006, p. 139). As we have seen, a national shortage of secure beds resulting from the decisions to run down the provision meant that it was extremely difficult to find him a suitable place. Efforts to get the police to take him into custody failed, as they said there was no reason to do so (despite ongoing criminality), efforts were also made to get his probation order breached but Magistrates said there was no reason to do so (despite him causing criminal damage with a knife to a flat) and the department of health said they could not find a bed because there was no central record. Despite everything, Stone was admitted to De la Pole hospital in Hull on 29 November 1994. Whilst there he was described as a compliant, model patient.

The above is an extremely convoluted summary of the Stone case. His history is a combination of medical professionals disagreeing what to do with him, what his diagnosis should be, whether he should be treated in the community or in hospital, and what medication he should be on. All the time his behaviour fluctuated and was volatile and aggressive. He made various statements about wanting to kill people, especially children. In many of his interactions with professional staff, he was described as showing the classic signs of a schizophrenic illness. He was not a case who slipped through the net; indeed, he was seen regularly by a range of people and subject to a number of reviews and assessments. Five days before the murders, Stone told a nurse that he wanted to kill someone. The nurse telephoned the GP who changed the prescription and dosages without informing the specialists (Dyer, 2006, p. 670). In November 1994, Stone had been felt to be in need of compulsory admission to hospital due to his mental illness and danger to others, but was allowed to remain in the community unsupervised. When he was eventually detained, he was discharged quite quickly as *not* being mentally ill, however, the community mental health team were reluctant to be involved *because* of his perceived danger. Interestingly, and amazingly conclusively, considering the uncertainties in the case, the CEO of West Kent Health Authority said that the question was whether (Stone) was mad or bad, and he concluded that he 'was certainly not mad' (Dyer, 2006). He was eventually convicted of two counts of murder and one of attempted murder and is now serving three life sentences. Bearing in mind his extensive psychiatric history and frequent diagnoses of schizophrenia, it is interesting to note the differences in his case and that of Calocane mentioned above in terms of mental health and penal sentencing.

Stone has always proclaimed his innocence and his first conviction was overturned as unreliable. Some commentators have pointed to a complete lack of evidence for his conviction, such as no forensic evidence to link him to the scene of the crime, unreliable witness statements, both in the community and in prison and the physical differences between him and the person described as being seen near the scene. Stone has always refused to engage in the parole process saying this would be tantamount to admitting his guilt. At the time of writing, his case has been referred to the Court of Appeal by the Criminal Cases Review Commission on the basis of a new DNA test being available. The last case we will mention in this section is slightly different from the others in that the victim was a family member, rather than a stranger. Terry Wooton, 71, was murdered by his son Tony, 49, in September 2011. Tony had a long history of mental illness and schizophrenia, with 15 hospital admissions between April 1982 and May 2011. He stabbed his father 10 times, resulting in his death. This was far from the first time he had attacked his father. Rather like the other cases we have described in this chapter, Tony Wooton's medical history showed alternating periods of compliance (with treatment) and then non-compliance and relapse (Barry, n.d.), admission to hospital had invariably led to stabilisation and discharge somewhat inevitably to a relapse. Similar to the Clunis case, each violent incident was treated separately rather than as a continuing pattern. As the inquiry into the Wooton case reported:

> ...the NHS is structured to allow people with complex health issues to be managed across multiple services throughout entire episodes of care – there are benefits BUT it can lead to a loss of a long-term perspective, as each team focuses on the particular function of that part of the service – not considering the overall course of the illness over time. Barry (n.d.)

The investigation team believed, with echoes of Clunis, that Wooton's care was delivered as a response to individual episodes rather than a desire to achieve treatment goals which would improve his quality of life, whilst he coped with a chronic illness. There was no evidence to suggest that when he was well, he acted aggressively and violently. The investigation team concluded that the victim's death was avoidable and preventable, because the perpetrator should have been admitted before 11 September 2011. Their words suggest a chilling simplicity in explaining the final tragic outcome. They said that:

> ...given the pattern of the perpetrator's illness, his response to medication and that the threats to his father formed part of his illness rather than family dysfunctionality, the death was predictable from the 17th August, 2011, which is when he ceased taking medication and reasonable attempts to seek his re-engagement had failed. Barry (n.d.)

Whilst anxious to play down the popular myth that all people suffering from schizophrenia are dangerously violent, indeed that they are more likely to be socially withdrawn and a victim of crime, the report did list a number of factors where such a link may be important. These included:

- A history of previous violent behaviour
- Failure to take medication
- Disengagement from services
- Certain types of delusions, particularly ones which are both persecutory and grandiose
- Command hallucinations which tell them to harm others
- Substance misuse or alcohol misuse or addiction

A number of these factors have been present in our case examples and therefore, it may be understandable why the victims of the Calocane killings find the hospital disposal puzzling (and in their view unjust), whilst other similar cases have led to a prison sentence.

Responding to Rare Events

We have already noted that there are a number of myths associated with a perceived link between mental ill health and criminality, especially violence. We have also noted that the evidence does not particularly bear this out, with mental health patients posing more of a risk of harm to themselves. Yet these feelings remain potent among the public and are reinforced with every new case involving tragedy and either mental health patients or early-released prisoners. In all these instances the prevailing sense is that if action had been taken, in any form, tragedy might have been avoided – the predictability and preventability elements mentioned in the Wooton Case Review (Barry, n.d.). The Clunis and Stone cases exactly fitted the typology of mentally ill people committing awful crimes, seemingly in a random and therefore much more frightening fashion. There was deep public anxiety about these crimes which raised a number of issues for the government and medical professions. Paramount among these were notions of indefinite containment for those considered dangerous and mentally ill, and the conditions surrounding 'treatability' and the power the government believed this gave to psychiatrists rather that legislators.

Francis (2007, p. 41) said of Stone, 'It would have been difficult to find a person with a background more likely to fuel a debate about the protection of society from dangerously disordered individuals, than Mr. Stone'. The Home Secretary, Jack Straw was asked by Allan Beith MP, 'Does the Home Secretary believe that further measures will be needed to deal with offenders who are deemed to be extremely violent because of mental illness or personality disorder, but whom psychiatrists diagnose as not likely to respond to treatment? Is he aware that this concern has arisen not simply following the conviction of Michael Stone for those two brutal and horrible murders, but because there has been a tendency in recent years for psychiatrists to diagnose a number of violent people as not likely to respond to treatment?' (Francis, 2007, p. 42). Mr Straw was able to reply, no doubt on a theme he warmed to and which has gained in popularity ever since, namely attacks on professional expertise:

> Quite extraordinarily for a medical profession, the psychiatric profession has said that it will take on only patients whom it regards as treatable. If that philosophy applied anywhere else in medicine, no progress would be made in medicine. It is time that the psychiatric profession seriously examined its own practices and tried to modernise them in a way that it has so far failed to do.
> Francis (2007, p. 42)

What unfolded during the 1990s was a quite acrimonious debate among members of the health services, notably psychiatrists, and politicians. The debate centred around issues of treatability and public protection – the latter an increasingly important platform for politicians off all persuasions. Stone for example, had been described by a Judge in 1987 as 'an extremely dangerous man' and by a probation officer as 'the most dangerous man I have dealt with' (Francis, 2007, p. 41). To many members of the public, when they see people described in these terms, the obvious question seems to be, 'why aren't they locked up – forever?' However, for criminal justice agencies to do this requires a most serious offence and for mental health professionals to do so, it requires amenability to treatment. For both Clunis and Stone, the main issue was, why were they not detained in secure conditions, considering the behaviour they had demonstrated *prior to* the killings described in this chapter. It was evident that, what exactly constituted mental illness was at the heart of the matter. A diagnosed mental illness opened up possibilities for secure detention and treatment under the mental health act 1983. The difficulty was, however, that much of the behaviour exhibited by many dangerous offenders was believed by the psychiatric profession to be unrelated to mental illness, but instead was a result of severe personality disorder.

It was this issue in particular that had fuelled Home Secretary Jack Straw's ire. In private correspondence with Tyrer (2021, p. 276), he said, 'I thought...that it was irrational that whether someone really dangerous could be detained in hospital depended not on any objective analysis of the risk posed to the public, but on the state of psychiatric understanding and diagnosis for the time being'. The importance attached to risk assessment ensured that the debate remained firmly within the public protection field rather than a focus on treatment. It also served another purpose for the Labour Government of the time and Conservative governments since, to attack professionals and their knowledge if it does not accord with the politicians preferred view. With risk assessment a key feature of the training of psychologists it was therefore telling that Paul Boateng, who had been a minister of state for health and the home office, told a gathering of psychiatrists, 'if you won't play ball, we'll get the psychologists to do it' (Tyrer, 2021, p. 276). What this implies about the professional status of psychologists is perhaps best left to the imagination. There is widespread agreement that the government's determination to push ahead with the reforms stemmed from the public reaction to the Russell killings. However, in the words of former Home Secretary Ken Clarke, '...when public opinion gets sufficiently animated, new policies are introduced without ever having been thought through' (Tyrer, 2021, p. 275).

Kendell (2002, p. 110) said that although there had been pressure to resolve the issue of whether personality disorder should be regarded as a mental illness, the position had always been ambiguous. However, government proposals to deal with this group of offenders, named as Dangerous and Severe Personality Disordered (DSPD) by the Government, forced the issue much more into the spotlight. The government were clearly looking for ways to make the detainment of certain offenders within the mental health sector, easier. This meant confronting issues relating to human rights, with the Human Rights Act stating that detention of anyone not convicted was illegal unless of 'unsound mind', alcoholic, drug dependent, or for the prevention of the spreading of contagious diseases. This meant the government had to argue that those it wished to include in the DSPD provisions were of unsound mind, meaning that their personality disorder represented a mental illness. Up until this point, mental health legislation distinguished between mental illness and psychopathic disorder (Kendell, 2002, p. 110). The Government intended to abandon this distinction in favour of a new definition of mental disorder, covering any disorder of the mind or the brain, covering personality disorder and mental illness.

In Britain, because the tradition had been not to view personality disorder as a mental illness, it was often used as a reason not to admit to hospital or to treatment – the issue raised by politicians noted above. The proposals met with opposition from a number of quarters. For example, the Royal College of Psychiatrists expressed concerns over their members being turned into instruments of social control without therapeutic intent (Appelbaum, 2005, p. 398). Eighty organisations lobbied against the Act, forming the Mental Health Alliance. Patients groups had expressed concerns that the new powers could be used to detain people against their will. Much of the argument though, centred around professional roles and responsibilities, and what some might argue was an attempt to diminish professional power and dilute it to other, less qualified individuals. We have seen this process in many areas, notably policing, probation, and education. The government had proposed that professionals other than psychiatrists should take responsibility for detaining people with mental illness, such as senior nurses, psychologists, occupational therapists, and social workers. The alliance broke up when it was felt that the royal college of psychiatrists was actively campaigning against the involvement of other professionals. Tony Maden, a distinguished academic in the field, said that 'this was a power that was reserved for doctors and not many people give up power voluntarily. I think it was that simple and I think it was a terrible reflection on the profession' (Butcher, 2007, p. 118). The likes of Jack Straw may well have agreed with Maden, but others might point to the very considerable deprivation of liberty inherent in these powers and argue for as much medical (psychiatric) knowledge as possible in making these life-altering decisions. One of the proposals, later dropped, was that a DSPD order should not be dependent on a criminal conviction or amenability to treatment, allowing the state to detain people on the grounds of unsound mind (O'Loughlin, 2019, p. 619). However, governments were not keen to downplay their plans in this area and the 2001 Labour Party manifesto pledged to 'protect citizens from the most dangerous offenders of all', i.e. those with a severe personality disorder. It is interesting to note that American psychiatrists were watching these developments closely and urged caution, as events unfolded on this side of the Atlantic (Appelbaum, 2005, p. 399).

Despite the volume of criticism, the Government pressed ahead with its plans, albeit modified, and set about opening four secure units, two in HMP Whitemoor and Frankland for men and women in HMP Low Newton, alongside two secure hospitals, Broadmoor and Rampton. By 2009, there were 12 women and 216 men in high security DSPD units. New methods had to be devised to identify the population at risk and this became a combination of standard diagnostic instruments and risk assessment. Three criteria emerged:

(1) More likely than not to commit an offence leading to serious physical or psychological harm from which the victim would find recovery very difficult.
(2) Has a significant disorder of personality defined by the Psychopathy Checklist – Revised (PCL-R) and International Personality Disorder Examination (IPDE) and in whom.
(3) The risk presented appeared to be functionally linked to the personality disorder (Tyrer et al., 2015, p. 98).

Two new intervention programmes were developed for the DSPD patients/ inmates. CHROMIS was established at Frankland and regarded psychopathic traits as responsivity factors and assumes that those with high levels of psychopathy are affected by the same criminogenic risk factors as ordinary offenders, but are more resistant to treatment due to mistrustfulness and a low tolerance for boredom. There is not, therefore, an attempt to change these personality traits but instead work with them to encourage changed thinking and behaviour. The programme was forward thinking with participants taught objective decision-making and to think about the consequences of their choices (O'Loughlin, 2019, p. 625). In contrast, the TRAUMA programme at Whitemoor targeted trauma and attachment disorders, seeking to modify problematic personality traits. It was based on a holistic approach aiming to enhance overall functioning and well-being to reduce reoffending risk. Treatment focussed on a cognitive interpersonal model, beginning with psychoanalytic psychotherapy. We do not wish to go too much further into the details of the DSPD treatment programme, but instead have a really brief look at outcomes. There were perhaps two driving imperatives for the initiative, to gain power for politicians, via the criminal justice system, to respond to heightened public anxiety, and perhaps also to reduce the perceived costs of a policy which relied heavily on in-hospital treatment and the expense of that estate. We have seen that, by and large, the government managed to get around the treatability issue by creating new classes of disorder and allowing for treatments that did not require the involvement of psychiatrists. Indeed, this followed a period of almost open warfare between the psychiatric profession and government ministers. For example, the President of the Royal College of Psychiatrists said of Straw, 'we are not very pleased with him, but, even more important, we are appalled by his ignorance. The Home

Secretary cannot expect psychiatrists to do his dirty work for him' (Tyrer, 2021, p. 275). Tyrer himself was not slow to criticise developments when he said that, 'treatment was delivered almost entirely by psychologists using esoteric interventions without an evidence base – (the) outcome was not and never will be evaluated' (2021, p. 276). So much of these proposals, just as in criminal legislation, depended on an accurate assessment of risk of serious harm. We will discuss aspects of risk assessment later but suffice to say, there is little belief in its accuracy, particularly for the more unusual crimes and behaviours. Tyrer (2021, p. 277) quoted Buchan and Lee as saying, 'six people would have to be detained to prevent one violent act. So, to prevent such acts, five out of six people, would be inappropriately detained. This was a serious matter for human rights'. Tyrer et al. (2015, p. 99) quoted a study by Coid et al. (2013) that 'in the most psychopathic of individuals, the prediction of risk is no better than chance'. Added to the pessimism over risk assessment to select the target group, there continued to be doubts over the effectiveness of interventions for the DSPD group. To again quote from Tyrer et al. (2015, p. 100) when they said, 'a regime that only provides detention and denies any form of therapeutic intervention for this population, may be just as effective or even more effective, than the many well-meaning but unvalidated treatments'. They argued that there was no real evidence that drugs or psychological treatment is effective for this group. Writing from America, Appelbaum (2005, p. 399) said that 'given the low base rate for violence in society, even relatively accurate assessment will result in large numbers of people who are falsely identified as at high risk of violence'. He further suggested that cooperation with the process involved corrupting psychiatry's treatment orientation and making it subservient to the government's public safety agenda. The government had originally estimated that 2,400 prisoners would be eligible for DSPD programmes, but the Bradley Report (2009) had suggested that personality disorder effected 63% of the prison population. In really round figures, this might mean finding 2,400 prisoners out of say, approximately 48,000 suffering from PD in prison. It would require really exceptional risk assessment processes to do this effectively.

Throughout its lifetime, the DSPD programme was in a continual struggle. The opposition was consistent and focussed on medical objections and human rights. Aside from activists, lawyers and psychiatrists constituted a powerful lobby. Despite the identified need, over 90% of prisoners were said to be suffering from a form of personality disorder, with 70% having two or more (much higher estimates than in the Bradley Report); the available beds were not consistently full (Rutherford, 2010). The programme was very expensive. It was established in 2001 with a capital cost of £128 m and annual operating costs of £40 m per annum. By 2008, the bed capacity had increased to 400 and annual operating costs were up to £60 m. It should be remembered that the scheme was still a pilot at this stage and had no statutory basis. It is very difficult to tie down the costs of the DSPD pilot and even more so to get a sense of its effectiveness. According to Rutherford (2010), there has been no outcomes research on the programme despite promises that it would itself be grounded in research. However, Rutherford claims that the research base was lacking and the programme was instead, based upon extensive informal discussions. All the while, it is important to remember that the government was pushing for full implementation of the programme and its establishment on a statutory basis. They were determined to overcome the opposition of the psychiatric profession, who themselves were equally determined not to be pulled into what they saw as a criminal or coercive way of dealing with this offender (patient) group.

The issue for governments, Conservative and Labour, was purely a political one. What do with offenders whose offending appeared to be linked with a mental disorder of some kind, but for whom the criminal justice options had run out? In other words, prisoners at the end of their sentence who *had* to be released. The other issue concerned those who could not access medical care (or detention) because psychiatrists had said that their particular disorder was not treatable, and therefore they could not be detained under the mental health act, 1983. Politicians had pledged to make public safety and protection a priority and were clearly frustrated that the medical profession would not play ball. As O'Loughlin (2019, p. 623) suggests, the offender groups were reduced in this debate to the 'redeemable and treatable' and the 'irredeemable and untreatable'. The government had attempted various legal measures, for example, proposing that people could be detained against their will without having committed a crime or being amenable to treatment – an idea that was dropped. What was not dropped, however, was the ending of the treatability clause which had lain at the heart of this issue from the beginning. The new Mental Health Act, 2007, replaced treatability with a requirement that appropriate medical treatment be available to alleviate or prevent a worsening of the disorder; in so doing the threshold for involuntary commitment was lowered. It became clear to the government that a criminal justice pathway was more likely to achieve their objectives than a medical one, and this is the route they embarked on next.

The Offender Personality Disorder Pathway

In light of the high costs of DSPD programmes, the limited numbers it treated and the ambivalence around programme effectiveness (Tyrer et al., 2015, p. 97), the Government decided to order a review into services for offenders suffering from personality disorder. This culminated in the Bradley Report (DoH, 2009), which in essence concluded that funding might more effectively reduce risk and harm if re-directed to provide an active pathway of interventions to reach a larger population group. The locus of interventions would be within the CJS rather than the health service, with the anticipation of offering more interventions and lower cost (MoJ, 2022, p. 5). The new scheme was to be a joint initiative between NHS (Improvement) and Her Majesty's Prison and Probation Services (HMPPS) (NHS, 2023). The target group were those with complex mental health needs who posed a high risk of serious harm to others, the very group that politicians of all political hues had been concerned about throughout the 1990s. With a stocktake of provision in 2008, and the Bradley Report in 2009, the view was that funds allocated in particular to secure hospital provision, could be more effectively used within criminal justice. A newly created pathway might reach more people at lower costs. The Offender Personality Disorder Pathway would shift the emphasis away from intensive treatment for a small number of individuals, towards psychologically informed management of all individuals meeting high risk, high harm criteria with a personality disorder (MoJ, 2022, p. 5). The joint sponsors of the programme believed that opinions towards this offender group had shifted away from what was the negatively viewed 'untreatable' criteria. They argued that a consensus had emerged about successful treatment based on an integrated, structured, relational approach from a multi-disciplinary team, incorporating the holistic needs of individuals with the main interventions being psychological and social in nature (MoJ, 2022, p. 3). The overall aims of the strategy were identified by Joseph and Benefield (2012, p. 210) as follows:

- Improved and earlier post-sentence identification, assessment, and case formulation of offenders with severe personality disorder.
- Improved risk assessment, sentence planning, and case management.
- New interventions and treatment services, commissioned by NOMS and NHS in secure category B and C prisons.
- Improvements in high-security prison treatment units.
- New progression environment with post-treatment support.
- Workforce development and leadership training.

In many ways it might be argued that the ambitions for the programme are hugely ambitious. These included an aspiration for a more therapeutically minded and compassionate prison and probation service that will deliver the pathway's aims by making therapeutic use of relationships between people. The programme would involve psychologically informed practice embedded across the national probation service. The prison system should aim to understand offenders and create enabling environments, delivering opportunities for people to tackle their offending and improve mental health. Prison regimes should be 'relational environments', empowered by a reflective practice culture, with a psychologically informed consultant available to all probation practitioners. These grand intentions do not however sit easily alongside the type of headlines recently reported in the Guardian newspaper. For example, 'Calls for more prison funding drowned out by tough talk on sentencing' (Siddique and Syal, 2023). Compare the ambitions for therapeutic regimes with this headline concerning Feltham Young Offenders Institution, 'Psychologists having to talk to young offenders through cell doors'. A shortage of prison staff to safely unlock the offenders mean conversations were conducted through cell doors or on exercise (Syval, 2023). In her description of HMP Wandsworth, Syval had described rat infested cells built in 1851, incidents of up to 300 broken toilet seats each month and a jail at 170% of capacity – an additional 667 prisoners. The conditions had led the Chief Inspector of Prisons, Charlie Taylor, to declare that 1 in 10 prisons should be shut down (*Guardian*, 25/9/2023).

It is difficult to see programmes such as the OPD being successful in such conditions, yet there are positive signs. In a recent evaluation, offenders described their lives before the OPD interventions. They referred to a series of Acute Childhood Experiences (ACEs), difficulties relating to others, being overwhelmed by their emotions, unable to identify their feelings, bottling things up, being highly self-critical, having poor social skills, and struggling to cope under pressure. Following interventions, although some claimed they did not know they were being managed on a pathway (MoJ, 2022, p. 17), there was general satisfaction that ACEs had been discussed and recognised for the first time according to many participants in the evaluation study. They described a high level of support, being able to talk to staff, feeling comfortable approaching staff, understood rather than judged, staff being patient and not reactive, feeling respected and safe on the unit and of course they appreciated being involved in decision-making (MoJ, 2022, p. 18). A number of prisoners mention 'case formulation' as a positive in their treatment. At the heart of the programme are two ways of working which appear key to all that follows. These are case identification and case formulation. The initial phase is a screening (administrative and risk assessment), much of this work would be carried out by an offender manager. Of the initial screenings, up to 30,000 at any one time, approximately 45% go on to consultation and formulation (MoJ, 2022, p. 6). Case formulations are carried out by an offender manager and psychologist, and are split into three levels. Level one is the most basic, which is an attempt to organise the most relevant information and indicate patterns of behaviour. Level two, additionally included a developmental history and attempts to produce a psychological explanation of the problem. Level three formulations are for the most complex cases, factoring in how difficulties could be overcome, how to motivate the offender, and is where the psychologist takes primary responsibility. The OPD is meant to be a truly collaborative and multi-agency venture. It recognises that the problem of personality disorder cannot be managed by one agency alone. This approach is very well summarised by Skett and Lewis (2019, p. 168), who describe 12 underpinning principles of the OPD:

(1) Shared ownership, joint responsibility, partnership working (criminal justice and health)
(2) A whole system, community-to-community pathway
(3) Offenders primarily managed through the CJS, with offender managers taking the lead
(4) Treatment and management informed by a bio-psychosocial approach
(5) All services adopt a relational approach
(6) Staff have a shared understanding and clarity of approach
(7) Pathway is sensitive to individual needs, including protected gender and offence characteristics
(8) Service users have clarity of approach
(9) There is meaningful user involvement in design, delivery, review, performance management, and evaluation

(10) Ruptures and setbacks should be expected, understood, and responded to as part of a formulation-based approach
(11) Shared learning across the pathway, staff, and service users
(12) Services developed in line with the model and using an evidence-based approach, where evaluation continually informs services

We have already noted some of the positive comments on the programme from service users. Another important intended outcome was an improvement to staff performance in this area, perhaps particularly for criminal justice staff. In this light, one senior probation manager was effusive in his praise. Steve Johnson-Proctor, Director of Probation for South East and Eastern areas, said the 'OPD pathway has been one of the most successful and effective practice developments within probation in recent years. It has significantly improved the skills base of our staff group, provided access to expert advice in our offices and improved links with local community health providers in England and Wales' (Skett and Lewis, 2019, p. 170). It might be argued then, that the benefits fall on what might be termed the 'softer' side of the equation. Service users spoke of their ability to speak more easily about their mental health difficulties with staff. Criminal justice staff, in particular, thought they had learnt from psychology colleagues. Yet at the harder end, and for the government this might mean reoffending rates, there appeared to be too little if any significant impact. The National Evaluation study (MoJ, 2022, p. 27) found that for both violent offending and sexual offending, there were higher rates after referral and involvement in the pathway. However, the authors cautioned against seeing this as a programme failure, not least due to the short time that the programme has been running.

Summary

As we have seen in this chapter, mentally ill and personality disordered offenders have been something of a running sore for governments since at least the 1990s. Matching as they do so many media stereotypes, each serious but statistically rare case has served to amplify public fears and led to increasingly strident calls for government action. However, trying to tackle this issue took politicians into contested waters, with powerful government departments, notably health and criminal justice, each having different priorities and ethos, coming together to what was variously described as a public safety or public health issue. Our review presented in this chapter suggests that there were major attempts to pull health into criminal justice where mentally ill and disordered offenders were concerned. Naturally these efforts sat less well with psychiatrists than psychologists, the latter having been involved already for a number of years, notably in risk assessment practice and developing offending behaviour-related programmes. Both Conservative and Labour governments struggled to take on the psychiatric profession, who themselves stuck with a strict clinical/medical line. Various Home Secretaries, but most notably Labour's Jack Straw, twisted and turned in their efforts to get the medical profession to play ball with what was clearly, a highly political game. There were threats to parts of the newly enacted Human Rights Act – a recurring theme for Conservative politicians over the past 12 years as well – creating new definitions of mental illness, attempts to create a diagnosis which existed nowhere else in the world; DSPD, and threats to replace psychiatrists with psychologists. Alongside this, sat a considerable ratcheting-up of the powers available to the courts to deal with offenders assessed as dangerous, with particular emphasis on their eventual release.

The Valdo Calocane case with which we opened this chapter, shows that the issues surrounding mentally ill offenders has not gone away, nor has it seemingly undergone a process of refinement. In the Calocane case, there was little dispute that he had a diagnosable mental illness and this was confirmed by five psychiatrists. Yet following the sentencing Judge's decision to impose a mental health disposal, considerable arguments from victims' families, with public and political support, have surfaced over the place of punishment in such disposals. The families argued that the sentence was not 'tough enough' and did not reflect the severity, or in their view, barbarity, of Calocane's actions. This sentence is subject to review requested by the Attorney General as being unduly lenient – an argument that completely seems to ignore the very clear legal provisions for these cases. That said, as we noted, the Judge did resist the opportunity to impose a restriction condition alongside the hospital order. It is most unlikely that this issue will go away. Human beings will continue to behave unpredictably and erratically. Sometimes that unpredictability will result in extreme violence. There are however opportunities to perhaps change the course of events, *once the offender has come into the system*. The Offender Disorder Pathway does show some promising signs, at least perhaps for longer term behavioural change, if not immediate reductions in offending. It offers lessons for work more widely with offenders, such as the importance of time (no change is instant), of talking to others, of working *with* the service user rather than telling them what to do, of learning from the expertise of other professions and overarching all, no-one agency or person can help with all the issues presented by mentally ill or disordered offenders.

At the heart of many of the difficulties in this area however lies the issue of what do we mean by mental illness and what allowances should be made for it in people's behaviour? Added to this, is what might governments, or indeed the public, tolerate from people who appear to many to be 'mad' when they commit crimes. The Calocane case suggests a growing intolerance with the medical profession and its diagnoses in mental health. This case appeared to be clear, but has been somewhat hijacked by discussions about deserved and proportionate punishment, rather than mental ill-health. Victims have become increasingly influential in crime policy formation, albeit often with a significant time lag. The more articulate the family, of the more beautiful or 'innocent' the victims, the greater the likelihood of causes being successfully taken up. Whatever the outcome of this most recent debate, it is evident that any success in this field is dependent upon sufficient resourcing. As we have noted, it must be extraordinarily difficult to work effectively in the prison conditions described earlier. Years of austerity have led to an increase in non or lesser qualified staff taking on professional roles, or of attempts to shorten qualification periods as a means of saving money and solving recruitment crises. Across a whole range of public facing agencies, especially the police, probation and prison services, the average number of years in the job of front-line staff has reduced dramatically, with new entrants having few people to consult and learn from informally. Without resolving these issues for the longer term, the likelihood of recurring crises appears inevitable.

Chapter 6

Terrorism and Terror-Related Offenders

The majority of this book is concerned with offenders labelled potentially dangerous and posing a risk of serious harm to the public. These offenders have generally, but not exclusively, committed serious sexual and violent crimes. However, recently, a new group has entered the typology and is another that can strike fear into the hearts of the public, namely terrorism related offenders. Most nation states across the globe have experienced terrorist attacks often resulting in major loss of life. Just as the public fear a lone, predatory sex offender striking out at so-called 'innocent' victims, then so too, terrorist offenders are imagined to pose a danger to larger numbers of people, often in crowded public spaces. The linking factor between these two groups is fear of the unknown and the unexpected. A number of incidents in the UK and other countries has, in effect, brought terrorism to home shores, rather than it being viewed as something that occurred overseas. As a result, preventative and interventionist measures to combat this 'new' threat have been devised, with much of the approach mirroring that described in this book for dealing with potentially dangerous offenders. However, there is a distinction between these two groups of offenders, and that concerns the political nature of the subject. When, throughout this book, we have talked about politics and public protection, it has very much been in the vein of how potentially dangerous offenders and protecting the public from them, has been weaponised by politicians. In essence, this was in order to establish difference between party political responses and by so doing, try to gain political advantage. In the case of extremism and terror-related offending, politics is far more central. This is due to the fact that these offenders are committed to a political or ideological cause, which informs and drives their behaviour. This cause aims to overthrow and replace existing forms of governance and will use violence to achieve these aims. The response to what is a national threat should be a national and unified effort – consensus politics in other words. Whereas in other forms of public protection, politicians work very hard to extol their 'difference' from their opponents, a case of 'we are tougher than you', in counter-terrorist measures there should not be sides or gaining political advantage. However, consensus does break down, as the response to the Shawcross report (2023) has demonstrated (see below).

Dealing With Terrorism-Related Offenders

In this section, we will briefly outline the nature of the problem, before exploring the measures developed to tackle it, comparing this where we can, with more broadly developed public protection methods. It is often the number of victims and casualties caused by terrorist attacks that most shocks the public, alongside the nature of close-up violence in personal attacks, frequently shown in gory detail on social media platforms. The 9/11 attacks in the United States, undoubtedly the trigger for modern-day counter terrorism approaches, have seen almost 3,000 fatalities so far, with numbers set to rise due to those diagnosed with cancer following breathing toxins at Ground Zero. In the UK, 270 died in the downing of a Pan Am flight over Lockerbie, in Scotland. There were 56 victims of the London Bridge attacks and 23 deaths at the Manchester Arena explosion. The largest loss of life in the UK of course still relates to the conflict in Northern Ireland. Over 3,500 deaths were recorded between 1969 and 2001, with more than half of these civilian (Cain archives, accessed 27 March 2024). At the time of writing, a significant attack took place in Moscow, with almost 140 deaths and over 150 injured among concert goers attacked by four gunmen (Atkinson, 2023). Islamic state has initially claimed responsibility. It is the scale of these events, often when the victims are enjoying themselves or going to work, and seemingly coming 'out of the blue', that generates high levels of public fear and anxiety. Despite the rarity of these events, there will inevitably be government responses, nationally and internationally, often ill-thought out, responding to public fear and alarm. As with measures deployed against sex offenders, the trajectory of these responses is inevitably upwards, leaving increasingly little room for manoeuvre or more measured efforts.

Fishmongers' Hall

As a way in to discussing issues arising from terrorist and terrorism-related offending, we will describe events at Fishmongers' Hall, in London, to attempt to understand lessons that might be learnt and common concerns across a number of attacks. Much of the following information is derived from the Inquests into the deaths following the attacks by Usman Khan, in November 2019 (Judiciary.UK 3.11.2021). Usman Khan had been serving an indeterminate sentence for public protection (IPP), with a minimum tariff of eight years. As we have noted elsewhere, release from the IPP would have had to have been authorised by the Parole Board and dependent upon him being assessed as no longer posing a high risk of harm to the public. He and eight others had pleaded guilty to acts preparatory for terrorism, with plans to bomb prominent buildings in London, and was sentenced in 2012. Whilst in prison he was described as a leading extremist figure associated with bullying, violence, and radicalisation. When assessed under the Extremist Risk Guidelines (ERG22+) he was regarded as still strongly engaged with radicalism and that there was a high risk that he would be involved in terrorist related activity upon release. Khan and two others of his group decided to appeal their sentences and were successful, in that the original IPP sentence was quashed and substituted with a fixed-term sentence of 16 years. This resulted in automatic release after 8 years, equal to the original tariff period. Significantly, release under the new sentence meant that he did not have to prove a lowered risk before release was authorised and went through very little preparation for that release. Another significant event during his sentence was that he became involved in an initiative led by the University of Cambridge, where undergraduate students from the Institute of Criminology, worked alongside serving prisoners in an educational mentoring capacity. Khan was to eventually be considered a success of the scheme and featured as a case study in publicity literature.

Released under conditions of a 'normal' licence, Khan was still designated as a Category A, maximum security prisoner, one of the very few to be released under that category. His OASys assessment indicated a very high risk of serious harm and this was added to by two pieces of prison intelligence, suggesting that he would return to his old ways, and that he intended to carry out an attack. Upon release he was subject to MAPPA arrangements and supervised by an offender manager (probation officer). He had a condition to live in a hostel and wear a GPS tag. He was not expected to use the rail network or attend public gatherings without permission from his offender manager. Somewhat at odds with his licence conditions, he was invited by the Learning Together scheme at Cambridge, to attend a major event at Fishmonger's Hall in London in November 2019. This event was to include prominent national speakers. In the event, permission was granted although, despite some discussion at MAPPA, there appears to have been no officially recorded decision in this case. The Coroner found it concerning, that the risks inherent in this decision, appeared to have been so underplayed and that there was no formal MAPPA approval given, indeed the whole event lacked a proper risk assessment. Prior to leaving for London, Khan had purchased a number of kitchen knives and other material that he was to use to fashion a fake suicide vest. None of this was picked up by the security services, police or probation. Whilst under supervision he had created a good impression, to the point that his curfew conditions were slowly eased. However, following a MAPPA requested Prevent (see below) visit to his flat, ostensibly to view his DVD collection, he became very angry at what he saw as an invasion of his privacy. This outburst did not, however, appear to diminish the generally positive picture drawn of Khan by his supervisors. Upon arrival at Euston he was met by Learning Together staff. He was already wearing his fake suicide vest under his clothing, which he had put on during the trip, and had knives in his bag. No search of his bag was made upon arrival. Whilst at the conference, Khan fatally stabbed two young people associated with the Learning Together programme and also stabbed and injured three others as he made his way out of the venue. He was eventually shot to death by police on London Bridge.

The Inquest following the killings and subsequent investigations revealed a number of failings common to others we have discussed in this book but also some that are unique to terrorist offenders. Perhaps the most important aspect of the case for this section of the book concerns communications, in particular, between MI5 and the supervising probation service (MAPPA). This led to a situation whereby many of those dealing with Khan were unaware of the risks he posed or chose to disregard them, preferring instead to accept his self-presentation as a reformed individual. For example, the offender manager, in discussion with the senior probation officer, decided to reduce Khan's risk status from 'very high' to 'high'. There were clearly issues concerning sharing information held by the security services with other professionals involved in supervision and management of Khan. The chair of the MAPPA panel supervising Khan had only limited security clearance, and had not been made aware of a covert priority investigation by the Security Services and West Midlands police, based on intelligence that he was planning an attack. In his report, the Coroner made clear his view that, 'it is vital that decisions on the management of terrorist offenders should take account of relevant security intelligence information'. Further recommendations included a greater use of forensic psychologists in risk assessments, a new police power to search without specific legal grounds and that efforts should be made to ensure mentoring arrangements for offenders do not suddenly stop. In Khan's case this happened due to a contractual dispute between the Home Office and the provider. Khan's case is not unusual in its failings. In short these can be summarised as an under-estimation of risk of harm, a failure of communication, a tendency to believe self-presentation and silo thinking around security information and activities. Within this, also, is an issue of trust, particularly concerns among security and counter-terrorism staff, about sharing information with non-security cleared members of MAPPA boards; a group with a very broad constituency of public, private, and occasionally charity sector agents.

What Is the Nature of the Problem?

According to Jonathan Hall, KC, in his review of MAPPA arrangements for terrorist risk offenders (Hall, 2020):

> ...the number of terrorist risk offenders is tiny compared to the number of sexual offenders managed in the community and tiny compared to the number of individuals identified by MI5 as posing a terrorist risk, but who have not yet been convicted of any offence.

However, as one member of a public protection team reported to Disley et al. (2016, p. 19), 'It's not just that there may be a very small number of people, it's also that the results could be catastrophic if they reoffended'. It may though, be the case, that it is less the actual numbers involved or even the frequency of real events, which causes public concern, but rather, the fear generated by the *possibility* of large scale, seemingly random events, about which little can be done. This is also not helped by a sense that public life is increasingly fractious and divided, with a resultant blurring of the distinction between legality and illegality, between what is considered morally right and what is not. This takes us into the territory of hate and extremism, which are not in general classified as terrorism, but are increasingly associated with harmful actions and as fostering terrorist-related activities. We will briefly discuss this topic, before moving on to discuss practical measures taken by the UK government.

The Terrorism Act 2000 defines terrorism as the use or threat of action, where the threat is designed to influence the government or intimidate the public or a section of it and/or the threat is made for the purpose of advancing a political, religious, or ideological cause. These actions include serious violence against a person, serious damage to property, endangering a person's life, creating a serious risk to the health or safety of the public or a section of the public and action designed to seriously interfere or disrupt an electronic system. Importantly, to be convicted of terrorism, people do not actually have to commit a terrorist attack, but can be convicted for planning, assisting, or collecting information on *how* to commit a terrorist attack. These issues are undoubtedly clearer than those involved in responding to and dealing with those who hold and espouse hateful and extremist views, where the levels of tolerance, of what is allowed under the law, is much greater and therefore, almost certainly, more confusing to the public. For example, Khan and Rowley (2021, p. 14) argue that 'the nature and scale of extremist activity that is currently allowed in Britain is shocking and dangerous'. Examples they give include glorifying terrorism, which is lawful, *provided* there is an avoidance encouraging, commissioning, preparing for or instigating acts of terrorism. It is lawful to stir up racial hatred so long as abuse, threats and insults are avoided. Therefore, it is legal to form a neo-Nazi extremist group which persistently praises Adolph Hitler and denies the holocaust. Khan and Rowley (2021, p. 16) believe that praising and glorifying terrorists...help create a climate that is conducive to terrorism. In examining the need for and indeed recommending, a new legal framework for extremism, they argue that to date, extremism has been examined through the lens of counter-terrorism, which they believe is futile and flawed. They suggest it is a distinct activity outside of terrorism and hate crime, defining it as follows, '(hateful extremism) is activity or materials directed at an *out* group, who are perceived as a threat to an *in* group, motivated by political, religious or racial supremacist ideology' (2021, p. 12). Of course, these are activities that promote arguments around human rights, notably those of free speech and lawful protest. It is in circumstances of protest that the public might question why the police do not act and the answer of course is that the activity is generally lawful. A number of issues have however prompted a government re-think, notably large-scale public disruption caused by climate protesters and the growing harassment of politicians, especially at their home and constituency offices, which has included the murders of two members of parliament. In a prelude to its new definition of extremism (Gov.Uk, 14.3.2024), the government said that, 'the threat from extremism has been steadily growing for many years...the pervasiveness of extremist ideologies in the aftermath of the terrorist attacks in Israel on 2nd October, 2023, highlighted the need for further action.' However, emphasising the acute political sensitivities in this subject, initial unbending support for Israel has become more nuanced in the face of their retaliatory military onslaught. The new definition states that 'Extremism is the promotion or advancement of an ideology based on violence, hatred or intolerance' that aims to:

- Negate or destroy fundamental rights and freedoms of others
- Undermine, overturn, or replace the UKs system of liberal parliamentary democracy and democratic rights or
- Intentionally creates a permissive environment for others to achieve the previous two points

Associated with these intentions, a range of behaviours were listed by the Government and these include:

- Using, threatening, inciting, justifying, glorifying, or excusing violence towards a group to dissuade them from using their legally defined right and freedoms
- Advocating that the UKs parliamentary democracy is not compatible with their ideology, and seeking to challenge or over throw it
- Using violent threats to dissuade citizens from participating freely in the democratic process
- Subverting the way public or state institutions exercise their powers in order to further ideological goals
- Using threats and behaviours against public officials, including the police, aimed at dissuading them from conducting their legal obligations
- Establishing a parallel governance

It is evident that the words used in the new guidance very much blurs the distinction between extremism and terrorism, not least with several references to the commission of actual acts of violence or threats and intimidation. This reflects other public protection measures where definitions have always expanded and never contracted. Unsurprisingly perhaps, the measures proposed by the government came in for considerable criticism from a broad range of individuals and organisations (The Guardian, 10 March 2024). The Arch Bishops of Canterbury and York said that the definition risked disproportionately targeting Muslim communities already experiencing high levels of hate and abuse. Other opposers of the measures included veteran campaigners such as Peter Hain and Peter Tatchell, who questioned, 'what are British values?' The National Secular Society and the Countryside Alliance were among others against the proposals. It is unlikely that opposition to these measures will disappear any time soon, nor indeed that the incidents giving rise to the need for such measures (in the government's view) will subside, as right-wing extremism flourishes across Europe and misogynous organisations increase rapidly (for example Incel culture) and online hate forums covering so many different causes (although please note below the government's attempts to effectively play down the threats from right-wing extremism).

The UK Government Response to Terror

The backbone of the UK government's response to terror attacks, notably following 9/11, was CONTEST (Home Office, 2023a, 2023b), a strategy to counter terror and consisting of four key elements. These were PREVENT – people from becoming terrorists or supporting terrorism, PURSUE – terrorists to disrupt plots, PROTECT – against attack and reduce vulnerability, and PREPARE – to mitigate the impact of any attack. There have been a number of iterations of the strategy since 2003, the most recent in 2023. We will focus on the first of the strands, PREVENT, as this most closely resembles the approaches taken with other potentially dangerous offenders described elsewhere in this book. At the heart of CONTEST lies an aim to strengthen the ability to work across departmental boundaries. This is most likely at governmental level, as lower level multi-agency working happens nearer to the ground in meetings such as MAPPA. The overall aims are to tackle the ideological causes of terrorism, enable earlier intervention to support those susceptible to terrorism, and to enable people already engaged to disengage and rehabilitate (Home Office, 2023a, 2023b). This process, of course, echoes work with potentially dangerous offenders, in that preventive strategies frequently rely upon 'pre-action' or 'pre-offence' assessments to trigger interventions. The sharing of information between agencies is a long-standing issue, not just in the UK (Wong, 2022, p. 219) and not least when some of that information is held by the security services. The case of Usman Khan brings this issue into sharp relief, demonstrating how information gaps can seriously impact on the supervision of offenders and the management of risk under MAPPA. At government level there are efforts to plug and avoid the gaps, for example, the Joint Extremism Unit (JEXU), is a specialist counter-terrorism unit of police, prison, and probation staff which aims to collaborate on the management of TACT offenders (those convicted under the Terrorism Act, 2000). These meetings are held bi-monthly and are complimented by-monthly PATHFINDER meetings of Police, Probation, Prison, Psychology, and Health staff aiming to share information, monitor ongoing risks, and devise strategies to mitigate those risks (Wong, 2022, p. 221). One feature to emerge from a number of reviews is the importance of co-working, co-location, and incorporation of specialist mental health staff.

As a part of the CONTEST strategy, the British government decided early on to engage with 'risky' communities and individuals, a process that is not only difficult but politically fraught, as it can be accused of stigmatising specific populations and profiling them. In some senses, the counter-terrorism 'caseload', might bear out this approach. According to Home Office (2023a, 2023b) figures, Islamist terrorism has been responsible for 67% of all attacks, constitute 75% of the caseload of MI5, and 64% of those in custody for terrorism related offences. The other significant numbers can be grouped under the heading of Extreme Right-Wing Terrorism, accounting for 22% of attacks, 25% of MI5 caseload, and 28% of those in custody for terror-related offences (this latter category a growing problem across Europe with a significant development in online hate forums). Since 2018, nine terrorist attacks have been declared in the UK with 7 deaths and

20 injured. Since March 2017, 39 late-stage attacks have been disrupted (Home Office, 2023a, 2023b). As a backcloth for intervention, a profile image of a terrorist offender was drawn up as follows: 'lonely, vulnerable, self-radicalised individuals who are drawn to extreme views, usually encountered and reinforced online, many with poor mental health' (Hall, 2020). PREVENT aimed to stop people getting into the way of life just mentioned, or to divert them away if they were already experiencing these issues. In simple terms, the intention was to stop people from becoming terrorists or supporting terrorism. This involved challenging extremist (non-violent) views and ideas and to stop people moving from extremist activity to terrorist related activity. It was felt that the threats were mostly from Islamists, but that the right wing were a growing problem. PREVENT has three objectives in Contest (Home Office, 2023a, 2023b):

(1) Tackle the ideological causes of terrorism
(2) Intervene early to support people from becoming terrorists
(3) To rehabilitate those who have engaged in terrorist activities

Possible thresholds seen as appropriate for PREVENT intervention were described as follows:

- Are accessing extremist materials
- Are espousing scripted ideological views
- Are demonstrating acute behaviour changes
- Have had potentially traumatic exposure to conflict zones
- Are showing signs of intolerance towards people from different ethnic backgrounds or other protected characteristics

PREVENT therefore became a strategy of community engagement, although this might be viewed as intervention. When she was Home Secretary, Theresa May said that the government... 'should engage with credible civic society organisations in order to encourage these organisations to challenge radical and extreme views in their local communities', because, she said, 'it is always better to be using those people to whom people look naturally to hear the message' (Massoumi, 2021, p. 967). Communities were viewed as part of a campaign to reject the ideology of violent extremism and to isolate apologists for terrorism – but communities were also understood as protagonists. Communities were therefore seen to be 'at risk' as well as 'risky'. The intention of Government was to work with the vast majority of people across all communities who reject violence. Funding was, however, most clearly directed towards Muslim areas, via the Preventing Violent Extremism Pathfinder Fund (PVEPF), launched in 2006 to fund community based, bottom-up projects. As such PREVENT funding found its way to training activities, education projects, sports and recreation, arts and cultural activities as well as debate and discussion groups. The most popular of these were discussions on violent extremism (Heath-Kelly, 2013, p. 403), but in his review of PREVENT, Shawcross (2023) had been shocked to hear the amount of violent, anti-Semitic views expressed at Channel meetings, something he did not believe worked towards lowering extremist and terrorist thinking.

Massoumi (2021) has written an interesting article on how both state actors and state-sponsored actors, have become involved in the 'communities' agenda, along the way becoming involved in what she terms 'soft repression'. This arises from the actions of an 'enforcement network' (Massoumi, 2021, p. 960), where conservative think tanks, counter-terrorism specialists, and civil society organisations come together to spread the government's anti-terror message. Recipients of funding were to be communities with 5% or more Muslims in the population or where there was a significant concentration in a few wards. The aims of the project funding were to win hearts and minds, engage with the community, build capacity and resilience. In its first iteration, Ruth Kelly, Labour Minister, said that the government would actively develop relationships with a wide network of Muslim organisations, including those who were 'less' critical of the invasion of Iraq. Initial funding in 2000 saw £60 m invested into Muslim civil society, but there was immediate criticism that organisations that were critical of the invasion were marginalised – and not funded (Massoumi, 2021, p. 963). By 2012, the Coalition Government moved away from direct funding of Muslim Civil Society and instead gave alternative, covert forms of support to disseminate pro-government messaging. For example, the Charities Commission was tasked with regulating the finances of Mosques and codes of practice through a charitable status registration drive, which gave greater powers to intervene in Mosques' activities. By 2011, the role of the charities commission was intensified, with powers given to investigate Muslim charities under the extremism and radicalisation code. The Charity Act, 2006 had already required all student unions to register with the Charities Commission which in turn subjected them to regulation. As a result, the commission has investigated extremist activities, literature and speeches at charity premises and events – very much as aspect of Massoumi's soft repression (Massoumi, 2021, p. 964). The Counter-Terrorism Act, 2015, created a statutory PREVENT duty for public bodies to pay due regard to prevent people being drawn into terrorism. The result of this, according to Massoumi, is the implementing of new policies by these bodies which indirectly constrain social movements, for example, restrictions on campus activism, with Universities developing information-sharing agreements with law enforcement agencies. She argues that as many organisations lacked knowledge and experience in this field, counter-extremism think tanks such as the Henry Jackson Society and Policy Exchange, have filled the void, giving them a platform to disseminate ideas and access to public institutions (Massoumi, 2021, p. 965). The collaboration between state and private actors constituted the 'enforcement network' referred to earlier. In 2007, a Research Information and Communications Unit (RICU) was established with the Home Office. One example of their activity, according to Massoumi, was to engage with a group called 'Making a Stand', an independent women's rights movement which aimed to empower women to stand up against extremism and help foster a reconciled British Muslim identity – the Sun newspaper (9 June 2018), for example, splashed a front-page picture of a Muslim woman wearing a Union Jack headscarf, under the title of Inspirational British

Muslims. The Government had also hired a PR firm to disseminate counter terrorism messaging, which was meant to be coming from Muslim groups.

It is clear then that the British government has tried a variety of 'soft' means to counter terrorism, alongside, of course, a range of terror related legislation. Because many of these measures rely upon identification of individuals and communities as a threat, then a means has to be devised to intervene in ways which are not seen as discriminatory. The adoption of risk methodologies is one way to achieve this, and has of course been successfully used in the management of high risk of harm offenders. In terms of combatting the discrimination label, risk methodologies can hide behind a thin veneer of scientific respectability. Heath-Kelly (2013) suggests that British counter-terrorism relied upon the invention of 'radicalisation' and related knowledge about transitions to terrorism, to undertake governance of communities rendered suspicious. They have made terrorism knowable and governable through conceptions of risk, making the future actionable (2013, p. 394). Again, this is familiar language in the world of potentially dangerous offenders, variously used to argue for a range of 'exceptional' measures for those who are assessed as posing a high risk of harm. However, as Heath-Kelly (2013, p. 396) notes, we do not really know why some young men resort to violent extremism and others do not, this not being helped by an indefinite understanding of radicalisation. According to Githens-Mazer and Lambert (2010, p. 901), radicalisation has become a tool and power exercised by the state and non-Muslim communities, against and to control, Muslim communities. It is as if there is a line drawn that connects radicalisation with terrorism, but there is little evidence for this – radical thinking does not have to lead to violent action. As Heath-Kelly (2013, p. 407) asks, when does a person make the transition from being a risk to risky? When are they said to have completed the process of radicalisation to being radicalised? There is uncertainty about when a person holding violent Islamist views might tip over to violent action, but being risky suggests a propensity to be dangerous. Being labelled as 'at risk' suggests a vulnerability to dangerousness – meaning that *they are always rendered as dangerous*. She suggests that any distinction between vulnerability and riskiness is defunct in PREVENT thinking (2013, p. 408). Finally, she suggests that radicalisation discourses should be considered as performative security knowledge – it is a discourse that actually produces the threats it claims to identify for the performance of governance, rather than reacting to the existence of such risks.

The Review of PREVENT

The independent review into PREVENT, led by government appointed (and according to Casciani, 2023, 'hand-picked') independent reviewer William Shawcross, believes that the PREVENT strategy has lost direction and focus, and is, in effect, too soft when tackling Islamism. Casciani (2023) described Shawcross as a well-known critic of Islamist political influence in Europe, and some of the findings in his review may not come as a surprise to his critics (Zara Sultana, MP said, at the presentation of the report to the House of Commons on 8th February, 2023, that 450 Muslim organisations and leading human rights groups such as Amnesty International, all boycotted involvement in the Inquiry). The report claimed that PREVENT had become synonymous with safeguarding, protecting those referred from harm and addressing their vulnerabilities. The report contrasted the approach taken with Islamist networks, described as narrow, and focussing on proscribed organisations, ignoring the contribution of non-violent networks to terrorism to that taken with ERWG organisations, described as broad, expansive, and inclusive. Shawcross believed that Islamist terrorism and extremism was underplayed within PREVENT, a result he said of a culture of timidity.

In presenting the report to Parliament, then home secretary Suella Braverman, said she intended to accept all of the report's recommendations. She opened her speech by saying that, 'terrorist attacks are not random acts of violence. They are inherently and necessarily ideological'. She particularly endorsed Shawcross's point about a lack of referrals concerning Islamist terrorism compared with right wing terrorism. She emphasised that 80% of live investigations undertaken by counter-terrorist policing, were concerned with Islamist terrorists, but only 16% of Prevent referrals concerned this group in 2021–22 (Hansard, 8.2.23). Perhaps, unsurprisingly for a Conservative Home Secretary on the right of the Party, there was little enthusiasm for what might be termed the supportive side of Prevent. She agreed with Shawcross that Prevent had shown cultural timidity and an institutional hesitancy to tackle Islamism, for fear of charges of Islamophobia. Braverman argued that Prevent had drawn in 'respectable right and centre right' organisations, when the threat from the extreme right was not the same in nature or scale as that posed by Islamism. She reminded MPs, that Prevent was a Security Service and not a Social Service. She also believed that the role of ideology in terrorism had been minimised within Prevent, with violence instead, being attributed to vulnerabilities such as mental health or poverty. Her summative comment might read as a rallying call for the Right wing of the Conservative Party, she said:

> William Shawcross has exposed a real problem; a cultural timidity, a blind eye being turned to extremism, a fraternisation with those who would do us harm, and a hesitancy to confront head-on and bravely, the threat of Islamist extremist ideology.

The report was not well received in many quarters, for example, in a press release linked to their own 'People's Review of Prevent' (Holmwood and Aitlhadj, 2023), the authors indicated that over 200 civil society organisations had called for the report to be withdrawn. In *The Guardian* (12/2/2023) reporter Mark Townsend, claimed that Shawcross had only visited six panel meetings in coming to his conclusions. He quoted Neil Basu, a former top counter-terrorism officer as saying, 'the report appeared to be inspired by right wing ideology and was insulting to professionals fighting to tackle extremism'. Amnesty International claimed that it 'was riddled with biased thinking, errors and plain anti-Muslim prejudice'. The 'People's Review' concluded that Prevent did not stop terrorism, that it curtails human rights and civil liberties and harms individuals who are innocent of any offence, particularly Muslim children. The report quoted Professor Conor Gearty, KC, who said, 'Prevent expands the frontiers of state power well past the crime, into that pre-criminal arena we used to call freedom' (Holmwood and Aitlhadj, 2023, p. 18).

MAPPA

The final aspect of the work with terrorism-related offenders that we wish to explore is MAPPA, the multi-agency public protection arrangements. Readers will recall that earlier in this chapter, we mentioned failings revealed concerning the MAPPA role in the Fishmongers' Hall attacks. MAPPA had been established in the Criminal Justice and Court Services Act 2000. This had followed on from an HMIP report in 1995 titled, 'Dealing with Dangerous People: The Probation Service and Public Protection' (Nash, 2006, p. 156). Home Office Minister Baroness Blatch commented that public protection had thus become the first priority of the probation service. The 1995 Report, among many recommendations, made two that were significant then and still today, in terms of the failings mentioned in Fishmongers' Hall Inquest report. One of these concerned risk assessments, with a requirement that one be carried out in *every* case – a huge bureaucratic demand. The other concerned information, with the report suggesting that it must flow more freely between agencies and organisations that deal with potentially dangerous offenders (Nash, 2006, p. 156). In brief, the public protection mandate gained strength and traction as both police and probation services, began to realise that they were is a new world of managing high risk offenders under the gaze of the public and politicians. Collaboration slowly became the norm as these two agencies found common ground and discovered, in a public protection context, that information could be shared. Kemshall and Maguire (2001, p. 248) found that it was as if the new language of risk bridged the ideological gap between police and probation staff. Across the country, a number of informal arrangements were established for police and probation to meet, share information, and consider risks posed by certain offenders. A pilot scheme which had been established in West Yorkshire acted as the model (Nash, 2006, p. 157).

Of course, one of the underlying concerns of these new sharing arrangements – voluntary in the first instance – was the extent to which organisational culture would inhibit progress. The 1995 report referred to earlier, had noted that there had been a growing realisation that police and probation were in the same business. Other work commented on the growing collaboration in a relatively positive light (see Bryan and Doyle, 2003; Nash, 1999a, 1999b; Kemshall and Maguire, 2001). Another HMIP report, 'Exercising Constant Vigilance: The Role of the Probation Service in Protecting the Public From Sex Offenders' (HMIP, 1998), hammered home the re-shaped expectations of the probation service, whilst legislative developments would, within just a few years, massively change the way in which the police would work with this group of offenders (see for example,

Thomas and Marshall, 2021). The informal sharing and working arrangements which had spread across parts of the country were formalised in 2000, with police and probation services becoming 'responsible authorities' under the new MAPPA arrangements. The 2000 Act required the two services to work together, to assess and manage the risks to the public, posed by potentially harmful offenders. Within three years, a new Criminal Justice Act (CJA, 2003) extended the responsible authorities to three with the inclusion of the Prison Service. Not only this, and in keeping with the idea of 'the more information the better', a number of other public bodies were included within MAPPA as 'duty to cooperate' agencies. These included Social Services Departments, youth offending teams, housing providers, health authorities including mental health services and victims' agencies. Public protection was therefore a duty for all and legislation would ensure that agencies would share their information and work together. In general terms this has been successful and cultural differences have not proved as obstructive as perhaps originally envisaged – indeed there are examples of 'cultural transference' between agencies (Nash, 2014).

In 2009, Secretary of State for Justice, Jack Straw, announced that MAPPA would now be involved in the supervision of terrorist-related offenders. They would join what was by then a well-established multi-agency process, backed by several hundred pages of official guidance. MAPPA has a considerable caseload, swelled hugely by the automatic inclusion of all registered sex offenders as required by the Sex Offenders Act, 1997. The size of the MAPPA has risen every year, unerringly, to reach 91,040 as at 31 March 2023: of these 58,357 were in category 1 (sexual offenders subject to notification) and 21,897 in category 2 (violent offenders sentenced to more than 12 months in custody) (Ministry of Justice, 2023). However, despite perhaps indicating a significant and risky problem, the vast majority of cases (98% or 89,489) were managed at Level 1 (this involves management by one or two agencies at most – usually police and probation, and for offenders posing a lower risk of harm). Terrorism-related offenders will be placed into a new category 4 (246 as at 31 March 2023). The numbers are not significant within the wider MAPPA framework, but, the ramifications of reoffending by terrorism offenders could be very considerable. Following the review of MAPPA and terrorist offenders by Hall, 2020, the Police, Crime, Sentencing and Courts Act, 2022, has now mandated that there will be *automatic* referral to MAPPA of all terrorism-connected offenders, no matter how minor the original offence. This follows another measure in the act which allows a Judge to define crimes as terror-related, even if they are not terrorism offences in law. The outcome of these two measures will undoubtedly see an increase in the numbers in MAPPA category 4. At the heart of MAPPA lies, in our view, a rather naïve assumption. This is that, by simply bringing professionals together, sharing and information flow will improve automatically. Part of this process also assumes that individual agency cultures will be broken down and greater trust will result. Although this should not be assumed as a default position, in the case of terrorism related offenders, there is an added information dimension, namely, security and secrecy. We have already mentioned that in the Fishmongers' Hall attack, the MAPPA chair was unaware of certain security related information, which impacted directly on Usman Khan's management. Undoubtedly, it is the broad constitution of MAPPA meetings which has led to information blockages, notably from the security services but also, at times, the police service. It was the Fishmongers' attack that led the government to establish an independent review into MAPPA and terrorist offenders (Hall, 2020), and we shall now briefly describe some of the issues arising from the Report.

In brief, Hall made a number of recommendations which covered aspects of MAPPA functioning, in particular, better identification of MAPPA (terrorism) offenders, additional powers for the police service, intelligence should be shared to aid better risk assessment and importantly, that MAPPA's periodic management meeting process should be replaced by active case management by a core group of security cleared police, probation, and prison officials (Hall, 2020, p. 2). In terms of risk, Hall makes interesting points concerning an over-reliance upon risk assessment tools, many of which are regarded as unhelpful for terrorist offenders due to their low base rate. In particular, he felt that the standard instrument used, ERG+22 (Extreme Risk Guidance) was overemphasised and that risk assessment should be based upon all available information, including security sensitive information. He said that 'the main focus he had observed (in MAPPA meetings), has been the identification and management of risk factors, rather than assessing the likelihood of an offender going on to carry out an attack'. This very much concerns issues around warning signs and imminence, factors which, as we say in the early part of this book, cause difficulties across the board in offender assessment. The standard risk assessment tools deployed by probation and prison services (the Offender Assessment System – OASys, and Offender Group Reconviction Scale – OGRS) show little merit, in that numbers of terrorist offenders from which to extrapolate offender baseline risk factors, are too low. Hall's view was these tools focus on the nature of the offence, criminogenic need and protective factors, with insufficient attention given to predicting risk and more to managing it. He believed that the ERG should be seen as a risk factor assessment, rather than a risk assessment. Assessments can of course lead to preventative measures and it has been an enduring feature of the dangerousness debate, that risk assessment is not good enough for this purpose. Hall felt that it was not sufficiently nuanced to identify the *type of harm* predicted. Echoing concerns of probation officers over many years, that prediction tools might more easily predict a further offence, but not necessarily a sexual or violent offence, Hall argued that 'the risk of committing a further terrorist offence is not the same as causing serious harm to the public' (Hall, 2020, p. 11). In other words, many terrorist-related offenders are many steps removed from causing actual, physical harm. He went on to say that there is an assumption that all terrorist offenders pose the same risk of serious harm. It is the crossover with extremism that causes difficulty for professionals, believing that extremism is only relevant to MAPPA when it indicates that the individual concerned may cause serious harm.

As noted above, active case management was a recommendation in the Hall review. This in place of the regular, periodic meetings system used by MAPPA. If a terrorist offender was assessed as posing a real and imminent risk of harm, the core group of security-cleared professional, professionals should meet on a day-to-day basis. He believed that the sharing of quality information, which may be held by security services, was crucial and this may require a major culture shift. In general, this was felt to be between the security services and MAPPA, in particular those 'duty to cooperate' agencies who sit outside of the core criminal justice system. However, in the early days of MAPPA, there was a feeling that the police would be reluctant to share information with probation officers, but this quite quickly became a non-problem. Hall spoke highly of the benefits of co-location as a means of breaking down barriers. There are clear benefits to that, although it is possible that agency distinctiveness can be eroded (Nash, 2014). Hall himself cautioning against the dangers of blurring roles between different agencies (2020, p. 37). Much about the role of MAPPA – and its core agencies – with terrorist related offenders is new. Although included since 2009 (Disley et al., 2016, p. 1), the numbers have been low, making the gaining of the right experience very difficult. In their research study, Disley et al., 2016, p. 10) believed that to share information effectively, a relationship of trust needed to be developed, as had been built up among core agencies over the years from 2001. They pointed out that Special Branch even had limited engagement with other parts of the police service.

Summary

The response to terrorism-related offending and extremism, echoes wider criminal justice efforts in assessing and managing potentially dangerous offenders. In short this involves identification and classification of 'risky' groups, risk assessment, and management of offenders from multi-agency organisations, the application of exceptional measures for exceptional offenders and the constant creation of new laws to tackle what are often quite rare occurrences. As we discussed earlier, politics, and party politics in particular, is central to public protection processes, but there are subtle differences where terrorist-related offenders are concerned. Protecting the public from harm is of course a key task of government and one which politicians and the public would share. Yet, somehow, public protection has become a contested area, not that it should be done, but more a case of how strong can the measures be made. It has been a wedge issue between politicians since the 1990s, a stick with which to beat 'soft' opponents to gain political advantage. The outcome of this process has been a constant stream of ever-tougher legislation, often in response to a single case, which has constantly drawn in a wider range of offenders and had a knock-on punitive and restrictive impact on a range of measures. The proximity of 'rights' debates to every discussion of public protection measures, ensures that its essentially political nature is maintained. Since the early 2000s, successive governments have decided that working together, a multi-agency collaboration between a range of organisations, has been the best way to protect the public. The well-established MAPPA process therefore seemed a natural home for supervising and managing those (mostly) convicted of terrorism and terror-related activities. The early days of MAPPA had been marked by efforts to encourage information-sharing between two agencies who had not been easy bedfellows previously, the police and probation services. However, as we have seen earlier in this chapter, additional community responsibilities for high risk of harm offenders, for both of these organisations, had overcome a number of doubts so that, at least, a professional sharing took place. The addition of terror-related offenders to MAPPA in 2009 is, on paper, a sound decision. It provided a well-established working process and a culture of sharing between agencies with at least some responsibility of offenders in the community. However, terrorism offenders brought with them new issues, namely the input and involvement of the security services. Not known for a sharing culture, even among law enforcement agencies, it is evident that it will continue to take a good deal of effort to ensure that collaboration happens and is effective. Several of the reports and reviews mentioned in this chapter comment on the importance of the security services working with other agencies.

In essence, public protection from any offender is about the prevention of serious harm. This is a difficult task, entailing as it does, an engagement with future and therefore mostly unknown events. This task is set against a background of some doubts expressed concerning the ability of multi-agency working to be effective. The College of Policing (2023, p. 1) noted that, 'there is no evidence to suggest that multi-agency interventions have a statistically significant impact on disrupting pathways from radicalisation to violence'. Others, however, are slightly more optimistic, for example Mazerolle et al. (2021, p. 78) argued that '...evidence suggests that building trust and shared understandings of missions and goals is central to multi-agency collaboration and that intelligence sharing is possibly the most valuable aspects of multi-agency collaboration'. This is undoubtedly true, but for us, the bottom line remains an ability to spot warning signs, to identify deterioration in behaviour or the sudden appearance of warning signs and triggers. In other words, systems can be refined as much as possible and protocols established to ensure information flow. All this helps, but the quality and ability of individual staff to work with difficult and driven offenders, remains paramount, and as much as systems can always be improved, equal attention needs to be given to the quality of training and opportunities to gain experience for front-line staff having to work with, what for many of them, will be a completely new challenge.

Part Four

Current Issues and Trends in Public Protection

Chapter 7

Serious Further Offending: Hindsight Bias and Political Scapegoating

On 12 March 2015, 18-year-old Conner Marshall was killed by David Braddon, a violent serial offender who was under the supervision of Working Links, a Welsh Community Rehabilitation Company (Morris, 2020). In January 2020, a Coroner's Inquest into the murder found inadequate practice in the following areas: oversight of staff, workloads and caseloads by team managers; management and supervision of staff; writing of the risk assessment and the implementation of its risk management plan; inadequate allocation and management of resources; an over-reliance on self-reporting and a lack of effective communication regarding a joint risk assessment management plan (https://www.inquest.org.uk/conner-marshall-inquest). Braddon committed what is called a serious further offence (SFO). Whilst fairly rare in the UK, SFOs have a devastating impact on the victims, their families and the wider community. So far, we have discussed the various criminal justice agencies and wider public sector organisations which all play a role in public protection. Unfortunately, as with all government agencies, things go wrong which sometimes lead to the commission of further offences, some of which are very serious. When these serious offences are committed whilst the offender is being managed in the community by the NPS and the police, it is understandable that questions are asked about the handling of the individual and why the supervising agencies were unable to stop them from reoffending. When the person on probation (PoP) is charged with a relevant offence as listed in schedule 15a of the Criminal Justice Act 2003, a mandatory internal SFO review is triggered that looks into key aspects of the PoP's risk management (MoJ, 2019). Examples of qualifying SFO's include murder, manslaughter, rape, assault by penetration or a sexual offence against a child under 13 years etc., and the internal SFO review attempts to provide an analysis of practice, including key contacts and meetings with the PoP, the risk assessment and risk of serious harm level assigned, risk management planning, significant events and so forth (HMIP, 2023a). Every year between 0.2% and 0.5% of PoPs are charged with an SFO. For instance, at the time of writing the latest published figures state that as of 31 December 2022, 240,431 PoPs were under probation supervision and that in the reporting year from April 2021 to March 2022, there were 529 SFO notifications made. In the period from April 2021 to March 2022, 288 PoPs were convicted of an SFO offence (Gov.Uk, 2024).

In 2008, we published what is still the only UK text on SFOs (Nash and Williams, 2008). In this book, we wanted to identify and explore some of the key reasons why SFOs occur, given that between 2005 and 2006, there were four high profile cases of murder which led to independent public inquiries by HMIP's then Chief Inspector Andrew Bridges. In each of these cases, serious failures were found within what was then the National Offender Management Service (NOMS changed to Her Majesty's Prison and Probation Service or HMPPS in 2017). In *The Anatomy of Serious Further Offending,* we were able to identify a number of common failures across the cases – from poor supervision, management and enforcement, inaccurate or poor risk assessments, problematic or weak decision making and failures in inter/multi-agency communication and effectiveness (Nash and Williams, 2008, pp. 217–221). These cases continued a long history of blaming and shaming against key agencies charged with protecting the public, starting most notably with the failings in the case of St Albans poisoner Graham Young in the 1960s and 1970s, who, having become a self-taught expert in poisons, proceeded to poison his father, step-mother, sister and school friend. Young was sent to Broadmoor on the basis of a psychopathic disorder diagnosis, only to poison inmates, be released on licence, obtain a job in a chemical factory – with no disclosure to his employers of his previous offences – where he proceeded to poison its staff (Aarvold et al., 1973; Holden, 1995). This case demonstrated the lack of clear and robust risk management systems for offenders released into the community, especially when suffering from mental health issues, as well as poor information sharing between agencies and various gaps or weaknesses in the legal frameworks (see Aarvold et al., 1973; Butler, 1975). Because the problems with the handling in the Young case allowed for SFOs to be committed, in 1972, the then Home Secretary, Sir Reginald Maudling, called for two public inquiries (HC, Jun 1972 col 1674). The first inquiry, led by Sir Carl Aarvold and published as the *Report on the Review of Procedures for the Discharge and Supervision of Psychiatric Patients Subject to Special Restrictions* (Aarvold et al., 1973), was created for a 'a searching examination of the arrangements for discharging and supervising restricted patients[...](and)[...]whether there are any further changes within the existing law that should be made' (HC, June 1972 col 1674). The second inquiry, led by Sir Richard Austen Butler and published as the *Report of the Committee on Mentally Abnormal Offenders* (Butler, 1975), was created as a wider 'fundamental review of the provisions of the criminal law relating to mentally abnormal offenders, and the facilities for the treatment of such persons' (HC, Jun 1972 col 1674). Both inquiries effectively kick-started the 'dangerousness debate' in the UK (Nash, 2006) and the move towards ever-increasing punitive sentencing, the continued tightening of licence conditions, the slow erosion of the social-work influence on offender management and rehabilitation because of its replacement with a managerialist approach (Tidmarsh, 2020) and the over-reliance on actuarial risk assessment methods (Forde, 2018; Nash, 2006). Phillips (2020, p. 64) tracks this as the beginning of the 'heterodox within the subfield of community sanctions' with probation officers beginning to lose their cultural, social and symbolic capital and drift from being a key voice within the heteronomous pole to an isolated one within the autonomous pole in that sub-field. This was one area missing from our 2008 *Anatomy of Serious Further Offences* text – a discussion of how successive governments had purposely removed these forms of professional capital and how political discourse, ideology and policy creation impacts the grassroots delivery of public protection. Because of this, we have decided in this chapter to focus on SFO's and the relevant political influence from Labour's Offender Management Act 2007, which removed the monopoly of the then Probation Boards and allowed for a wider range of service providers to be commissioned. We have shown in the chapter on probation and TR how this opening was exploited by the Coalition government's TR policy and the privatisation of large sections of the probation service in 2014. We have started at this point as it is a clear manifestation of the neo-liberal policies of managerialism, marketisation and privatisation of criminal justice in the UK: policies which have mostly had a detrimental impact on public protection and serious further offending. This chapter is slightly different from the previous chapters as it involves our own data created through a thematic analysis of HMIP independent SFO reviews. It begins with an exploration of what SFOs are and the key aspects of the notification and review process. This includes a critical review of the latest SFO statistics. Finally, we discuss some of the political issues behind independent inquiries and review some of the key themes within the HMIP SFO reviews that link directly to the politics of public protection.

Understanding SFO's, Notifications and Reviews and Inquiries

What is always emphasised in SFO reports is the impact that they have on public protection and public confidence in the criminal justice system. What is rarely highlighted is the impact that political decision making and policy has on the ability of the criminal justice system to protect the public. This aspect has become especially relevant since the Coalition/Conservative led TR part-privatisation of probation (discussed in Chapter 4). Indeed, politicians are extremely adept at insulating themselves from criticism, when they should equally bear the brunt of the wrath that is usually directed at a solitary probation officer, trained by and working within the current political system which seems to have done it's best to deconstruct what was a fairly robust public protection system. Indeed, a key reason for our inclusion of an SFO chapter is that we believe that political decision making should not be divorced from understanding when things go wrong. Cases such as Anthony Rice, who murdered Naomi Bryant (HMIP, 2006b), Damien Hanson and Elliot White, who murdered John Monckton (HMIP, 2006a), Leroy Campbell, who murdered Lisa Skidmore (HMIP, 2018) and Joseph McCann, who kidnapped, falsely imprisoned and raped a number of victims on 9 December 2019 (HMIP, 2020a, 2020b) have all rightly caused public outrage because each of these offenders had been released from prison and were being managed on licence by the probation and police services. These are SFOs and are defined as such when the following criteria are met (see HMPPS, n.d.c, p. 3).

Supervised Individual Eligibility

- Supervised individuals who are under any form of supervision by the Probation Service (licence or post sentence supervision) on the date of the SFO (excluding however supervised individuals where a court or recall warrant had been issued three months or more prior to the date of the SFO).
- Supervised individuals who were under any form of supervision by the Probation Service including those who have been subject to recall and released at SED, which terminated within 28 days prior to the SFO.
- In cases of deferred sentences where sentencing is deferred to allow a supervised individual to comply with any requirements set by the court. Consideration of a discretionary SFO review would need to take into account the specific requirements set by the court and the management of the case by the probation provider during that period.
- Supervised individuals under supervision as above, who are charged with an equivalent eligible offence in another jurisdiction.

Offence Eligibility

- The list of eligible offences comprises serious violent and serious sexual offences and offences committed under terrorism legislation (as described in Annex A of SFO Policy Framework, see HMPPS, n.d.a) or an equivalent eligible offence in another jurisdiction.

The eligible offences follow the four categories of offenders used within MAPPA (Cat1, 2, 3 and 4 – Sexual, Violent, Serious Other and Terrorist offenders) and 'in addition to the substantive offences[...].aiding, abetting, counselling, procuring or inciting the commission, or conspiring to commit, or attempting to commit any of the listed offences constitutes a serious further offence' (HMPPS, n.d.a, p. 2). Until recently, eligible offences were listed under schedule 15 of the CJA 2003. However, this has now changed and the offence eligibility criteria is now placed in a hierarchy between automatic and discretionary offences, which has reduced the pool of SFO offences from 153 to 48 (although, it should be noted that any of the remaining 105 offences could become a discretionary SFO). We are unsure when or why this change took place, but we can speculate that it was during the privatisation period and, given it reduces the number of offences that fall in scope of the SFO criteria, is an attempt to manipulate the SFO figures by reducing the overall number of SFO notifications, reviews and convictions. We further speculate that this policy change could only have been created at the government/ministerial level. These speculations make sense given what we show below in terms of SFO notification and conviction numbers, which have become an embarrassment for the then Conservative government and further proof that TR was a failed revolution. The automatic eligible offences are outlined in *Annex A, Qualifying Offence List* from the *SFO Policy Framework* (HMPPS, n.d.a, pp. 2–8) but include offences such as murder, attempted murder, manslaughter, rape (adults and children), sexual assault (adults and children) and various sexual exploitation and terrorism offences.

The SFO criteria – being under the supervision of probation and committing a qualifying offence – are the important factors when measuring SFO's and are thus directly affected by political windsocks and policy changes. For example, prior to the implementation of the Offender Rehabilitation Act (ORA) in March 2014, offenders receiving a sentence of less than 12 months were not supervised by the probation service. This lack of community management and rehabilitation were some of the influencing factors impacting on the so-called 'revolving-door' offenders who committed the largest proportion of re-offences. Although the reason for this re-offending 'fact' is far more complex and heterogeneous once one digs beyond re-offence statistics, as we discussed in chapter four, the then newly elected Coalition government in 2010 and 2012 to use the revolving door argument to push its now famously failed TR revolution through Parliament. ORA was supposed to herald a new dawn in both public protection and rehabilitation despite the fact that these two ideas are not always compatible. After it's implementation in February 2015, all offenders receiving a sentence of at least one day and less than two years would be brought into probation's scope, meaning any new offenders who were convicted for an eligible SFO would now be reviewed and counted in the official statistics. However, before we briefly look at the SFO statistics, it is important to discuss what happens once someone has been arrested and charged with a qualifying offence, as this process directly influences these statistics.

The process is divided into *notifications* and *reviews* (see Fig. 1) and, as you would expect, follows a highly bureaucratic managerial process. A third type is the *independent review* which we will discuss in a separate section below. Once someone is charged with a qualifying offence, the notification part begins which contains three parts (HMPPS, n.d.b, pp. 2–3). Stage 1 is where probation service court staff should identify SFO cases at court and complete the stage 1 form, which includes information on the supervised individual (e.g. name, alias, DoB, PNC, CRO and CRN numbers, address, ethnicity and gender); court appearance date; SFO details; any co-defendants and SFO victim information (HMPPS, n.d.d, pp. 2–7). Stage 2 involves a review of the case allocation process. This reviews whether or not the allocation process was followed in terms of either pre-sentence or immediately post sentence, whether the case allocation tool was used appropriately and always completed, and whether the necessary papers were completed in a timely manner and communicated to the relevant organisations (p. 8). Once stage 1 and 2 are complete, the notification form is sent to 'the relevant manager in the region in line with local arrangements for completion of stage 3' (HMPPS, n.d.d, p. 9). Stage 3 examines the supervised individual's level of risk of serious harm and type, level of supervision received, details of the index offence and other offences/sentences (so a review of

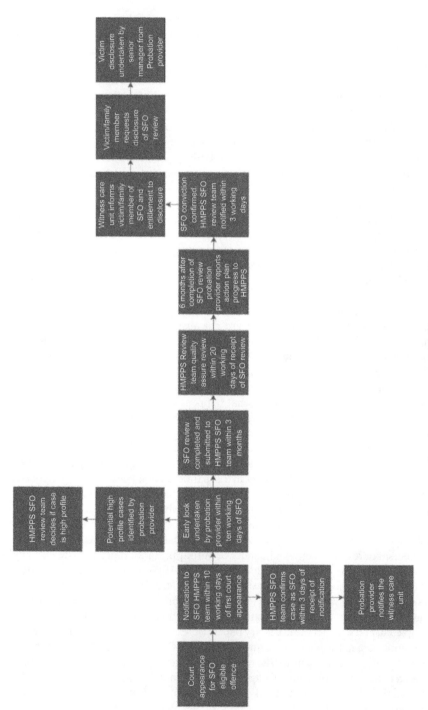

Fig. 1. The SFO Process (From HMIP, 2020a, p. 18).

pre-convictions) and so on (p. 10). Once the initial SFO notification paperwork has been sent and the SFO team confirms that it is indeed an SFO, an internal review is undertaken. One of the first things checked is whether the case is high profile or the potential to become high profile, which, obviously, can become a PR nightmare for HMPPS and the government and is perhaps one of the reasons why the focus tends to turn to a micro-analysis of the individual probation officer's practice. According to a HMIP thematic inspection (HMIP, 2020a, p. 19), the overall figure of high-profile cases is around 14%. The internal reviews tend to focus on the bureaucratic process and whether it was followed. This could mean any or all of the following areas:

- A review of the Offender Assessment System (OASys) risk assessment, it's quality and whether the various risk scores produced (through Offender Group Reconviction Scale [OGRS], OASys General Reoffending Predictor [OGP], OASys Violence Predictor [OVP], Risk of Serious Recidivism [RSR] and OASys Sexual Reoffending Predictor [OSP]) were accurately linked to low, medium, high or very high levels and the relevant management level;
- The level and quality of supervision undertaken such as number of meetings, types of rehabilitation programmes, compliance with programmes etc.;
- Where relevant, the quality and level of MA meetings and interactions;
- The licence-conditions and whether these were breached or tested by the supervised individual and;
- Identification of areas for improvement, or lessons to be learnt from the case.

With the odd exception, such as in the Joseph McCann case (MoJ, 2020), internal SFO reviews are not publicly available, so any understanding of the reasons behind such cases is usually only gleaned from the published HMIP independent reviews. Indeed, apart from low-level training every now and then, staff from probation and the wider multi-agency family do not often get the opportunity to receive training on the themes, failings and lessons across multiple SFO cases. Evidence of this can be taken from HMIP's own random sample of internal SFO reviews that are quality assured and which found that 50% of reviews under the learning standard received a rating of 'requires improvement' or 'inadequate' (HMIP, 2023a, p. 22). When, and if they do receive training, the quality and amount is likely to vary greatly across the 11 probation regions (although with the introduction of HMIP's Multi-Agency Learning Panels, we hope this will change). In fact, it was only recently that this quality assurance process was implemented, coming off the back of a thematic inspection and recommendation by HMIP itself:

> The ministry of justice should: Commission an external agency to:
> 1. Quality assure a proportion of completed SFO reviews each year to provide an independent view of the standard of work - with the results published on a regular basis. HMIP (2020a, p. 9)

The notion of independence is a tricky one in this context. SFO reviews are completed by a middle-manager within the same probation region where the SFO occurs. HMIP has questioned this operating model but to no avail (see HMIP, 2023a, p. 14), which is unsurprising given that HMIP's claims of independence can also be questioned. How (politically) independent can an organisation be when its chief is a career-civil servant and the inspection teams include previous employees of the probation service? We're not suggesting that HMIP doesn't provide thorough and objective investigation of SFO cases, but it would perhaps be better that these internal reviews and independent inquiries be undertaken by a truly independent body that has a mix of ex-practitioners, academic experts and members of the public, similar to the MAPPA lay person. This is something that the then HMIP inspector was against: 'Although we don't recommend that an independent body should take on the reviews themselves, we do recommend that there should be independent oversight of the quality assurance process' (HMIP, 2020a, p. 4). As it turns out, the external independent agency that was commissioned by the then Secretary of State for Justice, Robert Buckland, was HMIP, which published its first annual report of SFO reviews in September 2022 (HMIP, 2022a). HMIP takes a random sample of approximately 20% of SFO reviews and quality assures four main areas: (i) analysis of practice; (ii) sufficient or overall judgements; (iii) learning; and (iv) victims and their families (HMIP & HMPPS, 2021a). Each of these aspects are given a rating on a four-point scale, outstanding, good, requires improvement and inadequate, and a composite rating from all four aspects is also produced (HMIP & HMPPS, 2021b). For example, Fig. 2 below shows the characteristics of the outstanding and inadequate ratings (HMIP, 2022a, p. 11).

The quality assurance of reviews is important as it speaks to the ability of staff from all agencies involved in the supervision of someone convicted of an SFO and allows the identification of areas of good and bad practice. In the 2021–2022 period, HMIP quality assured 64 internal SFO reviews and in 2022–2023 that number rose to 86. In the latest report, HMIP found 'a disappointing reduction in the number of SFO reviews given a composite rating of 'Good' with only 49% of reviews reaching this standard in 2022–2023 compared to 66% in 2021–2022. They concluded that 'probation regions have not made progress in improving the overall quality of the SFO reviews (HMIP, 2023a, p. 11). A number of related factors were identified which explained this decline and many of these factors are a direct result of TR policy. For instance, resourcing and workload, the ability to professionally challenge at a senior and strategic level, learning opportunities and the lack of professional curiosity are factors that seem to be blamed on probation staff when things go wrong (HMIP, 2023a, pp. 11–12). Very little is said about how the organisational structure and culture is determined at the political level and how the degradation in criminal justice service provision greatly impacts staff's *agency*. Berger and Luckmann (1966) see the relationship between agency and structure as dialectical, arguing this is a continuous loop of *society–forms–individuals–individuals–form–society*. However, this is somewhat misleading as it ignores how agency within the structure is determined by those who hold power, and that top-down power dynamics impact on people's agency in different ways. Bourdieu's work on field theory is perhaps more insightful (see Bourdieu, 1986, 2000; Phillips, 2020). He uses the concepts of habitus, field and capital to examine the interplay between structure and agency, and, as we have demonstrated in the earlier chapter that reviews the impact of TR, these areas have been greatly weakened since TR.

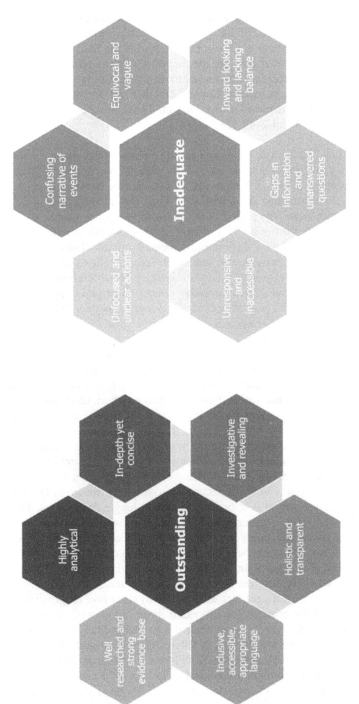

Fig. 2. Quality Assurance Rating – Outstanding and Inadequate.

It is understandable if at this point some readers are questioning the links we are attempting to make between SFO's, politics and public protection. Thankfully, it was a link that we did not have to construct or look too hard to prove, as the Government itself has stated that the number of SFO's committed is a key indicator of how well the criminal justice sector is doing. Consider this 2015 marketing claim from Andrew Selous, Conservative MP for South West Bedfordshire when asked about the impact that TR would have on safety and public protection (HC Deb, 2015, col 244WH):

> No. The hon. Lady will want to hear this because she made allegations about safety and so on. I know she will be reassured that the number of serious further offence notifications between 1 June and 30 September 2014 was 151. That was a reduction compared with same (sic) period of the previous two years, when the figure was 181 for both 2013 and 2012. All hon. Members will know - not least the two distinguished members of the Justice Committee who are present, the hon. Members for Hayes and Harlington (John McDonnell) and for Islington North (Jeremy Corbyn) - *that the level of serious further offences is an important indication of how well a probation service is doing. I hope that that reassures hon. Members [emphasis added].*

This really should not have reassured anyone at all and for a number of reasons. First, it was far too early to make this bold claim, given that probation had only been privatised on the 1st June. Second, it would have been more useful to use the SFO convictions figure rather than notifications or at least use them together for context. Finally, Selous was doing what many politicians do – play selective statistical confirmation bias to suggest that privatisation had made the public safer. Taking a date range of four months of SFO notifications (again not SFO convictions) is a poor sample size to base such an important claim on given what we're about to show in Fig. 3 and Table 2 below. There are a number of factors that impact on our ability to accurately assess how many SFOs are committed each year and why it is important to look at longer date ranges. The reporting year for most official criminal justice statistics is usually 1st April–31st March, and in any given reporting year, there will be a specific number of SFO notifications (i.e. a notification is sent to the relevant manager when a PoP appears in court and is charged with an SFO). However, the number of notifications is often considerably different from the number of actual convictions for that year, and this is due to different factors. First, many cases take longer than a year to process through the criminal justice system, so an initial notification may be made in one year but the conviction associated with that notification might be one, two or *nth* years later so will be in a different reporting year. Second, a number of those charged with an SFO offence will have their charges reduced to a lesser offence, for example, through a plea deal or because of a lack of evidence for the original charge. If these changes to the original charge(s) are not covered in the list of SFO eligible offences, they will therefore be removed from the SFO

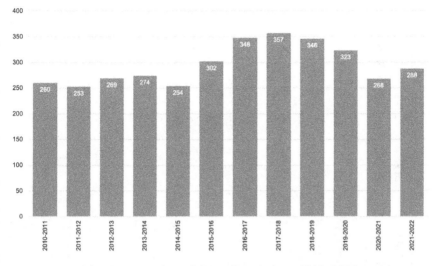

Fig. 3. Number of SFO Convictions 2010–2022.

counting. Finally, some offenders will be found not guilty of the charge and rightly be removed from the yearly figures. It is, therefore, quite difficult to follow the Government's reporting of SFO's and general reoffending, and when the figures are reported, they are usually from the previous year. For example, in researching this part of the chapter, we tried to find one source that would provide all required statistical information in terms of the following:

- Probation caseloads per year,
- The number of proven re-offences per year by offence type,
- The number of MAPPA and Non-MAPPA SFO notifications per year by offence type,
- The number of MAPPA and Non-MAPPA SFO convictions per year by offence type and
- All of the above in terms of all offenders and offences by risk and management level.

Such a source does not exist and even some of the items listed above are not publicly available, despite being important information that should be easily accessible. Indeed, it gets very confusing when looking into this. For instance, there are separate documents/sources that report probation caseloads, proven re-offences, the number of SFO notifications and convictions and by management level; the latter of which only reports those offenders who are managed by MAPPA which accounts for only a small percentage of all offenders managed by probation. We still cannot understand why there is such opaqueness in reporting criminal justice statistics and whether this is a deliberate political decision, which has then been carried out by the ONS, so that the general public are not fully

Table 2. Number of SFO Offences, NPS v CRC 2014–2019.

SFO Offence	2014 NPS	2014 CRC	2015 NPS	2015 CRC	2016 NPS	2016 CRC	2017 NPS	2017 CRC	2018 NPS	2018 CRC	2019 NPS	2019 CRC
Arson with intent to endanger life	14	1	11	4	16	0	18	2	16	2	19	1
Assault by penetration	17	7	13	17	17	18	18	19	6	9	10	12
Attempt or conspiracy to commit murder	31	15	18	36	22	38	34	51	36	43	31	51
Aggravated burglary	24	0	22	0	40	1	57	0	35	0	25	1
Causing death by dangerous/careless driving/aggravated vehicle taking	5	0	1	6	5	7	3	7	5	11	10	7
False imprisonment	11	0	9	1	24	1	29	0	17	0	19	2
Firearms offences including possession with intent	19	0	16	2	12	0	15	1	16	1	16	0
Kidnapping	22	1	11	4	12	2	21	1	28	0	23	1
Manslaughter	8	0	1	4	5	8	3	13	4	9	3	5
Murder	56	15	28	41	26	60	49	65	54	78	57	90
Offences under the explosive substances act	0	0	0	0	5	1	2	2	2	0	3	0
Other qualifying sexual offences	26	0	34	2	24	2	33	5	19	2	29	1
Other serious violent offence	1	0	0	1	0	0	2	1	3	0	1	0
Female genital mutilation	0	0	0	0	0	0	0	0	0	0	0	1
Other specified offence causing death	0	1	1	1	0	0	0	0	0	0	0	0
Rape	129	43	112	105	118	127	111	131	70	60	60	41
Robbery with firearm	8	0	11	2	8	0	15	0	12	1	10	0
Under 13 sexual offences including rape	20	7	22	12	16	9	15	17	15	8	13	2
Total	391	90	310	238	350	274	425	315	338	224	329	215

aware or do not fully understand the number of re-offences and SFO's that occur each year. In the latest *HMIP SFO Annual Report* (HMIP, 2023a, p. 6) Justin Russell, the then Chief Inspector reports that in the year 2021–2022, 529 SFO notifications were made from the 240,431 individuals under the supervision of probation, equating to 0.2%. Confusingly, rather than reporting the number of SFO proven convictions in the same year, he reports the number of convictions for a different year, 2020–2021, which stands at 245. Given this report was published in June 2023, we don't understand why he didn't report the proven convictions for the same year. If we look at the SFO notification to conviction conversion rate it hovers around the 50% mark: in 2019–2020, it was 50.1% (271 convictions from 536 notifications). At the time of writing, and for the sake of clarity, we have reported in Fig. 3 the proven figures for the number of SFO convictions taken from *GOV.UK's Justice Data* page which were published on 24 January 2024 (https://data.justice.gov.uk/probation/offender-management). As you can see, these figures are up to 2022, or 21 months old.

The above figure clearly shows an increase in SFO convictions since TR part-privatised probation and a decrease since 2021 when the service was re-nationalised (although they have slightly increased in the 2021–22 period). Indeed, this point was not lost on Labour MP Ellie Reeves of Lewisham West and Penge who, on the 7 July 2023 debate on His Majesty's Prison and Probation Service noted that:

> Between 2014 and 2019, during the privatisation years, the number of serious further offence convictions increased by more than a third, and the number of serious offenders on probation found guilty of murder increased by 123%. HC Deb (2023 col 755)

Whilst we are no fans of the neo-liberal and Conservative fetishistic drive for marketisation and privatisation, it would be remiss of us to not point out that what Ellie Reeves failed to mention is that this is the period of the introduction of ORA, which, as we have already highlighted above, brought more offenders under the scope of the probation service *ergo* the SFO inclusion criteria. Table 2 (HC Deb, 2020) shows the number of SFO notifications received between 1 January 2014 and 31 December 2019, by SFO offence, whether the offender was supervised by either (a) the National Probation Service (NPS) or (b) Community Rehabilitation Companies (CRCs). With more PoPs to supervise, it is entirely natural to expect to see more SFOs, especially if you consider that most SFOs are committed by those assessed as low and medium risk (HMIP, 2022a, 2023a; MoJ, 2023).

What these data clearly shows is an increase in SFOs for offenders managed by the CRCs. If we drill-down and sample some of the more prevalent SFO's (see Fig. 4), we find that for the offences attempted murder, murder and manslaughter, CRCs performed badly when compared to that of the NPS. These facts should be compounded by considering the CRC's were created to manage a large proportion of supposedly low and medium risk repeat offenders because of the Coalition

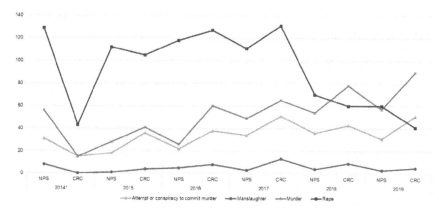

Fig. 4. Sample Comparison of SFOs – NPS vs CRC, 2014–2019.

government's incorrect belief that one of the main issues faced by the criminal justice system was that '57.6% for (sic) prisoners sentenced to under 12 months, with 17,560 re-offenders committing 83,107 further offences' (MoJ, 2013a, 2013b, p. 7); leading to fuzzy-logic that the lower-risk, revolving-door offenders can be managed differently through a competitive marketplace of providers and receive cheaper 'targeted rehabilitative interventions' (MoJ, 2013a, 2013b, p. 11). The SFO data shown in Fig. 3 and Table 2 illustrate what the opponents of TR had always feared in relation to the impact it would have on offender management (see the collection by Vanstone & Priestley, 2016 as well was the 2013 special edition of the *British Journal of Community Justice*): the majority of SFO's are committed by offenders who are assessed as low or medium risk (HMIP, 2020a, p. 25) and that supervising individuals in the community, regardless of risk their level, is far more complex and demands more specialism and experience than simply offering someone an employment appointment, an ergonomically friendly environment and a computer screen to apply for jobs (see Clift, 2018).

We decided to look more closely at the most serious types of this further offending, which produced some interesting results in the privatisation period. Apart from rape offences in the 2014–2015 and 2018–2019 periods, the CRC's produced more SFOs than NPS. In fact, for murder the situation was very concerning:

> In the four years since key parts of the probation system were privatised, there have been 225 charges of murder against offenders monitored by private probation contractors in the four years since their creation. That far outnumbers the 142 murder charges against high-risk criminals managed by the Government probation service over the same period. HC Deb (2019, col 573)

As shown in Fig. 4, the percentage in the number of SFO convictions between 2013–2014 (pre-privatisation) and 2014–2015 (post-privatisation) did decrease by 7.9% (from 274 to 254). However, it increased by 18.9% (from 254 to 302) in the following year and when there was a full year of comparable data (meaning a full year with the new TR structure operating). It gets even worse if we look at the comparisons between NPS and the CRC data from Table 2. Between the year 2015 and 2016 (again, really the first comparable year), there was an increase in NPS SFO convictions of 12.9% (from 310 to 350) whilst there was a 15.1% increase in CRC SFO convictions (from 234 to 274). If we are taking 'the level of serious further offences' as 'an important indication of how well a probation service is doing' the aforementioned Hon. gentlemen should have been honest and conceded that the CRCs were not doing a good job at public protection.

We believe that one of the key factors influencing SFO data over the last 10 years is the contradiction between cost-effectiveness and delivering a safe public protection product. It was Marx (1990) who first outlined that the key way to save money for any business is make its labour cheaper (as that's where most of the surplus-value is derived from). One strategy to achieve this is to deskill staff and/or have less experienced staff do more with less. As we have discussed in the TR chapter, privatisation removed a large proportion of staff that were experienced in risk management, public protection and who could mentor newly qualified staff – basically the expensive ones – leaving probation (and the CRC's) with little to no economic, cultural and social capital (Bourdieu, 1986). At the time of writing, the higher education sector is suffering in a similar way from the impact of the government's policies. Universities across the country are now run like private corporations, yet, at the same time, our 'markets' (i.e. students) have been highly regulated/restricted by government policies (in terms of caps on home student fees and visa restrictions for international students). This seems strange given the neo-liberal philosophy of a free-market economy. We're neither business owners nor economists, but it seems silly to us that you would purposely implement policies that restrict your key market (Laker, 2024). This can be seen as part of the wider Brexit effect with the UK Government placing "sanctions against itself."[1] Fundamentally, it boils down to the number of staff you have and unfortunately, this is one of the great lies of neo-liberalism: the unproven claim that marketisation and privatisation drives efficiency and that efficiency equals streamlining processes (Corcoran, 2020, pp. 16–23). What it actually means is doing more with less – or less staff doing more work. The fact that politicians play this neo-liberal game with people's lives for the sake of a few pennies saved is a dangerous game when it comes to public protection. SFOs prove this, and it's surprising that the families of SFO victims haven't demanded that politicians be held criminally responsible through some form of corporate manslaughter or US-style depraved indifference law. These are the individuals that should be held to account – not an overworked probation officer. It seems that this is recognised, albeit not admitted publicly, by policy creators and enforcers. In the new revisions to SFO policy and

---

[1] See James O'Brien, from LBC News, https://www.youtube.com/watch?v=GzplbEjvR-E.

practice (HMPPS, 2023a, 2023b, p. 2), there is an unusually honest admission that '*there are not enough people to do the job day-to-day of supervising people on probation [our emphasis]*.' Because of this, one of the central revisions was to restrict the focus of internal SFO reviews:

> The chronological entries will begin with the assessment in place at the start of the review period, followed by analysis of assessment, planning, reviewing and implementation practice *during the 6 months preceding the SFO [original emphasis]*. HMPPS (2023a, 2023b, p. 3)

What this basically means is that there aren't enough experienced probation staff to undertake a thorough review when an SFO occurs so change the process. This policy runs contrary to directions from the then Chief Inspector of HMIP, Justin Russell, who, in his last annual SFO report (HMIP, 2023a, p. 3) stated that 'more needs to be done to improve the quality of SFO reviews[...](and that)...the Probation Service needs to ensure that it produces high quality SFO reviews that *identify all available learning [our emphasis]*.' We do question how a high-quality review of an SFO that identifies all learning can be undertaken if you purposely restrict the time frame of analysis, therefore potentially missing crucial evidence, key warning signs and any subsequent learning. Despite this criticism, HMIP reports are very good at identifying failures with the operational management of public protection, so the remainder of this chapter focuses on these independent reviews.

The Politics of Independent Inquiries

So far in this chapter, we have briefly explored what SFOs are, the general process that is instigated once NPS are notified, the number of SFO notifications and convictions, and the process of internal SFO reviews. Along the way we have provided a political slant to our SFO analysis, highlighting where policy and political decision-making has impacted upon public protection. When discussing the review process, we noted that part of the problem with gaining a complete understanding of SFO's is the non-publication, with the exception of Joseph McCann (see MoJ, 2020), of internal reviews. Some of the reasons for this are understandable in respect of data protection issues, although we don't understand why this information cannot be redacted or removed to create a sanitised version for public consumption. We believe that a more transparent process would not only be in the public interest, but would also aid in putting together a much stronger training package. As it currently stands, there is no national programme for SFO training; in fact, there is no SFO training at all. Every once in a while, a probation region will run in-house training that might link with SFO's. For example, if there has been a sudden spike in SFO's linked to DVA perpetrators, someone from the SFO team might put together a presentation on the key aspects of the cases and possible learning points but that is as far as it goes. We happened to be presenting at a Hampshire probation career development day when one of the lead police investigators looking into the failures in the Danno Sonnex case presented some really interesting and useful findings to the group. It is quite clear that there is a need for more systematic enhanced training on SFO's and what can be learnt across all cases – not just a case study approach (although the new MALPs process will not do this either). Furthermore, as an outsider (and more objective) researcher, trying to gain access to internal reviews is almost impossible given the overly protective nature of the MoJ and their research application process. It is highly unlikely that they would grant access to undertake a rigorous study of internal reviews. So, from a research and learning perspective, the easiest way to understand SFO's is to look at the publicly available HMIP independent reviews. In this section, we take a look at some interesting findings from our thematic analysis of the nine HMIP SFO independent reviews. We undertook this analysis from a slightly different perspective than last time (Nash & Williams, 2008) by focussing on any aspects that link back to politics, public protection and TR. Before we explore some of these issues, it needs to be noted that even an analysis of these inquiries is fraught with potential difficulties. For example, there is no way to independently verify the accuracy of these reports, check the robustness of the methodology of the investigation or whether any information is reinterpreted or buried. As Alison Moss, the SPO in the Leroy Campbell case strongly argues (2021, pp. 65–70; 74–84), the independent investigation conducted by the then HMIP Chief Inspector, Dame Glenys Stacey, missed key details, contained inaccuracies, moved the blame over to her and, perhaps most worryingly, did not even interview her or other key personnel who were directly involved in Campbell's supervision. Indeed, Moss herself emailed Stacey: 'to inform her, very politely, that her investigative report into Lisa Skidmore's murder contained inaccuracies and that the crucial details about Campbell's disclosures to the covering probation officer had not been investigated properly' (Moss, 2021, p. 83). This issue points to the problem of methodology. Out of the nine published inquiries, none have a section that properly outlines the methodology used in the investigation. The closest we get to a methodology is a list of sources used in the investigation, and even then, this is only reported in five of the nine reports. For example, Table 3 lists the sources used in the Campbell inquiry (HMIP, 2018, pp. 8–9).

Lots could be said about this list, but we will stick to a few key issues. First, it is placed in a section entitled 'methodology'– which it isn't – it is simply a list of resources. We're not sure why it's called methodology given in the previous reports it has the better label of 'sources of information' (e.g. HMIP, 2006a, p. 8; HMIP, 2006b, p. 9). Whilst we appreciate that these reports are not academic papers, so there is no expectation/requirement to use a rigorous research design and method, the inclusion of an enhanced research/investigative methodology section would be beneficial. Second, this list misses perhaps the two most important people who should have been spoken too – the covering PO and the SPO overseeing the case. Why is this important? It's important because independent inquiries must search for the truth and facts must be precise. In the

Table 3. Sources of Information Used in the Campbell Review.

Case Records	Interviews
• ViSOR records • Parole Board decision letter • Parole dossier (a file of information about the prisoner) • Probation SFO review report, chronology, victim summary report and action plan • MSCR, action plan and summary report • Police internal management report (IMR)	• MAPPA Coordinator for the West Midlands • Probation Head of public Protection/Stakeholder Engagement and Chair of MAPPA Strategic Management Board • Parole Board Director, and Parole Board quality Assurance Lead • Head of Public Protection for the NPS, Midlands (responsible for conducting the SFO review) • Head and Deputy Head of the Local Delivery Unit (LDU) • Chief Executive Officer of the Fry Accord Housing Association • Head of Integrated Offender Management (IOM) with MAPPA Responsibilities, West Midlands Police • Head of Professional Standards, West Midlands police • Michael Spurr (Chief Executive Officer of HMPPS) • Sonia Crozier (Executive Director of NPS and Women) • Gordon Davison (Deputy Director HMPPS and Head of Public Protection Group) • Sarah Chand (Divisional Director, Midlands Division of NPS)

Campbell case, the inquiry report was quite scathing over the fact that his disclosure that he wanted to rape again was not acted upon:

> Once he confirmed that he had thoughts of rape, then it is beyond our comprehension that he was left to remain at full liberty. At that stage he could have been recalled to prison or else returned to the hostel to allow for close monitoring of his mood and behaviour.

These options should have been pursued, but they were not and we find that a very significant failing. HMIP (2018, p. 22).

This 'fact' was then used against the SPO – Alison Moss – who became the political scapegoat for Campbell's crimes and was sacked by probation although she had not known of the disclosure of the thoughts of rape at the time they were made and when they could have been acted upon (Moss, 2021, p. 83). Moss claims that Stacey did not know this, and once Moss informed her, she thought that the disciplinary proceedings against her smelt of a cover-up (2021, pp. 83–84). The decision by Stacey and her team not to interview the most relevant and important people is, therefore, bemusing but leads to an interesting third aspect. By simply reviewing processes and speaking to people in senior positions who usually fail to know the precise details of the case or, even worse, hide the truth to protect the organisation and, by extension, the government means perhaps the most important information in the case is missing. If we take a look at the list of sources in Table 2, the list of people interviewed were at least one-step removed from the offender management process, going up to high level executives who would have been in the difficult position of knowing about the problems that TR created for offender managers but were the ones forced to implement it because of government's failed TR revolution and the MoJ's coercive bureaucratic structure (Adler and Borys, 1996). With all due respect to them, why on earth do you interview the likes of Spurr, Crozier, Davison and Chand? The only areas they can possibly discuss is process, and this ultimately leads to them pushing their staff under the public protection bus when this process is not applied adequately enough in a particular case. We have observed and mentioned at various points throughout this book the huge negative effects that austerity has had on the running of the main criminal justice sector organisations. There is a wealth of research to support this (see Albertson & Fox, 2019; Hernandez, 2021; Irving, 2021; Mann et al., 2018). Yet, we are still left wondering how on earth someone is supposed to successfully undertake a process as complex as managing risky and chaotic individuals when they are not equipped with (a) the time to do this to a proper standard and (b) are not provided with the relevant tools to do so? We will talk more about the issue of processes below but it links to a fourth and final issue related to the problem with the methodology used: reviewing process paperwork. Obviously, this is important but it seems to us that, more often than not, this becomes a tick-box exercise to cover the organisation and the government from any responsibility. As Sjoberg and Miller (1973, p. 141) once concluded, 'hierarchy and control and the attendant matter of secrecy are central features of a bureaucracy's normative order.' Furthermore, and as we will discuss in more detail later, the cut-and-paste-style recommendations of these reports is to increase processes and bureaucracy and the training of staff to deliver them. Many public and private organisations, both large and small, tend to default to increasing processes *ergo* bureaucracy as the panacea for enhancing productivity and efficiency (see Jackson, 2001; Sjoberg & Miller, 1973). The problem is there is little evidence to support this. It seems counterproductive to us that inquiries usually recommend adding to bureaucratic processes when it's these very processes which might be hindering effective management in SFO cases in the first place. Finally, and before we move onto the inquiries themselves, we wish to highlight an interesting fact about the Campbell inquiry (HMIP, 2018) which might provide a reason behind the scapegoating of individual staff rather than the focus on systemic failures, which has actually been a useful feature of post-TR independent inquiries. The inquiry was the first major SFO case and independent inquiry since TR and privatisation. In that context it is not surprising that blame was directed towards staff rather than a failing system as that would have been embarrassing for the government. As we will show later, the consultation regarding the impact of TR that was being undertaken between the Campbell and McCann cases would have raised even more questions about the systemic failure of TR.

One thing that readers should be aware of is the sheer number of different agencies that produce internal reviews when serious offences are committed against people under their care and/or supervision. It's quite a lot given the net widening and dispersal of social control agencies that has been a feature of the UK's public protection system for the last 40 years (see Cohen, 1985). The majority of agencies that are involved in public protection have their own internal review processes and produce reports, some of which are made available to the general public. The list includes, but is not exhaustive of: (i) probation internal SFO reviews; (ii) HMIP independent SFO reviews; (iii) police MAPPA serious case reviews and domestic homicide reviews; (iv) LSCB child serious case reviews; (v) NHS combined serious case reviews and (vi) OIPC investigations. Most of these reviews examine the individual agency's involvement with a specific case and the effectiveness of their working practice. Where relevant, it will also consider the multi-agency working practice between any other agencies involved in the case. Sometimes there will be multiple reports produced by different agencies on the same case. Overall, we believe that it is not always helpful having layer upon layer of different reports as this can sometimes obscure the pathway to gaining a clear picture of all serious further offending across the multiple agencies. Furthermore, despite these numerous internal and external reviews, the different agencies do not regularly share their findings with each other and there is certainly little to no cross-pollination of learning. In fact, any understanding of the big SFO picture *is* obscured by different agency approaches, systems and reviews - none of this is joined up. For the remainder of this chapter we focus only on the HMIP independent SFO reviews but remind readers of the need to be careful with the use of such reports because of the potential for inaccuracies as identified by Moss (2021).

Pre-TR vs Post-TR

At the time of writing, there have been nine major independent reviews undertaken by HMIP since they were introduced as a response to the government's 2003 policy on *Inspecting for Improvement* (see HMIP, 2023b, p. 14).

We analysed all nine of these reports – four were undertaken in the pre-TR and five in the post-TR periods: (i) Peter Williams (2005); (ii) Anthony Rice (2006b); (iii) Damien Hanson and Elliott White (2006a); (iv) Jon Venables (2010); (v) Leroy Campbell (2008); (vi) Joseph McCann (2020b); (vii) Damien Bendall (2023c); (viii) Jordan McSweeney (2023d); and (ix) Joshua Jacques (2024). We do recognise that probation was unified in June 2021 but have decided to stick to the post-TR label because, upon examining the chronology of events produced in each of the five post-TR reports, it became clear that these individuals were managed in both the TR and unification phases. This cross-over means that the remnants of TR levels of staffing, experience and resources was still having an impact on the supervision of these PoPs in the unification phase. Each of these cases involves the most serious offences of rape, sexual assault and/or murder, committed by individuals who had extensive known histories of serious offending. One thing we noticed immediately was the change in the level of detail between the reports between those written pre-TR with those written post-TR. The mean number of pages per report has decreased by 39.21%, from a pre-TR mean of 69.75 (SD 34.39) to a post-TR mean of 42.40 (11.19). In fact, the last three HMIP reports were all under 40 pages in length which doesn't really allow much space for a thorough examination of all the problems within the case. There is also change between the reports in two phases when it comes to reporting wider systemic issues/ failures. These occur due to errors in the design, implementation, operation and maintenance of entire systems and, interestingly, the term was not mentioned in any of the pre-TR reports. The focus of these reports was on the individual failures to adequately manage the offending PoP, with blame being assigned locally. For instance, in the Damien Hanson and Elliot White case (2006), involving the murder of John Monckton and the attempted murder of Homerya Monckton in 2004, the theme of *doing the job properly* was used throughout to show the failures of the London probation area in not identifying the nature of risk (HMIP, 2006a, p. 3). The closest we get to a criticism of wider structural failures is in the Anthony Rice report (HMIP, 2006b, p. 4), where the principal finding discusses a *cumulative failure* of the whole process. The first mention of the terms *systemic issues* or *systemic failures* was in the Cambpell report, which initially got us excited until we read the entire sentence:

> In many SFO reviews the issues identified are systemic failures, whereas in this case we have identified points when practitioners and managers simply did not do what they should have done. HMIP (2018, p. 40)

Two things need to be mentioned about this claim. First, the previous reports do not fully look at systemic failures - they miss out the important elements of design and implementation. Second, the decision was purposely taken to not look at the wider systemic problems as this would point to the problems with the design and implementation of TR. We discuss some of the reasons behind this omission below. In later SFO reports, the term systemic issues is used and there is more of an attempt to widen the scope:

> *From McSweeney:* 'It is crucial that the service deals with these broader issues to address the practice deficits, and wider systemic issues identified in this independent review'. HMIP (2023d, p. 11)
>
> *From Jacques:* 'It is crucial that the service deals with these broader issues if it is to address the practice deficits and wider systemic issues identified in this independent review'. HMIP (2024, p. 18)

If these reports were produced by our students for marking, we would immediately penalise them for cut-and-pasting from previous work (what we call plagiarism). So, in the post-TR reports, more systemic failures or issues were identified in the reports which, of course, points to the continuing failure of the rehabilitation revolution promised by the Conservative government (HM Government, 2010; MoJ, 2013a, 2013b).

We undertook a thematic analysis of the nine HMIP reports using NVivo (Beazley and Jackson, 2013), and found some interesting results in terms of the politics of public protection. Fig. 5 shows the parent themes and their level of occurrence across the SFO reports. As you can see, the dominant themes are probation (120), management (89), offender (68), case (63) and assessment (57), all of which focus on the staff within the organisation and their case management of the supervised PoP.

By and large, these parent themes (nodes) include a large number of more specific child themes (NVivo calls them child nodes), all of which tend to be largely descriptive of the failure of staff to undertake or follow processes. It is not possible here to delve into all of the above themes and their respective child nodes so some examples will suffice. For the parent theme of *staff* this included the child themes of: *staff time, training, turnover* as well as *struggling staff, significant staffing issues* and (the lack of) *experienced staff*. Out of the many examples we could quote, the following from the Bendall case about *struggling staff* demonstrates the impact politics has had on public protection.

> The impact of unmanageable workloads at both the probation practitioner and senior probation officer levels resulted in reduced oversight of new or struggling staff, frequent role changes and sickness absence. This made consistency and continuity of practice challenging. HMIP (2023c, p. 3)

In the *staff turnover* child node, the following quote from the McCann case makes it abundantly clear that the design and implementation of the policies

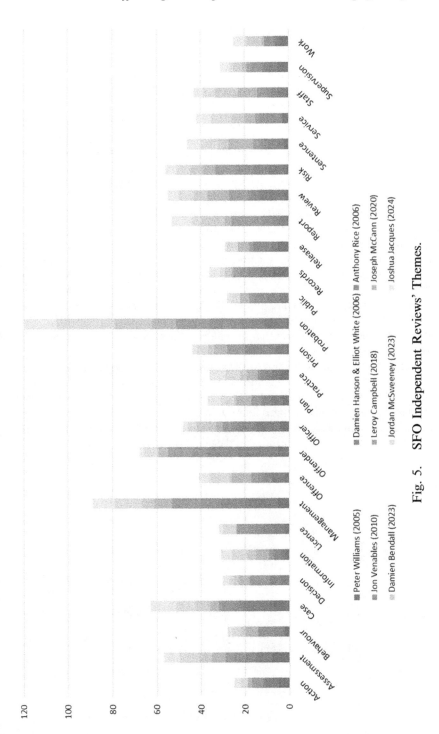

Fig. 5. SFO Independent Reviews' Themes.

within TR had had an immense impact on staff and their ability to operate a robust public protection system.

> High workloads and staff turnover were a factor in this inaction, but beyond management oversight, there was no process to ensure recall decisions were implemented. HMIP (2020b, p. 10)

Overall, the inquiries focus on the specifics of offender case management, therefore processes, bureaucracy and individual staff agency. Whilst this is understandable and we do not criticise HMIP at all for looking into deficiencies in practice, we do think that prioritising agency and process over wider structural issues is a misstep and can only be a result of the usual inability of any government organisation to admit when things go wrong. SFO cases are not simply a result of individual staff (and their own agency), but also happen because of problems within the structure. To blame individuals in terms of not adequately doing the process - a process which is complicated and takes time that the practitioners do not have - seems to us to be a political exercise in organisational scapegoating. In fact, the terms 'transforming rehabilitation' and 'community rehabilitation company/companies' were only mentioned 25 times across the 212 pages of the five post-TR reports (8 for TR and 17 for CRC). Even when these terms are mentioned, it is only in a descriptive way and did not consider the real impact that they had on the ability of staff to adequately protect the public in these cases.

Next, we were interested in the overall sentiments of the reports and the difference between negative and positive sentiments (defined as an automated process of coding, where NVivo interprets textual data and assigns it various positive or negative sentiment markers). NVivo assigns four sentiment markers - very negative, moderately negative, moderately positive and very positive. As to be expected (see Fig. 6), in all nine reports there is a larger focus on the negative, with 1,013 very negative and

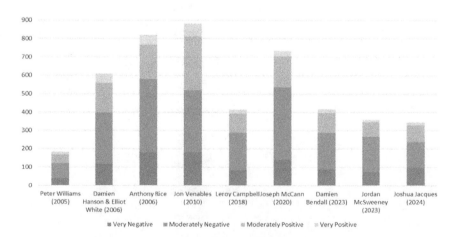

Fig. 6. Sentiment Markers for SFO Independent Reviews.

2,225 moderately negative markers assigned (3,238 negative references in total). There were 282 very positive and 1,246 moderately positive markers assigned (1,528 in total). However, the only statistically significant sentiment marker was the positive one - $t = 2.46$, $df = 7$, $p = 0.022$ with a large effect size of 1.65. This indicates that there were more very positive sentiments in the post-TR phase than the pre-TR one. As you can see from Fig. 6, with the exception of the McCann inquiry, there is a greater level of negative sentiments in the pre-TR reports (mean average of 405.00, SD 203.75) compared with post-TR reports (mean average of 323.60, SD 121.66); although this difference is not statistically significant ($t = 0.749$, $df = 7$, $p = 0.478$ with a medium effect size of 0.502). It does seem on the figure of the number of markers assigned alone that post-TR reports are less negative than pre-TR.

We also undertook a micro-analysis of the findings and recommendations in each report and, where available, the press statements released when the report is published. These yielded some interesting results. There tends to be much more detail in the post-TR summaries, despite generally being shorter reports overall. Once again, the focus is primarily on problems with the administrative and procedural, assessment and evaluation, and case management of the PoP being supervised, but there is much more focus on these aspects in the post-TR phase - with a total of 133 references for these themes in pre-TR reports as compared with 308 references in the post-TR reports (see Fig. 7).

As we have previously discussed in the chapter on TR, one of the government's marketing claims when pushing forward with their rehabilitation revolution was that privatisation would enhance public protection and make it more efficient (HM Government, 2010; MoJ, 2010, 2012, 2013a, 2013b). Of course, the extensive amount of evidence against such claims led to the embarrassment of the 2021 reunification. It was of interest to us to see if any of the post-TR reports were critical of TR. Whilst the post-TR findings and recommendations and press releases do sometimes mention wider organisational issues, very little is said about the impact that TR had on the SFO cases themselves. In fact, TR is only mentioned twice in the findings and recommendations (once in Campbell's and once in Bendall's) and it is not even mentioned in the press releases. Across the five reports, it is only mentioned eight times, and even then, it is only used in a descriptive/contextual manner. For example, take a look at the following quotes from the Campbell, Bendall and Jacques cases:

> *From Campbell:* 'But also identifies the problems that occurred following the Transforming Rehabilitation restructuring. In particular, the new PO, an experienced officer, had been given a full caseload of high risk cases. It is reported that prior to LC's oral hearing, the new PO had limited time to read through all the historic files. The SPO was also new to all cases and was relying on file records rather than personal knowledge of the case'. HMIP (2018, p. 23)

180 Politics and Public Protection

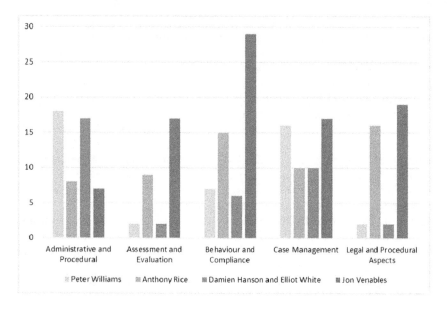

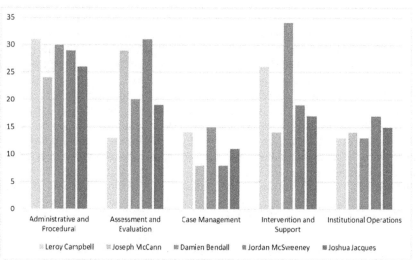

Fig. 7.   Findings and Recommendations Comparison, Pre vs Post-TR.

From Bendall: 'Inspectors found that high workloads and staff shortages in the Swindon office impacted on the ability of probation practitioners to undertake high-quality work. Inspectors heard that this was a long-standing issue that they had experienced since the changes introduced with Transforming Rehabilitation'. HMIP (2023c, p. 12)

From Jacques: 'Probation services underwent a major change in the summer of 2021. In 2014, the government's Transforming Rehabilitation programme split probation services into two. Services were then unified in June 2021 into one Probation Service. Preparations for, and the implementation of, this unification took place while services were disrupted by the Covid-19 pandemic'. HMIP (2024, p. 5)

The fact that critical commentary regarding TR is missing indicates that HMIP were not providing as full an independent assessment of the cases as one may think. If they were, we would expect a more thorough critique of the impact that TR had on these SFO cases. We can only speculate that this lack of a thorough critique of TR is because of ministerial oversight guiding the direction of this independent body. Remarkably, there was no mention of TR anywhere in the McCann report, which was one of the most visible and horrific of all these cases. We believe that both the 2018 Campbell and 2020 McCann cases are useful for understanding conservative politics of public protection and why the government finally admitted defeat and unified the probation service in June 2021. McCann was sentenced to 33 life sentences in December 2019 'for seven counts of rape; rape of a boy under 13; three counts of sexual assault; causing a boy under 13 to engage in sexual activity; seven counts of kidnap; 10 counts of false imprisonment; attempted kidnap; and two counts of offending with the intention of committing a sexual offence' (HMIP, 2020b, p. 5). These offences took place between 21 April 2019 and 5 May 2019, and it is not hyperbole to suggest this was a 14-day rampage by McCann, yet TR is not mentioned in either the MoJ's *Probation Serious Further Offence Review* (MoJ, 2020) or HMIP's *Independent Review of the Case of Joseph McCann* (HMIP, 2020b). We think this was because of the politically sensitive timing of the case. Probably because of the problems identified in the Campbell case, 'the government launched a consultation in 2018 on the future of TR and, in May 2019, announced a new probation service' (Johal & Davies, 2022, p. 2). Given all this was going on at the time McCann went on his horrendous rampage, it is unsurprising that TR was not mentioned in the 2020 MoJ and HMIP reports. The government also had enough on its plate with Covid and lockdown so it was probably thankful that media and public attention switched to a crisis that wasn't entirely of their own making. As we have discussed in the chapter on TR, probation and CRCs were eventually unified in June 2021.

A final area we want to discuss when it comes to the SFO inquiry reports is the recent introduction of the term *professional curiosity*. This means having a strong desire to know about something within the professional setting of probation practice (HMIP, 2022b, pp. 8–12) and has been officially defined as:

> A process of always questioning and seeking verification for the information you are given rather than making assumptions or accepting things at face value. By doing this you can avoid some common pitfalls in practice: being 'professionally optimistic' by focussing on positive and not identifying where things are not improving or risk is increasing; making a judgement about new information without verifying it with other agencies involved; accepting an offender's level of compliance and not exploring if this could be 'disguised compliance'; allowing crisis/chaotic behaviour to distract you from risk management work and accepting this as normal. HMPPS (2020, cited in HMIP, 2022b, p. 5)

This term has only started to appear post-TR, starting with the Campbell case (one reference); McCann (five references); Bendall (five references); McSweeney (seven references); and Jacques (12 references). In these reports the focus is, of course, on the individual probation officers and wider multi-agency staff and the failure to be professionally curious by asking probing questions to their PoP's:

> *From Jacques:* There was a notable absence of professional curiosity across all areas of probation practice from court through to sentence management, and a failure of the probation practitioners overseeing the case and their manager to meet fully their expected responsibilities. HMIP (2024, p. 3)

> *From McSweeney:* A critical omission in the case was the failure to apply sufficient professional curiosity and management oversight to ensure all available information was analysed to assess the risk posed by Jordan McSweeney. HMIP (2023d, pp. 8–9)

> *From Bendall:* Probation practitioners did not demonstrate sufficient professional curiosity when receiving allegations of domestic abuse. HMIP (2023c, p. 19)

It is interesting that professional curiosity has recently become the latest buzzword used to scapegoat staff and direct attention away from the cumulative effect of the problems created by successive governments' austerity policies and the failed transforming rehabilitation revolution. Traditionally, this concept was operationalised in the child safeguarding area and was key to social work practice

(Phillips et al., 2022, p. 555). It is somewhat ironic that when revamping the qualification for probation in 1996 and 1997 both the conservative and labour governments took the decision to remove the social work qualification as a requirement within this training despite concerns raised at the time (Tan, 1996). By focussing training within a solely psychological and criminal justice framework of risk management, it seems a really important facet of professional practice was lost despite it being obvious that it should never have been removed in the first place. This has been a common trend in recent years, purposely de-skilling professional practice through a coercive bureaucracy (Adler and Borys, 1996). Unfortunately, this has been a problem known for a while, as indicated in the Campbell report:

> The nature of the challenge facing the NPS has, however, changed since Transforming Rehabilitation. There are fewer opportunities for new staff to develop their skills by working with lower risk offenders. The span of control of front line managers has not reduced, but they must now be skilled in identifying and prioritising risky situations and cases from within a caseload where few present no risk. HMIP (2018, p. 39)

Ignoring those who work in public protection who are inexperienced and, in some cases incompetent (which we imagine is a fairly small number), having a skilled workforce who have the time to be professionally curious is costly. Public protection is costly because it takes time and expertise to get it right. It's a common feature that conservative/right-policy favours political ideology over science and expertise and whatever expertise they do follow tends to agree with their ideology. We are certainly in the age of the death of the expert (Hofstadter, 1963; Mooney, 2005; Storr, 2013): Expertise takes people and time, and this all costs money, which successive governments over the last 14 years have been unwilling to provide.

Summary

This chapter explored SFOs such as murder, rape and assault, and the internal reviews conducted by the probation service as well as the publicly available HMIP independent reviews. When things go wrong in public protection the primary agency is, and should be held accountable. In the case of SFO's, the probation service takes the brunt of the criticism in the independent reviews as well as in the media. The framing of these SFO inquiries is a wonderful exercise in hindsight bias which publicly blames individuals working under immense pressure and worsening conditions, primarily due to systemic failings in the government's public protection policies over the last 10 years. We explored some of the political elements surrounding this contentious issue and highlighted how SFO numbers were used to claim that the public were safer under TR, when the data showed the exact opposite. We then contrasted nine major independent inquiries conducted by HMIP, split into pre - and post-TR periods. Despite probation unification in June 2021, the post-TR label is retained due to overlaps in management phases observed in the analysed reports. Notably, post-TR reports exhibit reduced detail, with a 39.21% decrease in average page count compared to pre-TR reports. A shift in focus is evident, as pre-TR reports primarily address individual failures, while post-TR reports increasingly highlight systemic issues, reflecting shortcomings in TR's design and implementation. This transition is exemplified by the introduction of terms like *systemic issues* in later reports, signalling a departure from previous omissions. The persistence of systemic failures underscores the failure of TR to deliver on its promised rehabilitative revolution. Thematic analysis using NVivo reveals dominant themes revolving around probation, management, offenders, cases, and assessments, emphasising staff and case management within the organisation. This analysis sheds light on the politics of public protection, revealing ongoing challenges despite policy reforms. The thematic analysis identified various parent themes and their child nodes, revealing a predominant focus on staff failures to adhere to processes within the probation system. Noteworthy examples include staff struggles with workload, turnover, and experience, reflecting the impact of political decisions on public protection. For instance, in the Bendall case, overwhelming workloads led to reduced oversight, role changes, and inconsistency in practice. Similarly, in the McCann case, high workloads and staff turnover hindered effective action, highlighting the repercussions of TR policies on staff capability and public safety. While the inquiries primarily scrutinise individual staff actions and bureaucratic processes, the absence of thorough critique on wider structural issues, particularly regarding TR's impact, raises concerns. Despite evidence against claims of enhanced public protection through privatisation, criticisms of TR are sparse in the reports, suggesting potential ministerial influence. This lack of comprehensive assessment of TR's role in SFO cases implies a political agenda rather than independent scrutiny. Furthermore, the introduction of the term *professional curiosity* post-TR underscores the emphasis on individual staff accountability, deflecting attention from systemic problems exacerbated by austerity policies and TR reforms. Ironically, the removal of social work qualifications from probation training has hindered holistic practice, focussing solely on risk management within a criminal justice framework. This trend reflects a broader pattern of deskilling professional practice through bureaucratic mandates, neglecting the expertise required for effective public protection. In conclusion, the reports highlight the complex interplay between political decisions, staff capabilities, and systemic challenges in ensuring public safety within the probation system. By prioritising individual accountability over structural reform, policymakers risk undermining the effectiveness and integrity of public protection efforts, perpetuating a cycle of inadequate responses to complex social issues.

Chapter 8

Civilian-Led Public Protection: The Public's Response to Bad Public Protection Politics

In 2010, an online video called *1 boy 2 kittens* went viral. It showed the horrendous torture and murder of two kittens by Canadian Luke Magnotta and was followed by other videos of him drowning a cat and feeding one to a snake (Bruney, 2019). It was right that these videos caused online anger and outrage but they also led to another online response – a group of sleuths started an online investigation to try to identify and track him down. Using clues from the video and some quite sophisticated investigative techniques and networking across the Internet, he was finally identified and in 2019, Netflix released a documentary series based on the case called *Don't Fuck with Cats*. In an interesting yet unsurprising twist, it later transpired that the killing of the kittens was simply a prelude to the sadistic murder of Lin Jun (Warmington, 2022). By the criteria reviewed in our first chapter, Magnotta is certainly an extremely dangerous person; however, our focus in this chapter is not on the dangerous individual, or the official criminal justice response, but on the public's response and how we have moved into the era of civilian-led policing and public protection.

In the preceding chapters, we have spent a great deal of time exploring historical and contemporary links between politics and public protection, hopefully demonstrating the windsock nature of public protection policy. We have also shown that the political rhetoric of the five Conservative Prime Ministers since 2010 have talked tough on crime but have delivered what is essentially a de-prioritised public protection system. Evidence of this has been shown in our discussions of the political choice of austerity and the TR agenda, which had an immense detrimental impact on the three statutory criminal justice agencies charged with protecting the public (police, prisons and probation). In previous chapters, we have also shown the intended and unintended consequences of this politicised de-prioritisation of public protection. In this chapter, we take what some readers may regard as a strange tangential diversion into one of these unintended consequences by exploring the murky waters of what we are calling civilian-led public protection (CLPP). In recent years, and with the help of new Internet-based technologies (e.g. Facebook, YouTube and TikTok), there has been growing numbers of online and offline assemblages – heterogeneous ensembles of actors, collectives, materials and social aspects (Farias, 2011) – who undertake their own versions of public protection by engaging in investigations, identifying perpetrators and making their identities and crimes visible to potentially the whole world. We have also suggested that public protection has become embedded within a penal-populist political discourse on law and order (Pratt, 2007), with each political party consistently trying to up-the-ante regarding which party is tougher on crime. Unfortunately, this type of rhetoric costs money in practice, and successive conservative governments since 2010 have not matched their level of rhetoric with the same level of funding of public services. As we have previously mentioned (e.g. see Chapter 4), austerity as a political and economic choice has left criminal justice, as well as related wider public services, decimated to the core. With lower numbers of experienced workers, lower levels of training and fewer resources to do the job effectively, is it any surprise that members of the public lose faith in the system and decide to take action?

So, what happens when sections of the public no longer believe that criminal justice agencies can adequately protect them? Throughout history, members of the public, either on their own volition or through pseudo-official channels, have taken matters into their own hands and engaged in actions to investigate and bring suspects to justice. Sometimes, this has involved the dishing out of punishments by the groups themselves. Whilst there are numerous explanations for such actions, they tend to be tied to the perception that there is a policing and criminal justice vacuum and that the current criminal justice system is not up to the job of protecting the public. It is, therefore, up to civilians to take action. This chapter provides a micro-analysis of one such type of action – vigilantism and its online variant digital vigilantism (or digilantism). We focus on the issue of vigilantism and its more recent development, online vigilantism through the case study of paedophile hunters and their informal public protection (IPP) against perpetrators of online sexual grooming of children. It covers some of the core definitions and models of vigilantism, using historical examples throughout, moving onto an examination of the development of online social activism and vigilantism. In doing so, we hope to entice the reader to consider CLPP as one of the unintended consequences of the politicised de-prioritisation of the public protection agenda.

Defining Vigilantism

Before we explore contemporary developments linking the politics of public protection with civilian-led movements, it is important to discuss the complexities of the definitions and types of vigilantism that exist. Whilst we do not suggest this section offers an exhaustive account of vigilantism, it provides the important definitional parameters that sets the context influencing the public protection agenda in the coming decade (and beyond). To begin, consider the following definitions taken from some of the classic studies on vigilantism:

> The vigilante tradition, in the classic sense, refers to organised, extralegal movements, the members of which take the law into their own hands. Brown (1975, pp. 95–96)

> Consists of acts or threats of coercion in violation of the formal boundaries of established socio-political order which, however, are intended by the violators to defend that order from some form of subversion. Rosenbaum and Sederberg (1976, p. 4)

> (i) Planning and premeditation by those engaging in it; (ii) its participants are private engagement is voluntary; (iii) it is a form of 'autonomous citizenship' and, as such social movement; (iv) it uses or threatens the use of force; (v) it arises when an established order is under threat from the transgression, the potential transgression, or the imputed institutionalised norms; (vi) it aims to control crime or other social infraction assurances (or 'guarantees') of security both to participants and to others. Johnston (1996, p. 222–223)

> Vigilantism typically emerges in 'frontier' zones where the state is viewed as ineffective or corrupt...It is a form of self-help, with varying degrees of violence. Abrahams (1988, p. 4)

The common themes across the above definitions are as follows: a set of organised actions; these actions are undertaken by non-State *ergo* civilian actors; they often entail the use or threat of coercive force and/or violence; the behaviour is crime control oriented and it arises when then is a real or perceived ineffectual state/criminal justice response to real/perceived crime or moral transgressions. As Abrahams (2002, pp. 26–30) has noted, the concept has been indiscriminately used, becoming a form of criminological shorthand that makes it difficult to develop a descriptive definition or taxonomy that encompasses the wide range of phenomena it has been applied to. Despite such conceptual problems, in many countries across the world throughout history there have been countless examples of civilians engaging in collectivised, non-state sanctioned crime control behaviours. For instance, the Sungusungu anti-raiding groups in Tanzania, who break their targets' ankles and joints (Heald, 2006); the use of necklacing (extrajudicial summary execution) in South Africa, led by groups targeting anyone from regime collaborators to common thieves (Smith, 2017) and even the sale of beef in Uttar Pradesh, India, which led to vigilantism against the sellers (NPR, 2015). In all of these examples, groups have organised against a real and/or perceived threat to the dominant social order, engaging in crime control behaviours which attempt to maintain that social order. However, vigilantism can also be used as a way to question traditional norms and values, as in the case of the Gulabi Gang in India. Led by a group of females, the Gulabi Gang fought against traditional forms of gender and caste injustice, retaliating against men accused of gender-based violence. They were known for their hot pink saris and use of bamboo *lathis*, which were used as a 'symbol of courage and battle-readiness' (Walters, 2015).

More recently, examples of newer types of vigilantism have led some to re-evaluate the term, what it means and the methods used to undertake such collective action. Consider these definitions:

> Vigilantism as the collective use or threat of extra-legal (sic) violence in response to an alleged criminal act. Moncada (2017, p. 6)

> Rituals in which participants are mobilised to transform fear and righteous anger into purposive (premeditated or more or less immediate) reactive or preventive unlawful violent action to punish violations or moral imperatives to restore or uphold the moral community. Asif and Weenink (2019, p. 3)

> Vigilantism as the extralegal prevention, investigation, or punishment of offences (sic). Bateson (2021, p. 926)

These definitions have similar components to the ones explored above; however, they clarify the involvement of the non-state actor by introducing the term *extra-legal*. Also, terms such as prevention, investigation and punishment are all factors linked with our understanding of the term public protection, which we have discussed across various chapters in this current text. Despite the similarities across the old and newer definitions, there has been an effort to develop the definitional and conceptual frameworks to allow for contemporary changes to the forms that vigilantism has taken. Moncada (2017) provides a conceptual analysis of vigilantism that identifies areas of conceptual discord, suggesting that vigilantism is a contested concept and that a reimagining of the root concept is required. He outlines (2019, pp. 2–5), conceptually, how this can be achieved through exploring three aspects of conceptual discord (context-specific contextualisation, indeterminate core dimensions and attributes and the lack of sustained conceptual debate). In a way, an unintended consequence of the popularity of Johnston's 1996 article and his six definitional components was that it created a situation where this became the criminological shorthand that subsequent research has quoted without engaging in the type of critical and sustained conceptual debate identified by Moncada. Importantly, he discusses the following five core definitional dimensions of vigilantism and the range of attributes for each dimension (2019, pp. 5–6): (i) social organisation; (ii) targets; (iii) repertoires of violence; (iv) justification and (v) motivational. As we will show below, these components help to explain many types of historical and contemporary forms of vigilantism. What is useful about conceptualising vigilantism in Moncada's way, is that the root concept – vigilantism – acts as a starting point that allows for numerous applications under different conditions as it enables researchers to use the concept for various theoretical and empirical ends. This has been useful for our conceptual linking of CLPP to public protection as CLPP has developed within the socio-legal condition of legal legitimacy (Asif and Weenink, 2019, p. 11). Within this condition, civilians view legal authority as lacking, weak or missing and seek different ways to address violations in moral imperatives and/or the criminal code. Before expanding on this issue, we think it would be useful to provide a wider, albeit brief, historical background to vigilantism.

Calling the Hue and Cry – A Brief History of Vigilantism

It is broadly accepted within modern society that the ownership/jurisdictional boundary of public protection lies with the statutory agencies (police, prison and probation) and the wider multi-agency family (or duty to cooperate agencies such as third sector/voluntary community sector organisations, social services, child services, housing, NHS/mental health, etc.). As part of the social contract (Rousseau, 1968), the government attains its right to exist and to govern by the consent of the governed, and in turn, we agree to give up certain freedoms in order to be safe and secure. Part of these lost freedoms include the move from self-policing and public protection – within a framework of what Durkheim (1991) called mechanical solidarity – to a highly organised system of organic solidarity, in which the state takes jurisdictional control of policing and public protection (Garland, 1991, 2001). However, at various times throughout history, members of the public have either been *called-to-arms* to help the police maintain the moral and legal boundaries of the collective conscience (Durkheim, 1991); or they have decided to act on their own. Such boundary maintenance activities have sometimes been called *vigilantism* (Abrahams, 1988; Brown, 1975), which has a long, varied and sometimes racist/xenophobic history. This brief section on the history of vigilantism focuses primarily on the UK and USA, although where relevant, we have made reference to global examples. One certainty is that vigilantism is a global phenomenon and not just a modern Western one.

Most people make no distinction between vigilantes and lynch mobs, and as Abrahams (2002, pp. 26–30) has pointed out, the term 'vigilante' is itself a contested concept. Historians separate the two by the formers' longevity and organisation and draw a further distinction between *classical vigilantes* who targeted criminals on the US frontier and *neo-vigilantes*, who targeted 'aliens' (e.g. Catholics, Jews, African-Americans or labour leaders) for socio-political reasons (Brown, 1975). However, once one moves beyond the vigilantes' form of organisation to the desire for instant and informal justice, one can see why the popular conflation prevails. The justifications offered by lynch mobs are not that dissimilar from the universal motives that Abrahams argued exist and which can be detected from the original *Regulators* to today's cyber variants (Abrahams, 1988, p. 5). If Brown's thesis that vigilantism could only be understood through recognising a tradition of violent conflict resolution in the USA was correct, it becomes even more difficult to draw distinctions between the two forms of lynch law. Despite this, early types of vigilantism included the *classic vigilantes* in America (Brown, 1975, pp. 95–97), which 'arose as a response to a typical

American problem: the absence of effective law and order in a frontier region' (1975, p. 96), and so were created in order to 're-establish, in each new settled area, the civilised values of life, property and law and order' (1975, p. 97). The American vigilante tradition started around 1767 and, until 1900, was a constant factor with as many as 500 movements known originally as *regulators* but also as *slickers, stranglers* and *committees of safety* (1975, p. 97). The latter term is of special interest given that one of the key aims of public protection and a central part of the political public protection discourse is safety (see HM Government, 2010). Vigilante groups such as the *South Carolina Regulators, Iron Hills, Indiana Regulators* and the *Comites de Vigilance* tended to be short-lived movements of less than a year, although some lasted over a year. Many of these groups were led by 'local community leaders' (Brown, 1975, p. 97) using the common term *vigilance* within their name (e.g. 'Vigilance Committee' or 'Committee of Vigilance'), echoing Temperance and Vigilance moral crusade movements that were widespread in the UK and USA in the 18th and 19th centuries (see Boyer, 1978; Bristow, 1977; Gusfield, 1986). These vigilante groups tended to grow organically in response to varying types of frontier disorder, where 'the law was often absent or ineffectual' (Brown, 1975, p. 100). For example:

> Beginning with the first significant vigilantism in the gold-rush metropolis of San Francisco in 1849, and continuing for 53 years down to 1902, there were at least 210 vigilante movements in the West. Brown (1975, p. 100)

As Brown points out (1975, p. 115), these groups worked within an ideology of vigilantism that created the illusion of legitimacy as many were aware that their activities were largely illegal. This ideology consisted of three elements: (i) an economic rationale; (ii) the doctrine of vigilance and (iii) a philosophy of vigilantism. In respect of the economic rationale, many frontier towns lacked the economic means to support even the most basic form of criminal justice response, such as constables, policemen and sheriffs (1975, pp. 112–13). The resulting policing vacuum led to numerous vigilante groups forming for crime control and boundary maintenance purposes. As we will show later in this chapter, the economic rationale – in the form of criminal justice austerity policy – has been one of the drivers for the development of CLPP. The second element of the vigilante ideology is the doctrine of vigilance (1975, pp. 114–115). In order for vigilantism to thrive as an alternative to mainstream criminal justice methods, a fairly widespread belief in the necessity of vigilance is required. This entails being aware of the numerous risks in rapidly changing environments: 'to be vigilant in regard to all manner of things was an idea that increasingly commanded Americans [...](and)...provide a powerful intellectual foundation for the burgeoning vigilante movements' (Brown, 1975, p. 114). Again, we will demonstrate later in the chapter how the doctrine of vigilance from US frontier vigilantism is present in contemporary forms of CLPP, for example, when considering how the growth in Web 3.0 (Naik & Shivalingaiah, 2014) technologies has increased our capacity to be both reactive and proactive civilians when it comes to public protection. The final element of the vigilante ideology identified in Brown's review (1975, p. 115) is a general philosophy of vigilantism and consists of the three components of *self-preservation*, *the right of revolution* and *popular sovereignty*. In particular, by the middle of the 19th century, US vigilante groups were 'routinely invoking "self-preservation" or "self-protection" as the first principle of vigilantism' (Brown, 1975, p. 115). Despite creating a narrative of self-preservation, vigilante groups were more than aware that their activities were illegal so required more claims to justify their actions. One of these was the *right to revolution*, with groups such as Louisiana's *Comite de Vigilance* claiming that it was a 'revolutionary movement', whilst other groups formed themselves into revolutionary tribunals under the name of 'regulators' in order to 'deal with horse thieves and counterfeiters' (Brown, 1975, p. 116). Finally and, according to Brown (1975, p. 116), the most vital component of the philosophy of vigilantism was 'the democratic idea of popular sovereignty' – a deeply held political belief by many Americans which specified that:

> [...]the people of this country are the real sovereigns, and that whatever the laws[...][if they]...are found inadequate to their protection, it is the right of the people to take the protection of their property into their own hands, and deal with these villains according to their just desserts. Mott (1859, pp. 15–18 cited in Brown, 1975, p. 117)

As we will show below, the right of the people to take care of themselves when the law does not (or fails completely), is often a central rationale used by contemporary vigilante groups. Of course, the US has not been the only country in history to generate vigilante justice and protection. There are many examples from other countries around the world that could be examined but, given the focus of our book, a look at the historical links between vigilantism, civilian-led policing and current forms of CLPP in the UK is perhaps a more fruitful way forward.

England has a very strong tradition of civilian-led policing and justice delivery. Whilst it is not within the remit of this chapter to provide a full historical analysis, the elements most closely associated with delivering CLPP are the *hue and cry* and *rough music*. A pivotal point was 1285 and the signing of the Statute of Winchester by King Edward I, so a long time before a professional police force was established. This Act is one of the earliest recorded pieces of legislation regarding law enforcement in England and introduced the concept of the *hue and cry*. Its central aim was to establish measures for maintaining public order and apprehending criminals, so the hue and cry system was a rudimentary form of community policing and law enforcement but was centred around the issues of safety and public protection (Rawlings, 2003; Williams, 2015). Whilst most hue and cries were bespoke to local needs and justice responses, five key elements of how it worked can be identified: (i) requirement to raise the hue and cry; (ii) community response; (iii) pursuit and apprehension; (iv) responsibility of the hundred and (v) penalties for failure to respond (Hobbs, 1989; Rawlings,

2003). The *requirement to raise the hue and cry*, as embedded within the statute, mandated that if a crime occurred, particularly serious crimes like murder, theft or assault, any witness or victim was obliged to raise an alarm by shouting 'hue and cry' to alert others in the vicinity (Williams, 2015). This issue highlights the importance of *awareness* and *visibility*, both of which, as we will show later in this chapter, have become one of the key components of online vigilantism/ activism (Trottier, 2016, 2017). This raising awareness of a crime instigates a *community response* where members of the community were expected to join the pursuit of the criminal. This communal obligation meant the responsibility for apprehending wrongdoers fell not only on law enforcement officials but also on ordinary civilians (Hobbs, 1989; Williams, 2015). Third, part of the community response was *pursuit and apprehension*, which was the expectation of those hearing the hue and cry to join the pursuit and assist in capturing the perpetrator. This collective effort was crucial in the absence of professional police forces as we know them today (Reiner, 2010). A fourth aspect was known as the *responsibility of the hundred*. Given that some members of the public were reluctant to dish-out justice to people in their districts, the Statute of Winchester also assigned responsibility to the '100' – an administrative division in each mediaeval English district, charged with ensuring that the hue and cry was raised and responded to effectively. The hundred was expected to organise and oversee the process of pursuit and apprehension within its jurisdiction. Failure to heed the hue and cry and assist in the pursuit of criminals could result in *penalties for failure to respond*. For individuals who neglected their duty, this could include fines or other forms of punishment (Williams, 2015).

While the hue and cry system was an important component of medieval law enforcement and public protection in England, it had its limitations. It relied heavily on the willingness and ability of communities to respond swiftly and effectively to criminal activity. Moreover, it primarily targeted crimes that occurred in public spaces and often struggled to address more complex forms of criminal behaviour. However, the visibility and raising awareness actions of the hue and cry certainly had the effect of ensuring civilians were in charge of delivering localised policing, justice and public protection. The historian E. P. Thompson's work on *rough music* brings a cultural Marxist framework to understanding aspects of hue and cry and how civilians attempt to protect the public through asserting their own social values (1993). Thompson introduced the concept of *rough music* in his influential work *Whigs and Hunters: The Origin of the Black Act* (1977), and then again in his excellent *Customs in Common* (1993). Rough music – also known as *charivari* or *skimmington* – refers to a form of popular protest or social control that emerged in pre-industrial English villages and towns:

> The term which has been generally used in England since the end of the seventeenth century to denote a rude cacophony, with or without more elaborate ritual, which usually directed mockery or hostility against individuals who offended against certain community norms. Thompson (1993, p. 467)

In short, it refers to a collective and often raucous form of protest or ridicule directed towards individuals who violated community norms or committed socially unacceptable behaviour. This could include instances of adultery, domestic abuse, breaches of community standards or perceived injustices (Thompson, 1993). Thompson's theory of rough music offers insights into the dynamics of power, resistance, politics and social order in rural communities during the early modern period. Rough music was characterised by its ritualistic nature and symbolic elements. Typically, participants would create loud noises using pots, pans, drums, horns and other instruments to create a cacophonous procession through the streets of the village or town (Ingram, 1984). They might also use effigies or symbolic representations of the target of their scorn. As with the hue and cry, *community participation* was key to a rough music as it was a communal activity, involving a broad cross-section of the local population. It was not orchestrated by any formal authority but emerged organically as a response to perceived grievances or transgressions within the community. Both men and women, across different social classes, could participate in rough music events (Ingram, 1984; Thompson, 1993). Thompson (1993) argues that rough music served as a mechanism for *social regulation* and *discipline* in pre-industrial communities. By publicly shaming individuals who deviated from accepted norms of behaviour, rough music reinforced social cohesion and upheld community standards. It functioned as a form of informal social control, deterring others from engaging in similar conduct. In this sense, the visibility and awareness through public shaming acted as an expression of *popular justice* or *vigilantism*, where communities took matters into their own hands to address perceived wrongs or injustices. In the absence of centralised legal institutions or effective law enforcement, rough music provided a means for ordinary people to assert their values and hold others accountable.

Thompson (1993) suggests that rough music declined in significance with the rise of industrialisation, urbanisation and the development of modern legal and judicial systems. As communities became more fragmented and centralised authority grew stronger, the need for rough music as a means of social control diminished. Over time, as centralised law enforcement agencies developed and professionalised, the hue and cry and rough music apparatus gradually became less prominent (Reiner, 2010; Savage, 2007; Williams, 2015). However, remnants of hue and cry and rough music rituals and traditions persisted in some rural areas well into the 19th century. Their principles of community involvement and shared responsibility for maintaining public order and safety have left a lasting legacy in the history of policing and public protection in the UK. Thompson's theory of rough music offers valuable insights into the politics and dynamics of community life, social control and resistance in pre-industrial England. It highlights the importance of collective action, symbolic rituals and informal mechanisms of justice in shaping the behaviour and values of early modern societies. We will argue below that the community fragmentation and creation of a centralised police force has been affected by the development of the Internet, WWW and numerous technologies. Developments such as Web 2.0 and 3.0 (Naik & Shivalingaiah, 2014) have brought community power back into the justice and public protection arena, reducing community fragmentation and providing widespread awareness and visibility to issues that go way beyond what any 19th century rough music ever achieved. We have reviewed the above elements to US frontier vigilante groups and the UK's hue and cry and rough music to demonstrate that throughout history, civilians and vigilante groups have played a key role in policing, justice and public protection and have always invoked a number of very strong justifications and raison d'etres for their existence. Most of these reasons fall within the right to defend and protect themselves and their property from criminals and restore social stability by protecting the public and enhancing public safety. These activities and justifications, as we will demonstrate in the remainder of the chapter, have taken on a new emphasis in recent times producing what has been called informal criminal justice (ICJ). We would take this further and suggest digilantism is also a form of IPP.

Informal Justice and Public Protection

Anyone interested in public protection should consider examining the field of ICJ. The old forms of public protection through community involvement, such as the hue and cry and rough music discussed above, were replaced from the late 19th century with a more formalised control culture; with its organisation of the criminal justice into key agencies who engage in control and confinement activities (see Garland, 1991, 2001). As Cohen (1985, pp. 32–36) noted, starting around the 1960s there was the movement towards the professionalisation of the control culture, characterised by the net-widening of agencies and the dispersal of state power to new sites (also see Garland, 2001; Hillyard and Gordon, 1999). This was accompanied by the increase in the use of new and developing technologies aimed at preventive surveillance (e.g. the growth in CCTV in the 1990s after the tragic murder of James Bulger). Zedner (2007) labels this the move from post-criminology to pre-crime or from reactive to preventive criminal justice. Indeed, new technologies play a crucial role at various sites and points in the criminal justice and public protection process, adding more informal approaches to investigations, trials, punishment and public protection. Instead of the tendency for criminal justice and public protection agencies to widen their jurisdictional boundaries (Abbott, 1988; Cohen, 1985) or 'grab more ground and to impose unity' (Feenan, 2002, p. 2), many individuals and grassroots organisations have embraced new Internet and social media technologies to undertake their own forms of ICJ, vigilantism and popular justice (2002, pp. 1–5). This is what we call IPP, and it has gone digital.

Digital Vigilantism, Online Activism and Civilian Led Public Protection or a Bit of Both

To provide a contemporary context to the last point above and to what was outlined in the previous sections, consider the case of Liam Stacey, who was prosecuted for posting racially offensive comments on Twitter following the collapse of footballer Fabrice Muamba during a match in March 2012 (Stone, 2012). During a football match between Tottenham Hotspur and Bolton Wanderers on 17 March 2012, Bolton midfielder Fabrice Muamba collapsed on the field due to a cardiac arrest. The incident received widespread attention, and Muamba was hospitalised in critical condition. Stacey, a student at Swansea University at the time, posted racially offensive comments about Fabrice Muamba on Twitter shortly after the incident. His tweets sparked outrage and condemnation from other Twitter users, many of whom reported Stacey's comments to the police (Morris, 2012; Stone, 2012). These tweets were investigated as aggravated public order offences. Stacey was arrested and subsequently charged with inciting racial hatred. In June 2012, he appeared before magistrates in Swansea and pleaded guilty to the charges against him. He was sentenced to 56 days in prison for his offensive remarks and was suspended from his university course. The case garnered significant media attention and ignited debates about freedom of speech, the responsibilities of social media users and the limits of online expression (Shahi, 2012). It also provides a perfect example of what we are calling a *cyber rough music* or *cyber hue and cry* (Marx, 2013), with Twitter users calling out Stacey's actions by raising awareness and visibility of his racist comments and reporting him to the police. The above case is just one of many that has seen a challenge to the jurisdictional boundaries of mainstream criminal justice agencies (Abbott, 1988). In recent years and through no fault of their own, these agencies appear to have lost a firm grip on their public protection responsibilities due to the last 10 years of political austerity policies. This challenge manifests itself in a variety of ways such as public protests but also in terms of digital vigilantism and activism. The primary focus for the rest of this chapter is to consider how both a perceived (and sometimes real) failure of criminal justice agencies to adequately protect the public from all sorts of offences has helped fuel the rise in digital vigilantism. Of course, we do not condone any illegal activities that take place during the commission of digital vigilantism. However, as critical criminologists using our criminological imaginations (Barton et al., 2007, pp. 3–8), we understand how history, individual biographies and structural positionality has led to both civilian led policing and public protection. Our duty is to follow Walters (2007) suggestion and produce *deviant knowledge*, which we hope to achieve through an examination of the case study of the growth in paedophile hunter groups and show how their digital vigilantism is a type of online rough music that is often framed through the rationalisation of protecting children (who are members of the public) from online sexual groomers.

As Martin (2007, p. 124) once wonderfully put it, 'vigilantism is always as old as the newest frontier, and digilantes saddled up in the earliest days of the Wild Wild Web'. Online, cyber or digital vigilantism is sometimes referred to as digilantism and denotes the use of digital platforms and social media by individuals or groups to take action outside of the formal legal system and in response to perceived injustices or wrongdoing (Loveluck, 2020; Trottier, 2017). Trottier (2017, p. 56) uses Martin's term digilantes to describe digital vigilantism as 'a process where citizens are collectively offended by other citizen activity, and coordinate retaliation on mobile devices and social platforms'. Byrne (2013, p. 71) uses the term digilantes to describe individuals and groups who 'mete out extrajudicial punishment to cybercriminals such as scammers, hackers, and paedophiles', although it should be noted that digilantism has spread to many other forms of criminal and pseudo-criminal behaviours. Fundamentally, this form of action allows the widespread public sharing of evidence of alleged criminal acts and the shaming of those suspected of committing these offences. Indeed, visibility 'as manifest through the public and open distribution of a target's personal details, stands as a central feature of contemporary vigilante campaigns' (Favarel-Garrigues, 2020, p. 189). In a more recent review of the general concept of vigilantism, Moncada discusses the following five core definitional dimensions of vigilantism and the range of attributes for each dimension (2017, pp. 5–6):

(1) *Social Organisation* - referring to how the social ties shape 'coordination and execution of vigilantism and can 'run from formal to informal forms' (p. 5).
(2) *Targets* - which signifies that vigilante/digilante groups direct their attention to individuals who have engaged in behaviour that violates some moral or formal legal order that is punishable by the state (p. 5).
(3) *Repertoires of Violence* - which denotes the use or threat of the use of physical violence and can include verbal or psychological violence (p. 5).
(4) *Justification* - referring to how groups 'publicly legitimise their behaviour' and acts as the performative part of the collective action (pp. 5–6).
(5) *Motivational* - this tends to signify the reasons why individuals engage in vigilante activities (p. 6).

The above conceptualisation is especially useful when applied to understanding digilantism as a form of public protection. The considerable growth in digilantism over the last 10–12 years, is largely thanks to the enabling intersection between austerity-driven criminal justice vacuums, developing user generated Internet and communication technologies (ICT) and net-widening laws attempting to catch-up to dangerous offences which are now also facilitated by technology. As we have briefly discussed elsewhere (Williams, 2023), ever since the late 1990s the development of ICT - including the World Wide Web, the Internet and various hardware technologies - has provided society with huge benefits in terms of enabling easier and quicker ways for people to communicate, work, collaborate, share information and create content. Naik and Shivalingaiah (2014) summarise these technological developments within three distinct phases which they label as Web 1.0, Web 2.0 and Web 3.0. Web 2.0, known as the Social Web, facilitated interaction between web users and sites, and Web 3.0 (also known as the semantic web), encompasses 'meanings, connecting knowledge and putting them to work' (Naik & Shivalingaiah, 2014, p. 2). Within this last iteration, social media companies - initially driven by Twitter (now X) and Facebook - have blossomed, creating the direct and immediate communication between users, as well as the sharing of information and user-generated content. The ability to instantly react and share not only stories but our own productions in terms of videos and pictures, has enabled the public to be another potential site of criminal justice and public protection through different forms of digilantism. There are lots of different examples of this activity across the globe - both good and bad. Cases can range from unorganised individual victims wishing to make visible what the system of public protection tries to avoid, by naming the perpetrator and describing their offence(s), to the police asking for social media help in investigations, right through to organised global social movements. An example of the former is Savannah Dietrich from the US, who in 2012 defied a gag order and tweeted the names of two sixteen-year old boys who had sexually assaulted her. These dangerous individuals removed her clothing whilst she was drunk and unconscious, 'digitally raped her and took photos of the abuse' (Salter, 2013, p. 229). Unfortunately, and something which continues to happen in such cases, the offenders avoided jail and were only sentenced to 50 hours community service, with the prosecutor telling Dietrich to 'get over it and see a therapist' and that 'jail was for "real" rapists, murderers and robbers' (Gye, 2021, cited in Salter, 2013, p. 230). Dietrich took offence to this and tweeted the offenders' identities, despite knowing she faced a contempt charge and possibly jail time. Thankfully, news of her tweets and the threat to her liberty spread through social media, popular websites and blogs, generating immense media attention and eventually forcing the courts to rescind the contempt of court motion. As Salter (2013, p. 231) recognised, 'Dietrich's case can be seen as an example of the ways in which individual acts of protest against gender injustice can take on a counter-hegemonic dimension where it reaches sympathetic online counter-publics'. We would perhaps interpret this case in simpler terms as being a powerful public protection tool, as it allowed the visibility of these two dangerous offenders which ultimately empowers the public to better protect themselves from them, i.e. being informed so you can then make a decision as to whether or not you'd attend the same party as these offenders. Disclosure to victims and the wider community in certain cases is seen as good public protection practice as it allows the public to manage their own risks. The case also forced a change in the position of courts regarding the leniency of the original sentence, as they were forced to complete a sex offender treatment programme and were no longer able to apply to get their records expunged (2013, p. 231).

The Dietrich case is just one of many examples where a single victim has used the power of social media to make the invisible visible by naming individuals and showing to the wider public exactly what they have done. It also acts to highlight the often lenient sentences for what are often serious offences. The case of 19-year-old Australian Ashlee Savins is another example of this trend. Savins was assaulted by her then-partner and was left with significant facial injuries (Wood et al., 2018). Her friend, Ellie Sutton took photos and posted them on Facebook and, in a second post, named the perpetrator. This 'intimate partner violence (IPV) survivor selfie' eventually forced the police to take the case seriously and it was 'only after the pictures went viral that authorities took action to prosecute the perpetrator' (Wood et al., 2018, p. 2). Such cases tend to be about individual issues and cases where victims or those close to them feel let-down by criminal justice and public protection agencies. However, sometimes the system itself acts for online help, as in the case of the 2011 Vancouver riot, when approximately one hundred thousand people converged in downtown Vancouver after the Vancouver Canucks lost in the playoffs to the Boston Bruins (Trottier, 2014, p. 89). The ensuing riot led to the police crowd-sourcing user-led surveillance, with riot-themed groups emerging on Facebook and posting images and videos of the rioters which the police used as intelligence sources of information and evidence used in their investigation (Trottier, 2014, pp. 89–90). Finally, some types of digilantism lead to full-blown social movements, as in the case of the #metoo movement, with some of its more famous participants calling for the movement to create a 'transformative justice process to address this problem' (Wexler et al., 2019, p. 47). In 2017, after the collapse of the original Bill Cosby rape and sexual assault trial, a large number of women made allegations of sexual harassment and assault against Harvey Weinstein (Wexler et al., 2019, p. 47 and Banner, 2019, p. 201). This led US actress Alyssa Milano to tweet the following:

> Suggested by a friend: If all women who have been sexually harassed wrote "Me too" as a status, we might give people a sense of the magnitude of the problem. If you've been sexually harassed or assaulted write "me too" as a reply to this tweet. Cited in Banner (2019, p. 201)

This built on previous hashtag campaigns but soon exploded into a global social movement, with the 'hashtag posted as a Facebook status 12 million time's in the movements first 24 hours' (Banner, 2019, p. 203). Soon reports flooded in to various social media sites about all different forms of sexual harassment and assault, especially those that take place in the workplace (Wexler et al., 2019, p. 50). It is clear that the #metoo movement empowered victims of sexual harassment, assault and even rape to talk about their experiences, enhance the visibility of the issue and seek justice. It is, of course, not known the impact such movements have had on public protection but we can surmise that it's considerable: not only because of the cases that have been brought to courts and the subsequent convictions, but also because the visibility over the issue would hopefully have acted as a control mechanism to change the behaviour happening in the first place.

Regardless of their composition or focus, forms of digilantism or cyber activism tend to share key elements in terms of being user-led investigations and surveillance activities (Trottier, 2014, 2016) that lead to mediated visibility or digital exposure (Dennis, 2008; Thompson, 2005) that becomes weaponised (Trottier, 2017) towards achieving cyber/virtual justice and/or revenge (Salter, 2013; Wood et al., 2018). This is largely achieved through the generation of the politics of outrage through trial by media (Greer & McLaughlin, 2010, 2012). We now turn to a more focused example of digilantism by exploring the case of paedophile hunters and they use both the motivational and justification elements (Moncada, 2017, pp. 5–6) of public protection and safety when catching individuals who sexually communicate and groom children online for the purposes of meeting children to sexually assault and rape them. We believe that the digilante phenomenon of paedophile hunting offers a seminal example of civilians undertaking online IPP, or what we're calling CLPP.

Case Study – Hunting Paedophiles

Paedophile hunters have become a common phenomenon for more than a decade, occurring in many different countries including the UK, US, Canada, Russia and Australia (Favarel-Garrigues, 2020; Hussey et al., 2022; Williams, 2023). The bulk of this section focuses on the UK groups and some of the online ethnography conducted by one of the authors of this current text. Despite some slight variances between the groups and their member composition, they all involve adult members creating false online profiles pretending to be children under the age of 16, usually between the ages of 11 and 15, although there are cases where the decoy profile age is younger. These decoys then wait to be messaged using a variety of social media applications such as Facebook, Snapchat, WhatsApp, KIK, Tik Tok, Instagram, Baboo and Whisper. Once a suspect groomer has approached the decoy online, they engage in conversation that usually (quickly) turns sexually inappropriate, which is an offence under the s15 of the Sexual Offences Act 2003 and s67 of the Serious Crime Act 2015. The decoys record all of the communications they have with the suspect groomers and a meeting is organised. At this 'sting' meeting, the suspect is met by the team members which usually consists of a lead, members of the hunter group, the decoy they've been communicating with and security for the group. The meeting is recorded and depending on how the group like to operate they will either live-stream the sting (e.g. Facebook, Tik Tok or Instagram) or upload the recording to the social media app of choice at some point afterwards. During the sting the police are usually called and the groups hand over their evidence package once the suspect has been arrested. Sometimes, the groups will post an update on the case, which involves a picture of a letter received from the CPS and/or police detailing what the suspect has been charged with; or a picture of the offender and the result of the court case. In recent years, we have noticed that these groups have started to build an entire network assemblage (Farias, 2011) by working together. It is not uncommon to see sting videos posted with the title *Wolf Pack Hunters Uk - Sting by our Friends at COBRA UK*. This enables groups to collectively work together to sting someone who lives far away. For example, it might be that a decoy for a group in Portsmouth is speaking to someone in Newcastle, so instead of having to travel 350+ miles, the group can ask if another local group can conduct the sting on their behalf. This description is a typical example of what the groups do but, given there are approximately 100–150 groups operating at any given time in the UK (sometimes more, sometimes less), there is some variance between the groups. For instance, in our online ethnography, we have observed that some groups will live-stream the stings, whilst others wait until the suspect has been convicted of a grooming and/or other sexual offence before they name and shame him online (it's usually a him) (Williams, 2023). In terms of public protection, there is clear evidence that these groups are engaging in their own contemporary versions of the hue and cry and rough music - they are simply playing out these elements both in the online and physical worlds. In recent years, groups have begun to advertise that a sting is about to occur, or what we suggest is the groups calling for an online hue and cry. These Facebook posts, asking their audience to attend the live sting, is then supplemented by waiting for the audience to join them, demonstrated by the following quote from one of the sting videos examined:

> I'll let (the) audience build before I start talking properly. You've got 7000 people watching you right now. By the way, you're live all over Facebook. We expose people like you.

As mentioned above, rough music has been a traditional element of working-class culture for hundreds of years and usually involves 'directed mockery or hostility against individuals who offended against certain community norms' (Thompson, 1993, p. 467). We found elements of rough music in all of the online stings analysed, demonstrating how groups hunt down the alleged offender, mock them and, more often than not, are verbally hostile towards them. Consider the following examples taken from the analysed sting videos:

> You're a disgusting (sic), you're a fucking nonce. You're a fucking paedophile, ain't you? That's what you are, a fucking paedophile.
>
> Do you send all of your friends naked pictures of yourself? Of your penis, which by the way I think you should go to the GUM clinic and get checked out.
>
> It's taking all my might not to kick off because people like you repulse me and you don't seem to care.
>
> Move your fucking hands please. I'll tell you what, don't put your hands on me, because I will fucking…and I will fucking bend you up, yes.

During the research into these groups, it became clear that an argument could be made that they were engaging in what we call CLLP. Similar to ICJ, the activities of the groups are primarily focused on two aspects. The first is investigating or detecting online child sexual grooming of children, or what Hadjimatheou (2019) and Holmes (2022) call citizen-led (digital) policing. There is a burgeoning literature on citizen-led policing and its related field of nodal governance (Burris et al., 2005). Ever since the 1991 Morgan Report recommended a partnership approach to crime and disorder (Home Office, 1991, p. 14), successive neo-liberal governments and their criminal justice policies have both created the conditions for and encouraged the pluralisation of governance, which includes the fields of policing and public protection. As Shearing and Wood (2003, p. 403) have argued, this has led to some unanticipated consequences, resulting in a broadening of official and private nodes of governance. Paedophile hunters can be seen within this decentralised private nodal framework, although we prefer the more politically sensitive term civilian-led. Evidence of this can be seen when applying Moncada's (2017, pp. 5–6) justification and motivational dimensions, as the majority of hunter groups in the UK make it abundantly clear that they are engaging in the (public) protection of children. These sting video quotes are just five examples of many that illustrate this aspect of hunter activities:

> I'm a child protection enforcer.
>
> We're an online child protection team.
>
> We're protecting our children from people like you.
>
> Trying to protect children, not putting them at risk.
>
> I'm protecting children, that's all I'm doing.

These types of justifications were also found by the large Independent Inquiry into Child Sexual Abuse, headed by Professor Alex Jay. In the report *The Internet* (IICSA, 2020, pp. 63–64), Jay and her team discussed the issue of Internet child sexual abuse and how online child abuse activist groups or OCAGs assist in uncovering online child grooming. OCAG is the official term used for paedophile hunters and was created by the police in 2018 (see NPCC, 2019). In interviewing Dark Justice, the group were clear of the public protection element of their work: 'they were seeking to assist the police "in an area where they do not have the expertise, understanding or resources to act properly or at all, to protect children from sexual abuse"' (IICSA, 2020, p. 64). Unfortunately, OCAGs have ruffled a few feathers in the mainstream control and public protection cultures, especially with the above suggestion that the police do not have the expertise in the field of online investigations. In a wonderful example of confirmation bias, Chief Constable Simon Bailey gave an example of an OCAG group who had live-streamed a sting involving a man who they claimed had shown up to meet a 14-year-old. The man, of course, denied this and claimed he thought he was meeting a 48-year-old. Having reviewed the evidence, the police found that there was 'no evidence to suggest that the male thought that he was meeting a 14 year old child....there was nothing to show that they had said that they were 14 years of age' (IICSA, 2020, p. 64). Yes, perhaps in this case, but that's the problem with confirmation bias - there are hundreds of other cases where OCAG evidence has been used to convict online groomers (BBC, 2018). In our own ethnography, observing and analysing over 150 online sting videos, the hunter groups usually make the claim that the decoy stated the fake age towards the very beginning of the online exchange, as that is how they are able to quite easily confirm that the individual has sexually communicated with a child which is contrary to s67 of the SCA 2015. Furthermore, in recent legal appeals against convictions based on OCAG evidence, it is clear that their evidence has been accepted by the court. For example, in *Sutherland v Her Majesty's Advocate (Scotland)* [2020, UKSC 32], the Supreme Court dismissed the appeal from Sutherland, who tried to argue that allowing the OCAG evidence was in direct violation of Article 8 of the European Convention on Human Rights (everyone has the right to respect for his private and family life, his home and his correspondence). In dismissing the appeal, the Supreme Court argued that Article 8 couldn't be applied to private, non-state actors and, as OCAGs were not working on behalf of the state the ECHR provision did not apply. Holmes (2022, p. 219) has suggested that the decision in *Sutherland* amounts to tacit approval of proactive private paedophile hunter investigations and 'opens up the prospect of the state circumventing the accused's Article 8 privacy rights'. It seems then, that whilst the official policy of the police is to not encourage OCAGs, they still have to respond when a call is received informing them they have a sting suspect under citizen's arrest and the courts generally do not have a problem with the evidence they provide.

The second focus of the group's sting activities is to ensure that the invisible becomes visible, as the performative nature of the online sting places an emphasis on raising awareness through not only online masculine mockery (Hussey et al., 2022), but also naming and shaming the suspect and detailing what these suspect groomers have been saying and doing online. This is another key facet to the cyber rough music and feeds directly into wanting to keep children safe by 'lighting up' (exposing them online) the suspects. Under the child node *exposure and visibility* we found the following examples:

> You are going to be uploaded to the internet tonight, you'll be exposed for everybody to see, all over…Also your information is published online.
>
> When this is published online, I mean we attract over 3.3 million people, views, a week, it's not going to look good on you.
>
> This information, this footage here and here is also uploaded to Facebook.
>
> It's all there, logged up, waiting to go on the internet. Every fucking piece. Every dirty fucking picture is ready, when he gets home to press that button and put it all over the internet. And I hope your life is destroyed. I hope you are fucking ruined. And that's before you get to fucking jail. Fucking dirty paedophile scum.
>
> Get all this uploaded, start destroying him and then ring the police.

Most of this is done to make people aware of the suspect and their activities so they can protect themselves:

> All I need is for you people out there to get this shared with all these other groups, I'm going to upload them later, put them on my page. They all need sharing. The public needs to be made

aware. People in the nearby vicinity need to print his picture. Yes, we need to get flyers going round.

We have found that the two areas discussed above, *naming and shaming* and *public protection,* go hand-in-hand for the OCAGs. They tend to view this issue in the following terms - if they make these offenders visible, the general public has a better chance of protecting their children against them. Whilst we might not necessarily agree with their tactics, the motivations and justifications are compelling. Unsurprisingly, the official responses to the hunter groups has not been favourable and has been largely critical, especially from the main public protection agencies. The police in particular were very vocal with their claims that these groups were vigilantes and that engaging in vigilantism would only hurt investigative efforts to stop online child sexual grooming of children (IICSA, 2020; NPCC, 2019). This is nothing new as public protection agencies have always vehemently protected their jurisdictional boundaries and successive governments have shied away from allowing full public access to information held on the sex offenders register (with the exception of the robustly managed Child Sex Offender Disclosure Scheme - see McCartan, 2013). The advent of the technological developments mentioned above coupled with the creation of hunter groups has certainly and dramatically altered the public protection landscape. In 2018 the NPCC realised that these groups were here to stay for the foreseeable future and also had a large amount of public support (Tippett, 2022). They played quite a shrewd political game by creating a basic policy response towards the groups, reframing them from vigilantes to online child abuse activist groups, and placing them within a wider law enforcement typology of groups who respond to online child grooming (NPCC, 2019). They also outlined some of the reasons why OCAG activity may be unhelpful. We have reproduced these verbatim from the 2019 version (NPCC, 2019, pp. 6–7):

- *Untargeted:* OCAG's activity is not targeted. Total threat exceeds capacity – we must focus upon the highest threats. OCAG activity is (sic) does not consider the severity of harm and may divert activity from higher priority towards unassessed threat.
- *Inefficiency:* Response to OCAG activity is inefficient. Building prosecution cases from practice that is unregulated is less efficient than starting from a base of good operational practice. CJ partners are likely to require additional activity to remedy issues of disclosure and fairness.
- *Criminality:* Some OCAG activity may mask underlying activist criminality and it is difficult to discern this without effort. That effort (vetting or monitoring) is a diversion of resource in itself.
- *Lacking Safeguards:* OCAG activity does not routinely consider wider safeguarding and HRA issues relating to further uncontrolled offending post challenge; offenders may become vulnerable to self-harm or secondary abuse and extortion. As public bodies Law Enforcement agencies can't condone this.

- *Loss of Evidence:* OCAG activity risks loss of evidence where offenders are not effectively controlled post challenge. Poor disclosure and controls may jeopardise (sic) prosecutions.
- *Impeding LE Activity:* Poor trade craft has rendered some OCAGs visible to offenders. The lack of engagement has resulted in some OCAGs entrapping vulnerable adults who would not otherwise have engaged in inappropriate behaviour.

Whilst we appreciate that there may have been individual instances of all of these problems across various OCAGs, we certainly don't think this is common, and it is certainly another example of confirmation bias being employed to justify an argument. If we unpack some of the above, these arguments do not hold-up. The notion that it is unhelpful that OCAGs target anyone as the police should only target the highest threat is a very strange thing to say, given the police have a central role to play in public protection. So, does this mean bad luck to those victims groomed by the low-to-medium threats? It is clear that the NPCC have forgotten their own argument and which is the key reason why OCAGs engage in their own version of CLPP: when it comes to online sexual grooming of children, threat does exceed - indeed despairingly exceeds - capacity (NPCC, 2019, p. 6). In respect of evidence and inefficiency there is little doubt that there is a variance across the groups in the quality of the evidential packages handed over to the police. However, it is a sweeping generalisation to think it is common. There are examples on social media where the groups are actually praised for this part of their work. Furthermore, as the groups have continued catching online child sexual offenders, their practice has improved and developed. Interestingly, the directive from the NPCC (do not engage with OCAGs), seems to have largely been ignored by the rank-and-file, who routinely respond to calls, arrest the suspects at the hunter stings and use the evidential package to help secure a criminal conviction (see Gillespie, 2019).

The NPCC are not the only ones to highlight some of the problems with OCAG activity. Academic research has also identified some possible issues with this type of digilantism, not least the impact that it has on civilian-led policing and public protection as well as managing PoP's in the community (Hadjimatheou, 2019; Purshouse, 2020; Walton & Penfold, 2022). We of course, are not critical of most of this research, which usefully examines problems such as admissibility of evidence (Walton & Penfold, 2022), potential breaches of human rights (Holmes, 2022; Tippett, 2022), intrusive investigative methods and the threat to the procedural rights of suspects (Purshouse, 2020).

Unsurprisingly, politicians have largely shied away from discussing such groups, possibly because they are largely responsible for sowing the seeds for their creation. Consider the following: the potent mix of austerity policies which have depleted public protection agencies; the widening of online sexual offences laws (e.g. s67 SCA 2015) that require more of the very services they have depleted; and the immense failure to not regulate social media companies for facilitating online child sexual abuse and exploitation. All of these factors have helped create the public protection vacuum that has been filled by the hunter groups. In running a Hansard search for the terms 'paedophile hunters', 'online child abuse activist groups' and 'OCAG's' there was only one reference made about the groups in the last 10 years; and that was made in relation to a HMO and home ownership debate in the House of Commons. Labour MP Steve McCabe (HC Deb, 2020, col. 406WH) stated that:

> Again, ownership is unclear, but there are reports of frequent drug dealing and antisocial behaviour. Just the other evening, I learnt of a group of so-called paedophile hunters who turned up to deliver their vigilante justice at a property converted to bedsits for supported accommodation.

For the hunters, explaining why they do what they do is simple - the perception that the criminal justice and public protection system is broken:

> They go easy on people like you, you'll be protected, you always are, you always are.

> Half of the old bill can't be bothered to investigate things.

> He breached his order, he got sentenced to 12 months suspended sentence for 24 months back in May 2019. He's breached that. Got evidence on him for sexual communication with a child sending explicit pictures, and starting a meet.

Whilst the anger towards the public protection vacuum is understandable it should be noted that these vigilantes don't mete out punishment although you could argue that online visibility and exposure is a form of cyber-punishment (see Rowbottom, 2013). They hand the evidence over to the police and let the police and courts do the more standard functions of investigation, bringing cases to court and punishing these individuals. Because of this, it raises interesting questions about whether the term vigilantes is suitable and should be applied to groups conducting CLPP.

Summary

The chapter delved into the emergence of CLPP in response to perceived failures in traditional criminal justice systems, particularly exacerbated by austerity measures and political rhetoric. We explored some of the historical and contemporary context of vigilantism, tracing its roots from classical vigilantism in America to global manifestations. Definitions of vigilantism were explored, emphasising organised extralegal actions by civilians to address perceived threats to social order. In response to such perceived threats the hue and cry system in England and the tradition of rough music was created, which underscore the longstanding role of civilians in maintaining public order/protection. We then considered how historical vigilantism developed to contemporary forms of CLPP, facilitated by advancements in Internet technologies. We suggest that CLPP represents a form of IPP, driven by the same motivations of self-defence and social stability observed throughout history. Digital vigilantism and online activism represent modern forms of public protection, often emerging in response to perceived failures of traditional justice systems. The case of Liam Stacey, who faced legal consequences for racially offensive tweets about footballer Fabrice Muamba, exemplifies this dynamic. Social media users, outraged by Stacey's comments, reported him to the police, demonstrating a form of cyber vigilantism. Such actions, while not condoned, underscore a broader trend where civilians take justice into their own hands due to perceived inadequacies in formal systems. This phenomenon, termed *digilantism*, involves individuals or groups using digital platforms to address perceived injustices. Motivated by factors such as moral outrage and a desire for justice, digilantes engage in activities ranging from exposing criminal behaviour to coordinating online protests. Enabled by the proliferation of social media and advancing Internet technologies, digilantism has become increasingly prevalent. Examples such as the #metoo movement and paedophile hunter groups highlight the diverse manifestations of digilantism. While these actions empower individuals to seek accountability and visibility, they also raise ethical and legal concerns. Nevertheless, digilantism reflects a shifting landscape where the public plays an active role in shaping notions of justice and accountability, challenging traditional paradigms of public protection. The tradition of rough music within working-class culture, as outlined by Thompson (1993), has seamlessly transitioned into the digital realm and we provided a case study of the phenomena of paedophile hunters, who engage in online sting operations targeting alleged offenders, to illustrate this transition. These stings showcase a stark manifestation of directed mockery and verbal hostility against the accused, echoing historical practices. The vitriolic language hurled at these individuals underscores a form of modern-day rough music, where community norms are enforced through public shaming and confrontation. Embedded within these confrontations lies a dual purpose: CLPP and the exposure of perpetrators. Drawing parallels to ICJ, these groups, often referred to as online child abuse activist groups (OCAGs), undertake the role of detecting and investigating online child sexual grooming. Their self-proclaimed mission of protecting children resonates through their actions, as evidenced by their vocal justifications during stings and in official reports. Despite facing criticism from traditional public protection agencies, these groups persist in their efforts, propelled by a belief in the inadequacy of existing systems. The NPCC's cautious stance reflects concerns regarding the unregulated nature and potential drawbacks of OCAG activities. Yet, amidst debates over efficiency and legality, the undeniable impact of these groups in uncovering online predators cannot be dismissed.

Challenges notwithstanding, the rise of OCAGs signifies a shift in the landscape of public protection, with grassroots movements filling the void left by institutional shortcomings. Their actions, though contentious, shed light on systemic failures and prompt critical discourse on the intersection of digital vigilantism, public safety and the limitations of conventional law enforcement. Whether viewed as pioneers of digital justice or as contentious vigilantes, OCAGs continue to navigate a complex terrain, driven by their unwavering commitment to public protection through safeguarding vulnerable communities in the digital age.

Conclusion

We began this book by saying that we had rejected the idea of the Politics *of* Public Protection as a title and instead went with Politics *and* Public Protection. Having now written the book, we are convinced that we were right to do so, as identifying a coherent political line on this subject, or even a coherent understanding of what public protection means, has been next to impossible. It is simply not an entity to be grasped. Instead, it is an ever-changing, moving and slippery concept which promises much, but in reality, and not unexpectedly, cannot deliver it all. Government after government continue to reiterate the message that its 'first duty is to protect the public'. What does this mean in reality however? Armed forces may act as a deterrent to hostile neighbours, but it is being part of a larger group that is probably more effective. Intelligence can possibly give warning of organised terror threats, and a measure of success for counter-terrorism specialists is the number of threats that have been thwarted. Yet the public remains afraid of terror threats, not least because an increasing number appear to be 'lone wolf' attacks, so-called 'out of the blue' actions, which are as unpredictable as they are damaging. Therefore, an elite and highly specialist secret service can do a very good job in dealing with organised terror but may be helpless in the face of self or locally radicalised individuals who decide to act beneath the radar, so to speak. Organisations can act on previous behaviour patterns and current behaviour when it is known. They can do very little about Rumsfeld's unknown unknowns. In the recent global COVID-19 pandemic, it appeared as if no country in the world was prepared for a virulent new virus, with research scientists and health specialists racing to discover and develop an effective vaccine. Until that point, in the 21st century, medieval quarantine was the order of the day. Of course, when the government does act, it will find many among the public who will argue that it is interfering in freedom of choice, and it is overbearing and is, in effect, a nanny state.

In this book however, we have discussed a narrower, more specific threat and not something that impacts on the whole nation. That said, when we talk of potentially dangerous individuals, it is clear that there is a perception that anyone and everyone could be at risk or could be a victim. Of course, strictly this is true, but all the evidence from victim studies tell us that most violent and sexual assaults occur between those with at least some acquaintance, previous history or relationship. The random attack remains exceptionally rare, but media reports rarely stress this, and it is clearly 'good' journalism to sensationalise as much as possible. Public protection, from whatever threat or danger, offers the prospect, if not promise, of reducing the chances of serious incidents happening. It is essentially, therefore, preventative. Public protection therefore tends to be *reactive*. It kicks in when something serious has happened and acts to prevent a recurrence. It is almost certainly completely ineffective, when it comes to stopping those random attacks which generate so much public fear and anxiety. Politically, it is a situation where you are damned if you do and damned if you do not. It is an area where far-reaching promises are made, of safety and danger-reduction, but the means by which this safe space might be reached are ill-defined, and usually result from a reaction to the latest high-profile event rather than clear, evidence-based research and evaluation. Too often a new measure is proposed before the previous one has had time to bed in.

There are however votes and popularity to be had in offering protection to the public. Unfortunately, perhaps, this offer has become bound with punishment, and as a result, the process tends in an upwardly punitive direction rather than any alternative. Since the 1990s, law and order has been a contested political issue; contested not for *what* it should entail, but how *tough* it should be. We have discussed throughout the book the '*Bidding War*' between the Conservative government and Labour opposition throughout the 1990s. This was not a war about different sides of the argument however, it was about who could propose the toughest version of the same argument. It was around this time that public protection and tough sentences began to be merged in the same penal rhetoric. As a result, punitive measures evolved around ever-longer sentences, a significant increase in indeterminate sentences, restrictions on release, tougher monitoring and enforcement of community penalties, all producing significant cultural and professional changes to a number of criminal justice agencies. Notably sucked into this scenario was the probation service, a small but important criminal justice organisation which was vulnerable to the winds of political change. Perhaps more than any other organisation, its ethos and purpose has been transformed by public protection. As we have described, its origins in Victorian philanthropy are now consigned to penal history. Never popular with right-wing politicians and a populist-minded public, it had the misfortune to become a focal point for New Labour to display its tough credentials. To its opponents and detractors, a philosophy of 'advise, assist and befriend' could not sit with tough, realistic punishments and most certainly did not accord with public protection from potentially dangerous offenders. Ultimately, the probation service faced threats to both its overall survival as an organisation or to its identity with continued threats to merge with other, more punishment-oriented bodies. It was being shifted into becoming a more punitive and controlling organisation, and in many respects, resistance was futile.

There were risks, however, in adopting and adapting to what were a new set of values. These risks centred on more publicly known failures; successes being of little interest to those detractors. For example, as probation orders, originally in lieu of sentence, morphed into punitive sentences in their own right, success criteria became a reduction in offending rather than positive change in the offender. As we eventually learnt from the nothing works era, some things do work with some people some of the time. This, however, does not sit easily alongside tables of reconvictions, where an increase in funding for probation had not had a significant impact on offending; but equally there has not been significant increases. If offending rates were one yardstick by which to measure probation service effectiveness or ineffectiveness, the move into a more central public protection role, raised the stakes even higher. So-called failures of public protection, or serious further offences, were high profile, resulting in violence or death and very serious sexual assaults. Inevitably, the probation service, occupying such a central role, was a frequent target of public approbation. Their role in assessing risk of harm and the ongoing management of that risk, an extremely difficult task, became the public face of failure. *If* warning signs had been spotted earlier and *if* these had been acted upon, tragedy might have been avoided. This is of course partly true, but it is a simple interpretation of a complex problem based on the vagaries of human behaviour. Wrapped around these perceived failures are issues concerning resources, training, experience and skills. The supervision and management of high risk of harm offenders takes a good deal of time. It takes skills and experience to spot signs of deteriorating behaviour and escalating risk. It is not simply a case of form completion. A number of factors, including the COVID-19 pandemic and austerity measures, have left the probation service poorly placed to provide an effective service. Despite recent recruitment campaigns across the service, there is a shortage of experience with only 57% of probation staff in London having more than 5 years' experience, with substantial numbers under two years (HMPPS, 2023a, 2023b). In gaining access to internal probation documents, BBC News found that London Probation Service was operating at 127% of capacity, with nationally, 400 probation officers working at 160% (Symonds, 2023). With leaving rates across band 3 and 4 probation officers of approximately 10% and recruitment rates at about the same level (HMPPS, 2023a, 2023b), there appears to be little hope of relief, allied to a workload more likely to rise than fall. Another issue for the probation service and one identified by critics from the right in the 1990s, is the number of female staff. At a time when the service has been visibly pushed towards a more macho culture, the historic ratio of 2-1 in terms of males, has been reversed by 2023, to 2-1 in favour of females. This is not in itself a bad thing of course, but it does open up a number of issues which are very well covered by Tidmarsh (2023).

Given the widely acknowledged importance of the public protection task, it may surprise readers that key staff lack experience as much as they do, or even some core skills which have been squeezed out of professional training. Equally, they may be surprised that large numbers of civilian staff and lower-qualified tasks are involved in the process. For the police service, as we described, it appears to be a task on the periphery of police action, even though it involves working with the highest risk offenders and offers the opportunity to save lives. Depending on the organisation, staff may feel that the task is too stressful, or it is not worthy of their skills and professionalism, a remarkable thought. As with many public protection measures, questions why it might engender these feelings appear to be rarely asked. There is no doubt that the worries which might surround the commission of a further serious offence by someone under supervision are huge. However, much of this worry concerns a lack of time to conduct the supervisory process properly to give time for thinking, analysis and reflection. For us, it is the size of the public protection caseload which fosters fear and anxiety for probation staff and perhaps boredom for the police. As we have noted in various places throughout the book, public protection case numbers do not really go down. They are constantly fed not only by new legislative numbers but also by changes to that legislation. For example, more people might be placed under restrictive conditions, longer prison sentences will result in more parole reports and tougher enforcement rules will result in many more time-consuming breach procedures. Underlying all of this is of course risk assessment and management. If anything has contributed to the significant increase in workload, it is this huge, administrative nightmare.

Risk decisions underpin every aspect of public protection from probation officers' pre-sentence reports to Judicial decisions on sentencing, to prison allocation, parole release decisions, ongoing supervision and of course, breach and recall decisions in the event of failure. These decisions represent something of a battleground between professional discretion and the government's desire for standardised practice across various organisations. It is clear that standardisation and uniformity has won out to the extent that lesser qualified practitioners are able to complete forms which require limited professional knowledge. In part, a shortened risk assessment process is understandable on the basis of numbers alone. The routine requirement for risk assessments on almost every case, and the tendency to bureaucratically include offenders into the potentially dangerous (high-risk) category on offence classification alone, ensures the task remains daunting if not actually unachievable. Severe staff shortages brought on by austerity have not helped the situation. Politically, it now is more the case that completing a risk assessment has become more important than actually doing it right. For example, in the chapter on mentally ill and disordered offenders, we described the way in which psychiatrists had refused to play along with the government's proposals on dangerous severe personality disorder. Part of the dispute between them saw the government threaten to abandon psychiatric involvement in assessment, instead saying they would use psychologists, a profession more used to using standardised risk instruments – indeed that profession had developed many of them. There is also clear evidence of political interference in risk decisions that are reached which are entirely appropriate to the evidence and procedures governing those decisions, IF it is a decision that the government, in effect, does not like. A particularly good example of this has been government action concerning Parole Board decisions taken on all the evidence provided to it and considered by an experienced group of professionals serving as members. Again, what triggers this reaction is often the rare, highly publicised release of a prisoner sentenced for particularly nasty crimes and regarded as being let out 'early', when in fact many critics say they should not be let out at all. This is not about Parole Board decision-making as such, it is about sentences originally passed, and it is about retribution and punishment. If there is a process that is correctly carried out, it should be followed. The political side of public protection, with votes and popularity at stake, means that the process will be changed to make it fit better with the government's political ambition. Recent reforms to the Parole Board have very much taken it in the direction of greater political control.

Risk is inherently political. Governments continually pledge to reduce risks to the public, although they do, mostly, have the sense not to guarantee to *eliminate* risk. When incidents occur, especially if it is a serious crime by a known offender, risk management is inevitably seen as having failed. What this really means is that a person, a criminal justice professional, has somehow failed with either assessment or management. This attitude does however remove the offender's agency, their decision-making, choices, personal situation and context. It is they who commit the crimes; risk professionals can really only do three things concerning risk: assess it accurately, put in place measures to mitigate it and be aware of the signs that behaviour is deteriorating, or the management plan has been compromised. Those who apportion blame onto professionals need to know that effective risk management is more than form completion. It takes time and skill, and, in our view, the professional needs to *know* the offender. Whichever way this is wrapped up, it means that a relationship between offender and professional needs to be formed if feelings and thinking is to be recognised. Meetings need to be face-to-face, and staff should not be constantly stressed by the bureaucratic demands of the organisation. If governments are to deliver on their promises of protection, they need to ensure staff have the headroom in which to operate and they also need to stop adding to the dangerous offender population.

In this text, we have written about two specific groups of offenders who cause a good deal of fear and alarm, which is, mostly, at odds with the actual risks of harm that they pose. Mentally ill or disordered offenders can cause significant anxiety. It is perhaps the public sense that these offenders lack control of their actions and maybe hearing voices telling them what to do. It is the seemingly complete randomness of attacks perpetrated by some mentally ill people that gives the public the sense that they, or anyone, could be a victim. Despite the statistical unlikelihood of becoming a victim of a mentally ill or disordered offender, when it does happen it invariably triggers a debate about treatment and/or punishment. The Valdo Calocane case that we described earlier is a good example of how this debate can not only come to public notice, but also can be taken up and re-shaped by politicians, the media and victims' groups. In this case, a plea of diminished responsibility was accepted by the court on the recommendations of five psychiatrists and resulted in a hospital detention order being imposed. Although it was the correct sentence in law, the families of Calocane's victims believed that justice was not served because the sentence was insufficiently punitive. Faced with a high-profile media campaign and very articulate, claims-making victims, the government is likely to act and respond to calls to introduce a new category of second-degree murder. This is another example of how one, well publicised and horrific crime, can shape public protection thinking and legislation. The debate between care and punishment has raged for years, but this case may well alter its trajectory. In short, we appear to be entering a period when punishment must be a part of every sentence, but not only that, punishment that reflects the seriousness of the crime. At times there appears to be a very thin line between punishment and retribution. The Calocane case shows how decisions that are taken absolutely correctly according to legislation and procedures operating at the time can be challenged and changed as a result of the negative publicity that might attach to government. As a part of what may become a flurry of reaction, there will be impact on various agencies. Finally, in a fallout from this case, and amid numerous hearings for police misconduct and poor practice, it was revealed that police had shared extremely offensive comments about the case on a social media platform, echoing similar activity by Metropolitan Police officers following high-profile murders and assault in London (Sky News, 24 April 2024).

The other group we discussed were terrorism related offenders, a threat that has come to be regarded as very much a 'home' issue. Traditionally, terrorist offences were regarded as something which happened elsewhere – overseas and technically, out of mind. Even the home-grown terror offences related to the Northern Ireland situation were not regarded by the public as a threat to them (mistakenly so at times) but rather, aimed at military and police personnel. However, numerous attacks on the UK mainland, where there have been large civilian casualties, have added to the fear and alarm that the public feel over random, unpredictable events. So-called lone wolf attacks appear to slip under the intelligence radar and are much more difficult to thwart than larger events about which more information may be known. Although extremely rare, rather like attacks from mentally ill people, when these do occur, it is the uncertainty and unpredictability that increases fear and a sense that 'nothing can be done'.

It is these words, uncertain and unpredictable, that makes the whole public protection process difficult, if not impossible, to achieve. Almost every government uttering on the subject implies that efforts will be made to remove that unpredictability and replace it with as much certainty as they can in terms of protecting the public. Logically however, this almost falls down at the first hurdle. If a person is unpredictable in their behaviour, it is, by definition, extremely difficult to plan preventive action for something which may or may not happen at a time which is unknown. Of course, many of these attacks may not be as random as we have just suggested. There may be people who have seen clues in behaviour, words may have been spoken which reveal intent, or new interests in weapons, or religion or hate speech may all be saying something about a potential future crime. Yet, for these signs and clues to be picked up, someone has to know the person well enough to spot them. If by definition they are loners, this is unlikely to happen. So, the paradox of public protection is that the very people the public wish to be protected from are unlikely to even enter the system *until they commit their crimes*. Protection then, in our view, is as much about prevention of repetition as prevention more generally. To echo Donald Rumsfeld's sentiments mentioned earlier, it is next to impossible to predict 'unknown unknowns', but there is a chance with 'known knowns'. In other words, if a person is known to agencies, and what is known is not only good quality information, but is both historic and current, and supervisors are skilled at understanding its significance, there is a chance that offending patterns might be disrupted.

We have seen however that the knock-on effect of the public and political emotion that surrounds high profile, high harm cases, means that criminal justice agendas remain permanently punitive. Any alternative to imprisonment does, in itself, have to prove its punitive credentials and rehabilitation takes on a narrow focus. Unfortunately, due to the unpredictable nature of dangerous, criminal behaviour, legislation to tackle it becomes not only a catch-all, but changes with each new case that apparently shows a loophole or exposes a failing. Underlying all responses is the need for politicians to be seen to be doing something, and if that something results in headlines, then so much the better. The impact on legislation is twofold. The first is that sentences become longer and more people are drawn into longer sentences, or automatic indeterminate sentences (for example the changing rules over whole life sentences). The second impact comes when prisoners seek release. The new tougher regime means that the point at which release might be first considered is pushed further back into the sentence and, when that point is reached, and if release is authorised, it will become subject to stringent licence conditions – often such that a failure becomes almost inevitable. As we have also seen, the Parole Board, the independent body charged with assessing prisoners for early release, find themselves the subject of intense political and indeed media scrutiny for decisions taken in line with policy and procedure, but which the public, or politicians, or the media, simply do not like or agree with. We described the MAPPA caseload as the 'worry group' and indeed, the issue for public protection is that this group continues to grow, not least because it is becoming increasingly unacceptable to take someone *out* of the group. The fear of those making these decisions is that the person will go on to commit another serious crime, and *they* will be blamed for making the wrong decision. The scientific veneer of risk assessment tools is perhaps a cover for an illusion of accuracy said to be lacking in the clinical method, which, according to its detractors, too often sought causes outside of an offender's determination to commit a crime. Despite efforts to include a greater amount of dynamic risk information in the standardised assessments, the 'dagger at the heart' of good assessment (to ape Charles Clarke) is the lack of time needed to understand an offender. The ever-expanding caseload and list of restrictive conditions to enforce are hardly likely to make this situation any better.

The final two chapters explored the politics of blaming agencies when there are serious further offences and what has been a key contemporary public response to a breakdown in the faith of both public protection policy and in the agencies that implement that policy. SFOs have profound ramifications on society with key public protection agencies, most notably the probation service becoming the focal point of criticism in the aftermath, both in independent reviews and media narratives. However, we have suggested that such critiques often overlook the systemic failings ingrained within government policies, especially over the past decade, placing undue blame on individuals working under strenuous conditions. When looking into the political dimensions surrounding SFO inquiries, particularly in the context of *Transforming Rehabilitation* policies, there were clear discrepancies between claimed improvements in public safety under TR and the reality of what was happening on a day-to-day basis at the grassroots level. Thankfully, this has not been lost on HMIP, as contrasts between pre- and post-TR independent inquiries reveal a shift in focus from individual failures to systemic issues in later reports. However, much more could be said in terms of policy failure and government overreach. Political decisions, particularly those related to TR, have directly impacted staff capabilities and public safety. Examples such as the Bendall and McCann cases illustrate how overwhelming workloads and staff turnover hindered effective action, ultimately jeopardising public protection.

Despite evidence suggesting the failure of TR to enhance public safety, criticisms of the policy within the reports are scant, hinting at a less independent objective examination of the role that politics has played in making the public feel less safe. The absence of comprehensive scrutiny on TR's role in SFO cases and the emphasis on individual staff accountability deflect attention from wider structural issues exacerbated by austerity measures and policy reforms. However, it was found that in the post-TR HMIP inquiries, there were signs advocating for a shift in focus from individual accountability to structural reform within the probation system. We highlighted what many others have about this dreadful experiment; by warning against the perils of prioritising political agendas over effective public protection measures, emphasising the need for holistic approaches that address systemic challenges and help uphold, not delegitimise, professional standards within the field. Ultimately, the calls for a re-evaluation of policies that undermine the integrity of public protection efforts and perpetuate inadequate responses to complex social issues was eventually heard and the madness of the failed revolution that was TR is no more. The heart of public protection was resuscitated with reunification in June 2021. However, the damage this has caused in terms of a weakened, less experienced and demotivated staff will be felt for many years to come, and the picture is the same across all agencies which have a public protection remit. Is it any wonder that members of the public here in the UK, having suffered through years of poor governance that lines the pockets of private companies with public money have decided to do it themselves?

Civilian-led public protection is technically not new but in recent years, has become a response to the perceived deficiencies within traditional criminal justice systems, particularly those public protection areas exacerbated by austerity measures and political rhetoric. By tracing the historical roots of vigilantism, from classical forms in America to contemporary manifestations globally, we highlighted the enduring role of civilians in upholding public order and protection. CLPP emerges as a modern iteration of historical vigilantism, facilitated by advancements in Internet technologies, and we discussed a number of local and global examples of digital vigilantism and online activism to illustrate how civilians leverage digital platforms to address perceived injustices and failures of formal justice and public protection processes. While phenomena like digilantism empower individuals to seek accountability and visibility, they also raise ethical and legal concerns, challenging traditional paradigms of public protection. The transition of rough music traditions into the digital realm, exemplified by groups like OCAG's, showcases a modern-day form of community enforcement through public shaming and confrontation. Despite criticism from traditional public protection agencies, OCAG's persist in their mission to uncover online predators, highlighting systemic failures and prompting critical discourse on digital

Conclusion   217

vigilantism and public safety. The rise of OCAGs signifies a transformative shift in the landscape of public protection, where grassroots movements fill the void left by institutional shortcomings. While their actions may be contentious, they shed light on the limitations of conventional law enforcement and advocate for a re-evaluation of approaches to safeguarding vulnerable communities in the digital age. In essence, CLPP and digital vigilantism reflect a dynamic interplay between societal norms, technological advancements, and public protection imperatives, challenging established notions of justice and accountability. As these movements continue to navigate a complex terrain, their unwavering commitment to public protection underscores the imperative for ongoing dialogue and adaptation within the realm of criminal justice and public protection processes.

References

Aarvold, C., Hill, D., & Newton, G. P. (1973). *Report on the review of procedures for the discharge and supervision of psychiatric patient's subject to special restrictions.* Her Majesty's Stationery Office.
Abbott, A. (1988). *The system of professions: An essay on the division of expert labour.* The University of Chicago Press.
Abrahams, R. (1988). *Vigilant citizens: Vigilantism and the state.* Polity Press.
Abrahams, R. (2002). What's in a name? Some thoughts on the vocabulary of vigilantism and related forms of 'informal criminal justice'. In D. Feenan (Ed.), *Informal criminal justice* (pp. 25–40). Ashgate.
Adler, P. S., & Borys, B. (1996). Two types of bureaucracy: Enabling and coercive. *Administrative Science Quarterly, 41*(1), 61–89.
Advisory Council on the Penal System. (1978). *Sentences of imprisonment.* HMSO.
Albertson, K., & Fox, C. (2019). The marketisation of rehabilitation: Some economic considerations. *Probation Journal, 66*(1), 25–42. https://doi.org/10.1177/0264550518820122
Albertson, K., Cocoran, M., & Philips, J. (Eds.) (2020). *Marketisation and privatisation in criminal justice.* Policy Press.
Allen, G., & Carthew, H. (2024). *Police service strength.* House of Commons Library. https://researchbriefings.files.parliament.uk/documents/SN00634/SN00634.pdf
Allen, G., & Mansfield, Z. (2022, December 1). *House of Commons Library.* https://commonslibrary.parliament.uk
Allen, R., & Hough, M. (2007). Community penalties, sentencers, the media and public opinion. In L. Gelsthorpe & R. Morgan (Eds.), *Handbook of probation* (pp. 565–590). Routledge.
Anderson, R. (1907). *Crime and criminals: Some facts and suggestions.* James Nisbet and Co.
Angermeyer, M. C., & Matschinger, H. (2003). Public attitudes about schizophrenia and depression: Similarities and differences. *Social Psychiatry and Psychiatric Epidemiology, 38*(9), 526–534. https://doi.org/10.1007/s00127-003-0676-6
Annison, H. (2015). *Dangerous politics: Risk, political vulnerability and penal policy.* Oxford University Press.
Annison, H. (2020). Re-examining risk and blame in penal controversies: Parole in England and Wales, 2013-2018. In J. Pratt & J. Anderson (Eds.), *Criminal justice, risk and the revolt against uncertainty* (pp. 139–163). Palgrave Macmillan.
Annison, H., & Guiney, T. (2022). Populism, conservatism and the politics of parole in England and Wales. *The Political Quarterly, 93*(3), 416–423. https://doi.org/10.1111/1467-923X.13170
Antar, A. Y. (2023). Guilty or not guilty by reason of insanity? A comparative study of murderers referred for psychiatric assessment by court order. *Health and Justice, 11*(1). https://doi.org/10.1186/s40352-023-00230-z

References

Appelbaum, P. S. (2005). Dangerous severe personality disorders: England's experiment in using psychiatry for public protection. *Psychiatric Service*, *56*(4), 383–503.

Appleton, C., & Gilman, H. (2022). Sentenced to die in prison: Reflections on whole life orders. *Prison Service Journal*, *261*, 4–8.

Asif, M., & Weenink, D. (2019). Vigilante rituals theory: A cultural explanation of vigilante violence. *European Journal of Criminology*, *19*(2), 1–20. https://doi.org/10.1177/1477370819887518

Atkinson, E. (2023, March 25). BBC News.

Banner, F. (2019). *Crowdsourcing the law: Trying sexual assault on social media*. Lexington Books.

Bardsley, A. (2023, January 8). *The woman who bit pal's nose off in act of animal savagery*. Manchester Evening News.

Barry, G. (n.d.). *Domestic homicide review Alan/2011*. Kent Community Safety Partnership and Medway Community Safety Partnership. https://www.hundredfamilies.org/wp/wp-content/uploads/2013/12/TONY_WOTTON_Full_DHR.pdf

Barton, A., Corteen, K., Scott, D., & Whyte, D. (2007). Introduction: Developing a criminological imagination. In A. Barton, K. Corteen, D. Scott, & D. Whyte (Eds.), *Expanding the criminological imagination: Critical readings in criminology* (pp. 1–14). Willan Publishing.

Bateson, R. (2021). The politics of vigilantism. *Comparative Political Studies*, *54*(6), 923–955. https://doi.org/10.1177/0010414020957692

BBC. (2016). *Labour MP Jo Cox murdered for political cause*. https://www.bbc.co.uk/news/uk-37978582

BBC. (2018). *'Paedophile hunter' evidence used to charge 150 suspects*. https://www.bbc.co.uk/news/uk-england-43634585

BBC. (2024). *Nottingham attacks: Families anger as triple killer gets hospital order*. https://www.bbc.co.uk/news/uk-england-nottinghamshire-68087302

Beard, J. (2023, April 24). *Sentences of imprisonment for public protection research briefing*. House of Commons Library. https://researchbriefings.files.parliament.uk/documents/SN06086/SN06086.pdf

Beazley, P., & Jackson, K. (2013). *Qualitative data analysis with NVivo*. Sage Publications Ltd.

Beck, U. (2009). World risk society and manufactured uncertainties in F. Battistelli & Galantino, M. G. (2018). Dangers, risks and threats: An alternative conceptualisation to the catch-all concept of risk, *Current Sociology*, *67*(1).

Belanger, A. (2021). *What a 1970s report on recidivism reveals about modern-day misinformation*. Knight Science Journalism. https://ksj.mit.edu/news/2021/05/05/recidivism-misinformation/

Bell, E. (2014). There is an alternative: Challenging the logic of neoliberal penality. *Theoretical Criminology*, *18*(4), 489–505.

Berger, P., & Luckmann, T. (1966). *The social construction of reality: A treatise in the sociology of knowledge*. Penguin Books.

Blick, A. (2023). 'An obligation of means, not one of result': A historical overview and theoretical assessment of the whole life order sentencing regime in England and Wales. *Journal of Criminal Law*, *87*(5–6), 355–385. https://doi.org/10.1177/00220183231216169

Bonholm, A., & Corvellec, H. (2011). A relational theory of risk. *Journal of Risk Research, 14*(2), 175–190. https://doi.org/10.1080/13669877.2010.515313

Bourdieu, P. (1986). The forms of capital. In J. Richardson (Ed.), *Handbook of theory and research for the sociology of education* (pp. 241–258). Greenwood.

Bourdieu, P. (2000). *Distinction: A social critique of the judgement of taste.* Routledge.

Bowen, P. (2013). Digging up the grassroots? The impact of marketisation and managerialism on local justice, 1997 to 2013. *British Journal of Community Justice, 11*(2–3), 9–20.

Bowling, B., Reiner, R., & Sheptycki, J. W. E. (2019). *The politics of the police* (5th ed.). Oxford University Press.

Boyer, P. (1978). *Urban masses and moral order in America, 1820-1920.* Harvard University Press.

Bradley. (1990). *R v Parole Board, ex parte Bradley, Queens Bench Division 4 April, 1990.* https://vlex.co.uk

Bristow, E. (1977). *Vice and vigilance.* Gill and Macmillan Ltd.

Brown, J. (2021). *Policing in the UK.* House of Commons Library. www.commons library.parliamnet.uk

Brown, R., & Hobbs, A. (2023, April 25). *Trust in the police.* UK Parliament Post, Post Note 693.

Brown, R. M. (1975). *Strain of violence: Historical studies of American violence and vigilantism.* Oxford University Press.

Bruney, G. (2019). Netflix's Don't F**k With Cats tells the true story of one of Canada's most infamous murderers. *Esquire Online Magazine.* https://www.esquire.com/entertainment/a30308038/netflix-dont-fuck-with-cats-luka-magnotta/

Bryan, T., & Doyle, P. (2003). Developing multi-agency public protection arrangements. In A. Matravers (Ed.), *Sex offenders in the community: Managing and reducing the risk* (pp. 189–206). Willan Publishing.

Burke, L., & Collett, C. (2010). People are not things. What new labour has done to probation. *Probation Journal, 57*(3), 232–249. https://doi.org/10.1177/0264550510373957

Burke, L., & Collett, S. (2015). *Delivering rehabilitation: The politics, governance and control of probation.* Routledge.

Burke, L., & Collett, S. (2016). Transforming rehabilitation: Organizational bifurcation and the end of probation as we knew it? *Probation Journal, 63*(2), 120–135. https://doi.org/10.1177/0264550516648400

Burris, S. C., Drahos, P., & Shearing, C. D. (2005). Nodal governance. *Australian Journal of Legal Philosophy, 30*, 1–43. https://ssrn.com/abstract=760928

Butcher, J. (2007). Controversial Mental Health Bill reaches the finishing line. *The Lancet, 370*, 117–118. https://doi.org/10.1016/S0140-6736(07)61067-8

Butler, R. A. (1975). *Report of the committee on mentally abnormal offenders.* Cmnd. 6244. HMSO.

Byrne, D. A. (2013). 419 digilantes and the frontier of radical justice online. *Radical History Review, 117*, 70–82.

Cain Archives. (2024). *Northern Ireland conflict since 1969, conflict and politics.* https://cain.ulster.ac.uk/

Calder, S. D. (2013). Transforming rehabilitation: A fiscal motivated approach to offender management. *British Journal of Community Justice, 11*(2–3), 175–188.

References

Canton, R., & Dominey, J. (2018). *Probation*. Routledge.
Casciani, D. (2023, February 8). Prevent counter-terror scheme lambasted in review. *The Guardian*.
Casey, L. (2023). *An independent review into the standards and behaviour and internal culture of the Metropolitan Police Service. Final report*.
Cavadino, M., & Dignan, J. (1997). *The penal system: An introduction*. Sage.
Chalk, A. (2023, October 16). *The Government's approach to criminal justice*. Statement to the House of Commons.
Charman, S. (2018, January 12). From crime fighting to public protection: The shaping of police officers' sense of role. In *Perspectives on policing, paper 3. The Police Foundation*. https://www.police-foundation.org.uk/wp-content/uploads/2018/01/perspectives_on_policing_officers_sense_of_role-FINAL.pdf
Christofferson, M. (2018). Risk, danger and trust: Refining the relational theory of risk. *Journal of Risk Research*, *21*(10), 1233–1247. https://doi.org/10.1080/13669877.2017.1301538
Clift, S. (2018). *Transforming rehabilitation: The reconfiguration of risk within a community rehabilitation company*. Unpublished PhD Thesis. University of Portsmouth.
Cohen, S. (1985). *Visions of social control: Crime, punishment and classification*. Polity Press.
Coid, J. W., Ullrich, S., & Kallis, C. (2013). Predicting future violence among individuals with psychopathy. *British Journal of Psychiatry*, *203*, 387–388. https://doi.org/10.1192/bjp.bp.112.118471
Coid, J. (1994). The Christopher Clunis enquiry. *Psychiatric Bulletin*, *18*, 449–452.
College of Policing. (2021). Protective orders and civil orders. https://www.college.police.uk/guidance/violence-against-women-and-girls-toolkit/protective-measures-and-civil-orders
College of Policing. (2023). Multi-agency interventions to address radicalisation. https://www.college.police.uk/research/crime-reduction-toolkit/multi-agency-interventions-address-radicalisation
Corcoran, M. (2020). Market society utopianism in penal politics. In K. Albertson, M. Corcoran, & J. Phillips (Eds.), *Marketisation and privatisation in criminal justice* (pp. 15–29). Policy Press.
Courts and Tribunals Judiciary. (2023). *Rex v David Carrick*. https://www.judiciary.uk/wp-content/uploads/2023/02/R-v-David-Carrick-sentencing-070223.pdf
CPS. (2018, October 26). *The code for crown prosecutors*. CPS. Gov.Uk.
CPS. (2024). *Press statement: Man sentenced for killing of three people and attempted murder of three others in Nottingham*. https://www.cps.gov.uk/east-midlands/news/man-sentenced-killing-three-people-and-attempted-murder-three-others-0
Daily Mail. (2022a). Police have failed to solve a single burglary in nearly half of the country's neighbourhoods over the past three years. https://www.dailymail.co.uk/news/article-10933747/Police-failed-solve-burglaries-nearly-half-countrys-neighbourhoods-data-reveals.html
Daily Mail. (2022b). Police fail to turn up to 120 breaks-ins a day on average. https://www.dailymail.co.uk/news/article-11948027/Police-fail-turn-120-break-ins-day-average.html
Daily Mail. (2024). Police failed to take toxicology tests from Nottingham triple killer Valdo Calocane that could have led to a stiffer sentence. https://www.dailymail.co.

uk/news/article-13036707/police-failed-toxicology-tests-valdo-calocane-nottingham-killer.html
Deering, J., & Feilzer, M. (2019). Hollowing out probation? The roots of transforming rehabilitation. *Probation Journal*, *66*(1), 8–24. https://doi.org/10.1177/0264550518820119
Deering, J. (2015). *Privatising probation: Is transforming rehabilitation the end of the probation ideal?* Policy Press.
Dennis, K. (2008). Keeping a close watch - The rise of self-surveillance and the threat of digital exposure. *The Sociological Review*, *56*(3), 347–357.
De Vries, M., & Bijlsma, J. (2022). The elusive concept of dangerousness: The state of the art in criminal legal theory and the necessity of further research. *Criminal Justice Ethics*, *41*(2), 142–166. https://doi.org/10.1080/0731129X.2022.2102837
Disley, E., Pardal, M., Weed, K., & Reding, A. (2016). *Multi agency public protection arrangements to manage and supervise terrorist offenders*. Rand Corporation.
Domestic Abuse Commissioner. (2024). *Distorted police statistics downplay domestic abuse reports, says Commissioner*. https://domesticabusecommissioner.uk/distorted-police-statistics-downplay-domestic-abuse-reports-says-commissioner/
Dominey, J. (2016). Fragmenting probation: Recommendations from research. *Probation Journal*, *63*(2), 136–143. https://doi.org/10.1177/0264550516637244
Doughty Street Chambers. (2023). *(Stephanie Davin) A Court or an Advisor? Further proposed reforms to the Parole Board*. https://insights.doughtystreet.co.uk/post/102i8zy/a-court-or-an-adviser-further-proposed-reforms-to-the-parole-board
Downes, D., & Newburn, T. (2023). *The official history of criminal justice in England and Wales. Volume 4, the politics of law and order*. Routledge.
Drake, D. H. (2012). *Prisons, punishment and the pursuit of security, critical criminological perspectives*. Palgrave Macmillan.
Dunbar, I. (1985). *A sense of direction*. Home Office.
Dunbar, I., & Langdon, A. (1998). *Tough justice: Sentencing and penal policies in the 1990s*. Blackstone Press.
Dunn, B. (2017). Class, capital and the global unfree market: Resituating theories of monopoly capitalism and unequal exchange. *Science & Society*, *81*(3), 348–374. https://doi.org/10.1521/siso.2017.81.3.348
Durkheim, E. (1991). *The division of labour in society*. The Macmillan Press Ltd.
Dyer, C. (2006, September 30). Better care for Michael Stone might still not have prevented the killings. *British Medical Journal*, *333*. https://doi.org/10.1136/bmj.333.7570.670-b
End Violence Against Women. (2021). *Almost half of women have less trust in police following the Sarah Everard Murder*. https://www.endviolenceagainstwomen.org.uk/almost-half-of-women-have-less-trust-in-police-following-sarah-everard-murder
Evans, E. (2016). The expected impacts of transforming rehabilitation on working relationships with offenders. *Probation Journal*, *63*(2), 153–161. https://doi.org/10.1177/0264550516648392
Fanarraga, I. (2020). What's in a name? An empirical analysis of apostrophe laws. *Criminology, Criminal Justice, Law and Society, Criminology*, *21*(3), 39–68.
Farias, I. (2011). Introduction: Decentring the object of urban studies. In I. Farias & T. Bender (Eds.), *Urban assemblages: How actor-network theory changes urban studies* (pp. 1–24). Routledge.

Favarel-Garrigues, G. (2020). Digital vigilantism and anti-paedophile activism in Russia. Between civic involvement in law enforcement, moral policing and business venture. *Global Crime, 21*(3–4), 306–326. https://doi.org/10.1080/17440572.2019.1676738

Feenan, D. (2002). Re-introducing informal criminal justice. In D. Feenan (Ed.), *Informal criminal justice* (pp. 1–13). Ashgate.

Fitzgibbon, W. (2011). *Probation and social work on trial.* Palgrave Macmillan.

Fitzgibbon, W. (2013). Risk and privatisation. *British Journal of Community Justice, 11*(2–3), 87–90.

Floud, J., & Young, W. (1981). *Dangerous offenders and criminal justice.* Heinemann.

Flynn, N. (2002). *Introduction to prisons and imprisonment.* Waterside Press.

Forde, R. A. (2018). *Bad psychology: how forensic psychology left science behind.* Jessica Kingsley Publishers.

Francis, R. (2007). The Michael Stone inquiry – A reflection. *Journal of Mental Health Law, 41*–44. https://www.northumbriajournals.co.uk/index.php/ijmhcl/article/view/199/194

Fulford, LJ. (2021, September 30). *Sentencing remarks, Wayne Couzens.* www.judiciary.uk/wp-content/uploads/2021/09/Wayne-Couzens-Sentencing-Remarks-pdf

Garland, D. (1991). *Punishment and modern society: A study in social theory.* Clarendon Press.

Garland, D. (2001). *The culture of control: crime and social order in contemporary society.* Oxford University Press.

Gauke, D. (2018). *Prisons reform speech.* Royal Society of Arts, https://www.gov.uk/government/speeches/prisons-reform-speech

Gendreau, P., & Ross, R. R. (1987). Revivivification of rehabilitation. Evidence from the 1980s. *Justice Quarterly, 4*(3), 349–407.

Gibbens, T. C. N. (1983). Medico-legal aspects. In M. Shepherd & O. L. Zangwill (Eds.), *Handbook of psychiatry.* Cambridge University Press.

Gillespie, A. A. (1998). Paedophiles and the Crime and Disorder Bill. *Journal of Current Legal Issues, 1.*

Gillespie, A. A. (2019). "Paedophile hunters": How should the law respond? *Criminal Law Review, 12*, 1016–1034.

Gilligan, J. (2000). Punishment and violence. Is the criminal law based on one huge mistake? *Social Research, 67*(3), 745–772.

Githens-Mazer, J., & Lambert, R. (2010). Why Conventional wisdom on radicalisation fails; The persistence of a failed discourse. *International Affairs, 86*(4), 889–901.

Golding, B. (2010). Sex offender management in the community: Who are the victims? In M. Nash & A. Williams (Eds.), *Handbook of public protection* (pp. 234–255). Willan Publishing.

Gosling, H. (2016). 'All this is about is money and making sure that heads are on beds': Perceptions of payment by results in a therapeutic community. *Probation Journal, 63*(2), 144–152. https://doi.org/10.1177/0264550516637241

Gov.Uk. (2024). *Probation data: Offender management.* https://data.justice.gov.uk/probation/offender-management

Greater Manchester Police. (2022). https://www.gmp.police.uk/news/greater-manchester/news/news/2022/may/over-3000-visits-made-by-dedicated-sex-offender-unit-ensuring-gm-safe-from-re-offending/

Greer, C., & McLaughlin, E. (2010). 'Trial by media': Policing, the 24–7 news mediasphere and the 'politics of outrage'. *Theoretical Criminology*, *15*(1), 23–46. https://doi.org/10.1177/1362480610387461

Greer, C., & McLaughlin, E. (2012). Media justice: Madeleine McCann, intermediatization and 'trial by media' in the British press. *Theoretical Criminology*, *16*(4), 395–416. https://doi.org/10.1177/1362480612454559

Guiney, T. (2018). *Getting out: Early release in England and Wales, 1960-1995*. Oxford University Press.

Guiney, T. (2022). Ideologies, power and the politics of punishment: The case of the British Conservative Party. *British Journal of Criminology*, *62*(5), 1158–1174. https://doi.org/10.1093/bjc/azac031

Gusfield, J. R. (1986). *Symbolic crusade: Status politics and the American temperance movement* (2nd ed.). University of Illinois Press.

Hadjimatheou, K. (2019). Citizen-led digital policing and democratic norms: The case of self-styled paedophile hunters. *Criminology and Criminal Justice*, *21*(4), 547–565. https://doi.org/10.1177/1748895819880956

Hall, J. (2020). *Terrorist risk offenders: Independent review of statutory multi-agency public protection arrangements*. Ministry of Justice.

Halle, C., Tzani-Pepelasi, C., Pylarinou, N.-R., & Fumagalli, A. (2020, August). The link between mental health, crime and violence. *New Ideas in Psychology*, *58*.

Hansard (1988) *Lords Sitting, Miss Sharon Campbell*, December 1988, Vol. 502, cc 453–472.

Hansard, 21 January 1988 Gartree Prison (Escape) HC Deb vol 125 cc 785-6W.

Hare, R. D. (1993). *Without conscience: The disturbing world of the psychopaths among us*. Pocket Books.

Harrison, K. (2011). *Dangerousness, risk and the governance of serious sexual and violent offenders*. Routledge.

HC Deb (29 Jun. 1972) (839) col. 1674. https://hansard.parliament.uk/commons/1972-06-29/debates/9c1f080e-0eda-489e-86fe-d35f0e5aafae/GrahamYoung

HC Deb (13 Jan. 2015) (590) col. 244WH. https://hansard.parliament.uk/Commons/2015-01-13/debates/15011361000001/ProbationService?highlight=serious%20further%20offence#contribution-15011361000161

HC Deb (28 Feb. 2019) (655) col 573. https://hansard.parliament.uk/commons/2019-02-28/debates/822732A9-D2C2-480F-9E90-D7ACA22F9AC2/StDavid%E2%80%99SDay

HC Deb (02 Mar. 2020) UIN 23576. https://questions-statements.parliament.uk/written-questions/detail/2020-03-02/23576#

HC Deb (11 Nov. 2020) (683) col. 406WH. https://hansard.parliament.uk/Commons/2020-11-11/debates/20111119000002/SupportedAccommodationHmos?highlight=paedophile%20hunters#contribution-3EA4B3D3-0D69-4449-A122-E8E032387758

HC Deb (04 Jul. 2023) (735) col. 755. https://hansard.parliament.uk/commons/2023-07-04/debates/A48BEBE3-ED93-4E2F-8254-3D1E2FCAD991/HisMajesty%E2%80%99SPrisonAndProbationService

Heald, S. (2006). State, law, and vigilantism in Northern Tanzania. *African Affairs*, *105*(419), 265–283.

Heath-Kelly, C. (2013). Counter-terrorism and the counterfactual: Producing the 'Radicalisation' discourse and the UK prevent strategy. *The British Journal of Politics & International Relations, 15*, 394–415.

Health Quality Improvement Partnership. (2017). *National confidential inquiry into suicide and homicide by people with mental illness, annual report, 2017*. The University of Manchester.

Hernandez, T. A. (2021). The consequences of the austerity policies for public services in the UK. *Studies in Social Justice, 15*(3), 518–537.

Hillyard, P., & Gordon, D. (1999). Arresting statistics: The drift to informal justice in England and Wales. *Journal of Law and Society, 26*, 502–522. https://doi.org/10.1111/1467-6478.00138

HL Law (20 May 2013) (745) col. 661 and col. 662. https://hansard.parliament.uk/Lords/2013-05-20/debates/1305202000172/OffenderRehabilitationBill(HL)?highlight=transforming%20rehabilitation#contribution-1305206000111

HMCPSI. (2024). *An inspection of the Crown Prosecution Service actions in the Valdo Calocane case*. Publication no. CP001:1314. https://www.justiceinspectorates.gov.uk/hmcpsi/wp-content/uploads/sites/3/2024/03/2024-03-21-Calocane-report.pdf

HMICFRS. (2022a). An inspection of vetting, misconduct and misogyny in the police service. https://hmicfrs.justiceinspectorates.gov.uk/publication-html/an-inspection-of-vetting-misconduct-and-misogyny-in-the-police-service/

HMICFRS. (2022b). The police response to burglary, robbery and other acquisitive crime -Finding time for crime. https://hmicfrs.justiceinspectorates.gov.uk/publications/police-response-to-burglary-robbery-and-other-acquisitive-crime/

HM Government. (2010). *The coalition: Our programme for government*. HM Government.

HMIP. (1995). *Dealing with dangerous people: The probation service and public protection. Report of a thematic inspection*. HMSO.

HMIP. (1998). *Exercising constant vigilance: The role of the probation service in protecting the public from sex offenders. Report of a thematic inspection*. HMSO.

HMIP. (2005a). *Inquiry into the supervision of Peter Williams by Nottingham City Youth Offending Team*. Her Majesty's Inspectorate of Probation.

HMIP. (2005b). *Inquiry into the supervision of Peter Williams by Nottingham City Youth Offending Team*. Her Majesty's Inspectorate of Probation.

HMIP. (2006a). *An independent review of a serious further offence case: Damien Hanson & Elliot White*. Her Majesty's Inspectorate of Probation.

HMIP. (2006b). *An independent review of a serious further offence case: Anthony Rice*. Her Majesty's Inspectorate of Probation.

HMIP. (2016). *Unintended consequences: Finding a way forward for prisoners serving sentences of IPP: Thematic review*. Her Majesty's Inspectorate of Probation.

HMIP. (2018). *Independent review of the case of Leroy Campbell: Final report*. Her Majesty's Inspectorate of Probation.

HMIP. (2020a). *A thematic inspection of the serious further offences (SFO) investigation and review process: An inspection by HM Inspectorate of Probation*. Her Majesty's Inspectorate of Probation.

HMIP. (2020b). *Independent review of the case of Joseph McCann*. Her Majesty's Inspectorate of Probation.

HMIP. (2022a). *HM Inspectorate of Probation. Annual report 2022: Serious further offences*. His Majesty's Inspectorate of Probation.

HMIP. (2022b). *Practitioner: Professional curiosity insights guide.* His Majesty's Inspectorate of Probation.
HMIP. (2023a). *HM Inspectorate of Probation. Annual report 2023: Serious further offences.* His Majesty's Inspectorate of Probation.
HMIP. (2023b). *The history of HM Inspectorate of Probation - A short paper.* His Majesty's Inspectorate of Probation.
HMIP. (2023c). *Independent serious further offence review of Damien Bendall.* His Majesty's Inspectorate of Probation.
HMIP. (2023d). *Independent serious further offence review of Jordan McSweeney.* His Majesty's Inspectorate of Probation.
HMIP. (2024). *Independent serious further offence review of Joshua Jacques.* His Majesty's Inspectorate of Probation.
HMIPPS. (2008). *The indefinite sentence for public protection: A thematic review.* www.justiceinspectorates.gov.uk
HMIP, HMCPSI, HMICA, HMIP, &HMIC (2009). *Prolific and other priority offenders A joint inspection of the PPO programme.* Criminal Justice Joint Inspection. https://assets-hmicfrs.justiceinspectorates.gov.uk/uploads/prolific-and-other-priority-offenders-20090718.pdf
HMIP, & HMPPS. (2021a). Quality assurance standards for probation serious further offence reviews. https://www.justiceinspectorates.gov.uk/hmiprobation/wp-content/uploads/sites/5/2023/09/Quality-assurance-standards-for-probation-Serious-Further-Offence-reviews.pdf
HMIP, & HMPPS. (2021b). Rating characteristics for the quality assurance of serious further offence (SFO) reviews. https://www.justiceinspectorates.gov.uk/hmiprobation/wp-content/uploads/sites/5/2024/02/Ratings-characteristics-for-the-quality-assurance-of-Serious-Further-Offence-reviews.pdf
HMPPS. (n.d.b). *Policy framework - notification and review procedures for serious further offences. Annex B: Operational guidance.* His Majesty's Prison and Probation Service. https://assets.publishing.service.gov.uk/media/619fa348d3bf7f05 5eb9b6b4/annex-b-operational-guidance.pdf
HMPPS. (n.d.c). *Annex C: SFO notification.* His Majesty's Prison and Probation Service. https://www.gov.uk/government/publications/probation-service-serious-further-offence-procedures-policy-framework
HMPPS. (2021). *Offender management statistics quarterly, April to June 2021.* https://www.gov.uk/government/statistics/offender-management-statistics-quarterly-april-to-june-2021/offender-management-statistics-quarterly-april-to-june-2021
HMPPS. (2023a). *Workforce quarterly.* https://www.gov.uk/government/statistics/hm-prison-probation-service-workforce-quarterly-december-2023
HMPPS. (2023b). *Serious further offences: Revisions to policy and practice guidance.* His Majesty's Prison and Probation Services.
HMPPS. (n.d.a). *Policy framework - Notification and review procedures for serious further offences. Annex A: Qualifying offence list.* His Majesty's Prison and Probation Service. https://assets.publishing.service.gov.uk/media/619fa3368fa8f503 82034dcf/annex-a-sfo-qualifying-offence-list.pdf
HMPPS. (n.d.d). *Serious further offences (SFO) notification.* His Majesty's Prison and Probation Services. https://assets.publishing.service.gov.uk/media/619fa35ce90e070 4439f4217/annex-c-sfo-notification.pdf

HMPS. (1988). *Statement of purpose of the prison service*. MoJ. HMSO. Accessed on December 7, 2021.

Hobbs, D. (1989). *Doing the business: Entrepreneurship, the working-class and detectives in the East End of London*. Oxford University Press.

HoC. (2021). *Unification of probation services*. No. 9252. House of Commons Library.

Hofstadter, R. (1963). *Anti-intellectualism in American life*. Vintage Books.

Holden, A. (1995). *The St. Albans poisoner*. Black Swan.

Holmes, A. M. (2022). Citizen led policing in the digital realm: Paedophile hunters and Article 8 in the case of Sutherland v Her Majesty's Advocate. *The Modern Law Review, 85*, 219–231. https://doi.org/10.1111/1468-2230.12653

Holmwood, J., & Aitlhadj, L. (2023). *The people's review of prevent. A response to the Shawcross report*. www.preventwatch.org

Home Office. (1966). *Report of the inquiry into prison escapes and security*. HMSO.

Home Office. (1968). *Radzinowicz report 1968: The regime for long-term prisoners in conditions of maximum security. Report of the advisory council on the penal system*. HMSO.

Home Office. (1979). *Committee of inquiry into the United Kingdom Prison Service: Report (May Committee)*. HMSO.

Home Office. (1991). *Safer communities: The local delivery of crime prevention through the partnership approach*. Home Office.

Home Office. (1995). *New arrangement for recruitment and qualifying training of probation officers*. HMSO.

Home Office. (1996). *Protecting the public the government's strategy on crime in England and Wales*. HMSO.

Home Office. (1997). *Community protection orders: A consultation paper*. HMSO.

Home Office. (2006). *A five-year strategy for protecting the public and reducing re-offending*. HMSO.

Home Office. (2007). *Review of the protection of children from sex offenders*. HMSO.

Home Office. (2023a). *CONTEST. The UKs strategy for countering terrorism*. The Secretary of State for the Home Department.

Home Office. (2023b). *Independent review into the police-led management of registered sex offenders in the community*. https://www.gov.uk/government/publications/independent-review-of-police-led-sex-offender-management/independent-review-into-the-police-led-management-of-registered-sex-offenders-in-the-community-executive-summary-accessibe-version

Home Office. (2024). *Prime Minister launches retail crime crackdown*. Home Office. https://www.gov.uk/government/news/prime-minister-launches-retail-crime-crackdown

House of Commons Library. (2023). *Research briefing, sentencing bill 2023-24*.

Hussey, E., Richards, K., & Scott, J. (2022). Pedophile hunters and performing masculinities online. *Deviant Behavior, 43*(11), 1313–1330. https://doi.org/10.1080/01639625.2021.1978278

IICSA. (2020, March). *The internet. Investigation report*. The Independent Inquiry into Child Sexual Abuse. https://www.iicsa.org.uk/reports-recommendations/publications/investigation/internet.html

Ingram, M. (1984). Ridings, rough music and the "reform of popular culture" in early modern Europe. *Past & Present, 105*, 79–113.

Inside Time. (2023). *Labour set out alternative plan to overturn Parole Board changes.* https://insidetime.org/newsround/labour-sets-out-alternative-plan-to-overturn-parole-board-decisions/

IOPC. (2023). *IOPC launches multiple investigations into handling of reports about David Carrick.* https://www.policeconduct.gov.uk/news/iopc-launches-multiple-investigations-handling-reports-about-david-carrick

Irving, Z. (2021). The legacy of austerity. *Social Policy and Society, 20*(1), 91–110. https://doi.org/10.1017/S1474746420000500

Jackson, P. M. (2001). Public sector added value: Can bureaucracy deliver? *Public Administration, 79,* 5–28. https://doi.org/10.1111/1467-9299.00243

Janus, E. (2010). The preventive state: When is prevention of harm harmful? In M. Nash & A. Williams (Eds.), *Handbook of public protection* (pp. 316–334). Willan Publishing.

Jarvis, F. V. (1972). *Advise, assist and befriend: A history of the probation and after-care service.* NAPO.

Johal, R. & Davies, N. (2022, August). *Reunification of probation services.* IfG Insight. Institute for Government. https://www.instituteforgovernment.org.uk/sites/default/files/publications/probation-case-study.pdf

Johnson, D. (1981). Vigilance and the law: The moral authority of popular justice in the far west. *American Quarterly, 33*(5), 558–586.

Johnston, L. (1996). What is vigilantism? *British Journal of Criminology, 36*(2), 220–236. https://doi.org/10.1093/oxfordjournals.bjc.a014083

Jones, T., & Newburn, T. (2006). Three Strikes and You're Out: Exploring symbol and substance in American and British Crime Control Politics. *British Journal of Criminology, 46*(5), 781–802. https://doi.org/10.1093/bjc/azl007

Joseph, N., & Benefield, N. (2012). A joint offender personality disorder pathway strategy: An outline summary. *Criminal Behaviour and Mental Health, 22,* 210–217. https://doi.org/10.1002/cbm.1835

Judiciary UK. (2021). *Inquests arising from the deaths in the Fishmongers' Hall terror. Regulation 28 report on action to prevent future deaths.* https://www.judiciary.uk/wp-content/uploads/2021/11/Fishmongers-Hall-Inquests-Prevention-of-future-deaths-report-2021-0362_Published-by-Chief-Coroner.pdf

Karsna, K., & Kelly, L. (2021). *The scale and nature of child sexual abuse, review of the evidence.* Centre of Expertise on Child Sexual Abuse. https://www.csacentre.org.uk/app/uploads/2023/09/Scale-and-nature-review-of-evidence-2021.pdf

Kemshall, H., & Maguire, M. (2001). Public protection, punishment and risk penality: The multi-agency risk management of sexual and violent offenders. *Punishment & Society, 3*(2), 237–264.

Kemshall, H., & McIvor, G. (2004). *Managing sex offender risk.* Jessica Kingsley.

Kemshall, H. (2010). Community protection and multi-agency public protection arrangements. In M. Nash & A. Williams, *Handbook of public protection* (pp. 199–216). Willan Publishing.

Kemshall, H., & Wood, J. (2010). *Research report 32. Child sex offender review (CSOR) public disclosure pilots: A process evaluation* (2nd ed.). Home Office.

Kendell, R. E. (2002). The distinction between personality disorder and mental illness. *British Journal of Psychiatry, 18,* 110–115.

Kewley, S. (2017). Policing people with sexual convictions using a strengths-based approach. *Journal of Criminal Psychology, 7*(3), 168–182.

Khan, S., & Rowley, M. (2021). *Operating with impunity. Hateful extremism: The need for a legal framework*. Commission for Countering Extremism.

Kim, A. (2019). Crimes by people with schizophrenia in Korea: Comparison with the general population. *BMC Psychiatry, 19*(1), 1–12. https://doi.org/10.1186/s12888-019-2355-5

King, R. D., & Morgan, R. (1980). *The future of the prison system*. Gower.

King, R. D., & Wilmott, L. (2022). Unrealistic Politicians and Frustrated Probation Officers. *Probation Quarterly, 23*, 32–35. https://doi.org/10.54006/REGH1683

Laker, B. (2024). Major blow to U.K. universities: The decline of international students. *Forbes*. https://www.forbes.com/sites/benjaminlaker/2024/01/28/major-blow-to-uk-universities-the-decline-of-international-students/?sh=2a4a4b627996

Large, M., Smith, G., Swinson, N., Shaw, J., & Nielssen, O. (2008). Homicide due to mental disorder in England and Wales over 50 years. *The British Journal of Psychiatry, 193*, 130–133.

Law Report. (1996). *R v Secretary of State for the Home Department, ex parte NAPO*. Queens Bench Divisional Court. LJ Kennedy, Mr Justice Forbes.

Learmont, J. (1995). *Review of prison security in England and Wales and the escape from Parkhurst prison on Tuesday 3rd January 1995*. HMSO.

Leon, C. S. (2011). Sex offender punishment and the persistence of penal harm in the United States. *International Journal of Law and Psychiatry, 34*, 177–185.

Loader, I. (2006). Fall of the "Platonic Guardians": Liberalism, criminology and political responses to crime in England and Wales. *British Journal of Criminology, 46*(4), 561–586. https://doi.org/10.1093/bjc/azi091

Lord Carter's Review of Prisons. (2007, December 10). *Securing the future; proposals for the efficient use of custody in England and Wales*. House of Lords.

Loveluck, B. (2020). The many shades of digital vigilantism. A typology for online self-justice. *Global Crime, 21*(3–4), 213–241. https://doi.org/10.1080/17440572.2019.1614444

Mair, G. (2016). 'A difficult trip, I think': The end days of the probation service in England and Wales? *European Journal of Probation, 8*(1), 3–15. https://doi.org/10.1177/2066220316637389

Maloney, C. (2024). 'Deprived background' sentencing guidelines in force. *Law Society Gazette*. https://www.lawgazette.co.uk/news/deprived-background-sentencing-guidelines-in-force/5119260.article.

Mann, N., Devendran, P., & Lundrigan, S. (2018). Policing in a time of austerity: Understanding the public protection paradox through qualitative interviews with police monitoring officers. *Policing, 14*(3), 630–642. https://doi.org/10.1093/police/pay047

Martin, R. (2007). Digilante justice: Citizenship in cyberspace. *New Atlantis, 16*, 124–127.

Martinson, R. (1974). What works? – Questions and answers about prison reform. *The Public Interest, 35*, 22–54.

Marx, G. T. (2013). The public as partner? Technology can make us auxiliaries as well as vigilantes. *Security & Privacy, 11*(5), 56–61.

Marx, K. (1990). *Capital: A critique of political economy. Volume one*. Penguin Books.

Massoumi, N. (2021). The role of civil society in political repression. The UK prevent counter-terrorism programme. *Sociology, 55*, 959–977.

Mawby, R. C., Crawley, P., & Wright, A. (2007). Beyond 'polibation' and towards 'prisi-polibation'? Joint agency offender management in the context of the street crime initiative. *International Journal of Police Science and Management*, *19*(2), 122–134. https://doi.org/10.1350/ijps.2007.9.2.122

Mawby, R. C., & Worrall, A. (2004). 'Polibation' revisited Policing, probation and prolific offender projects. *International Journal of Police Science and Management*, *6*(2), 63–73. https://doi.org/10.1350/ijps.6.2.63.34466

Mazerolle, L., Chernay, A., Eggins, E., Hine, L., & Higginson, A. (2021). Multi Agency programs with police as a Partner for reducing radicalisation to violence. *Campbell Systematic Reviews*, *17*(2), 2–88. https://doi.org/10.1002/cl2.1162

McCartan, K. (2013). From a lack of engagement and mistrust to partnership? Public attitudes to the disclosure of sex offender information. *International Journal of Police Science and Management*, *15*(3), 219–236. https://doi.org/10.1350/ijps.2013.15.3.313

McPhee, D., Hester, M., Bates, L. Lilley-Walker, S. J., & Patsios, D. (2022). Criminal justice responses to domestic violence and abuse in England: An analysis of case attrition and inequalities using police data. *Policing and Society*, *32*(8), 963–980.

Mills, H. (2011). *Community sentences: a solution to penal excess?* Centre for Crime and Justice Studies.

Ministry of Justice. (2022). *Root and branch Review of the Parole System.* HMSO.

Ministry of Justice. (2023). *Offenders to be ordered to attend sentencing.* Press Release.

Ministry of Justice. (2024). Tough new measures to bolster landmark victims' bill. https://www.gov.uk/government/news/tough-new-measures-to-bolster-landmark-victims-law

MoJ. (2010). *Breaking the cycle: Effective punishment, rehabilitation and sentencing of offenders.* Ministry of Justice.

MoJ. (2011). *Competition strategy for offender services.* Ministry of Justice.

MoJ. (2012). *Punishment and reform: Effective probation services.* Consultation paper CP7/2012. Ministry of Justice.

MoJ. (2013a). *Transforming rehabilitation: A revolution in the way we manage offenders.* Consultation Paper CP1/2013. Ministry of Justice.

MoJ. (2013b). *Punishment and reform: Effective probation services summary of consultation responses.* Ministry of Justice.

MoJ. (2019). *Serious further offences.* Ministry of Justice.

MoJ. (2020). *Probation serious further offence review in the case of Joseph McCann.* Ministry of Justice.

MoJ. (2021). *Prisons strategy white paper.* CP 581. Ministry of Justice. https://assets.publishing.service.gov.uk/media/61af18e38fa8f5037e8ccc47/prisons-strategy-white-paper.pdf

MoJ. (2022). *Root and branch review of the parole system: The future of the parole system in England and Wales.* CP 654. Ministry of Justice.

MoJ. (2023). *Multi-agency public protection arrangements (MAPPA) annual report 2022/23.* Ministry of Justice. https://assets.publishing.service.gov.uk/media/653966ade6c968000daa9b26/MAPPA_Annual_Report_2023.pdf

MoJ, & HMPPS. (2021). *Policy name: Notification and review procedures for serious further offences policy framework.* Ministry of Justice and His Majesty's Prison and Probation Service. https://assets.publishing.service.gov.uk/media/619fa320d3bf7f05522e2e1b/sfo-policy-framework.pdf

Moncada, E. (2017). Varieties of vigilantism: Conceptual discord, meaning and strategies. *Global Crime*, *18*(4), 403–423. https://doi.org/10.1080/17440572.2017.1374183

Mooney, C. (2005). *The Republican war on science*. Basic Books.

Morris, S. (2012). Student who mocked Fabrice Muamba on Twitter 'massively sorry'. *The Guardian*. https://www.theguardian.com/uk/2012/may/22/muamba-twitter-abuse-student-sorry

Morris, S. (2020). Coroner: Supervision of Conner Marshall's killer 'woefully inadequate'. https://www.theguardian.com/uk-news/2020/jan/17/coroner-supervision-of-conner-marshall-killer-woefully-inadequate

Moss, A. (2021). *The Leroy Campbell case*. Independently Published.

Mydlowski, L., & Turner-Moore, R. (2023). Tensions between police training and practice for the risk assessment of registered sex offenders in England and Wales. *Journal of Sexual Aggression*, 1–14. https://doi.org/10.1080/13552600.2023.2190752

Naik, U., & Shivalingaiah, D. (2014). Comparative Study of Web 1.0, Web 2.0 and Web 3.0. In *Paper presented at the 6th International CALIBER 2008 Conference*. University of Allahabad.

NAO. (2019). *Transforming rehabilitation: Progress review*. National Audit Office.

Nash, M., & Williams, A. (2008). *The anatomy of serious further offending*. Oxford University Press.

Nash, M., & Williams, A. (Eds.). (2010). *Handbook of public protection*. Willan Publishing.

Nash, M. (1999a). *Police, probation and protecting the public*. Blackstone Press.

Nash, M. (1999b). Enter the 'Polibation Officer'. *International Journal of Police Science and Management*, *1*(4), 360–368. https://doi.org/10.1177/146135579900100404

Nash, M. (2006). *Public protection and the criminal justice process*. Oxford University Press.

Nash, M. (2008). Exit the Polibation Officer: De-coupling police and probation. *International Journal of Police Science and Management*, *10*(3), 302–312. https://doi.org/10.1350/ijps.2008.10.3.86

Nash, M. (2014). 'Scum Cuddlers': Police offender managers and the sex offenders register in England and Wales. *Policing and Society*, *26*(4), 411–427. https://doi.org/10.1080/10439463.2014.942855

National Police Chiefs' Council. (2024). *Violence against women and girls*. https://www.npcc.police.uk/our-work/violence-against-women-and-girls/

NHS. (2023, December 1). *The offender personality disorder (OPD) pathway: a joint strategy for 2023-2028*. NHS.

Nottinghamshire Police. (2024). *Timeline of our contact with Valdo Calocane*. https://www.nottinghamshire.police.uk/news/nottinghamshire/news/news/2024/january/timeline-of-our-contact-with-valdo-calocane/

NPCC. (2017). *New tailored approach to manage registered sex offenders introduced*. https://news.npcc.police.uk/releases/new-tailored-approach-to-managing-registered-sex-offenders-introduced

NPCC. (2019). *National Police Chief's Council: Responding to online child abuse activists*. https://npcc.police.uk/2019%20FOI/NPCC%20Miscellaneous/015%2019%20NPCC%20FOI%20Response%20Part%203.pdf

NPCC. (2023a). First violence against women and girls benchmark published. https://news.npcc.police.uk/releases/first-benchmark-of-police-performance-on-tackling-violence-against-women-and-girls-published

NPCC. (2023b). 1m officer hours saved with new approach to mental health. https://news.npcc.police.uk/releases/police-to-save-1-million-officer-hours-as-forces-adopt-new-model-to-ensure-specialist-care-for-health-incidents

NPR. (2015). Animosity flares up among religions over India's 'Sacred Cow' ban. https://www.cpr.org/2015/10/13/animosity-flares-up-among-religions-over-indias-sacred-cow-ban/

O'Loughlin, A. (2019). Deconstructing risk, therapeutic needs and the dangerous personality disordered subject. *Punishment & Society, 21*(5), 616–638.

Omand, D. (2010). *Omand review. Independent serious further offence review: The case of Jon Venables.* Ministry of Justice.

ONS. (2017, September). *Crime in England and Wales: Year ending September 2017.* ONS.

ONS. (2023a). *Crime in England and Wales: Year ending June 2023.* https://www.gov.uk/government/statistics/crime-in-england-and-wales-year-ending-june-2023

ONS. (2023b). *Homicide in England and Wales: Year ending March, 2023.* https://www.ons.gov.uk/peoplepopulationandcommunity/crimeandjustice/articles/homicideinenglandandwales/yearendingmarch2023

Osborne, S. (2018, February 7). Victims of John Worboys win right to challenge Parole Board decision to set him free. *The Express.*

O'Sullivan, J., Hoggett, J., Kemshall, H., & McCartan, K. (2016). Understandings, implications and alternative approaches to the use of the sex offender register in the UK. *Irish Probation Journal, 13,* 84–101.

Parole Board. (2018). *Professor Nick Hardwick responds to concerns about Worboys case.* Press Release. https://www.gov.uk/government/news/professor-nick-hardwick-responds-to-concerns-about-worboys-case

Pearson, G. (1983). *Hooligan: A history of respectable fears.* The Macmillan Press Ltd.

Phillips, J., Ainslie, S., Fowler, A., & Westaby, C. (2021). 'What does professional curiosity mean to you?': An exploration of professional curiosity in probation. *British Journal of Social Work, 52,* 554–572.

Phillips, J., Ainslie, S., Fowler, A., & Westaby, C. (2022) *Putting professional curiosity into practice. Academic Insights 2022/07.* Her Majesty's Inspectorate of Probation.

Phillips, J. (2020). Understanding the privatisation of probation through the lens of Bourdieu's field theory. In K. Albertson, M. Corcoran, & J. Phillips (Eds.), *Marketisation and privatisation in criminal justice* (pp. 59–73). Policy Press.

Pierre, J. (n.d.). *How does fear influence risk assessment and decision making?* https://www.psychologytoday.com/gb/blog/psych-unseen/202007/how-does-fear-influence-risk-assessment-and-decision-making

Pollard, C., & Lucas, J. (2018, January 15). Shrink who urges leniency for pervs backed rapist Worboys' release. *The Sun.*

Police Foundation. (2022). A new mode of protection. Realising policing and public safety for the 21st century. The final report of the strategic review of policing in England and Wales, *Chair Sir Michael Barbery,* March 2022.

PoliticsHome (2023). More than half of women don't trust police to keep them safe. https://www.politicshome.com/news/article/more-than-half-women-dont-trust-police-keep-them-safe

Potter, H. (2019). *Shades of the prison house: History of incarceration in the British Isles*. Boydell Press.

Pratt, J. (1997). *Governing the dangerous*. Federation Press.

Pratt, J. (2007). *Penal populism*. Routledge.

Price, D. (2000). The origins and durability of security classification: A study in penological Pragmatism or spies, dickie and prison. In *British Criminology Conference Selected Proceedings, Vol. 13*, Liverpool, July 1993.

Prime Minsters Office. (2023). Society's most depraved killers will face life behind bars with no chance of being released, under tough plans announced by the Prime Minister. https://www.gov.uk/government/news/pm-announces-new-plans-so-societys-most-depraved-killers-will-face-life-behind-bars#:~:text=26%20August%202023-,Society's%20most%20depraved%20killers%20will%20face%20life%20behind%20bars%20with,most%20horrific%20types%20of%20murder

Prins, H. (1988). Dangerous clients: Further observations on the limitation of mayhem. *British Journal of Social Work*, *18*, 593–609.

PRT. (2021a, October 4). *Dramatic rise in numbers spending 10 years of more in prison*. https://prisonreformtrust.org.uk/dramatic-rise-in-numbers-spending-10-years-or-more-in-prison/

PRT. (2021b). Long-term prisoners: The facts, England and wales, October, 2021. https://prisonreformtrust.org.uk/wp-content/uploads/2021/10/Long-term-prisoners_the-facts_2021.pdf

PRT. (2023a). *Prison: the facts, Bromley Briefings, June, 2023*. Prison Reform Trust.

PRT (2023b). *Prison Reform Trust Briefing – IPP action plan*. House of Lords.

Purshouse, J. (2020). 'Paedophile hunters', criminal procedure, and fundamental human rights. *Journal of Law and Society*, *47*(3), 384–411. https://doi.org/10.1111/jols.12235

Pycroft, A. & Gough, D. (Eds.) (2019). *Multi-agency working in criminal justice: theory, policy and practice* (2nd ed.). Policy Press.

R v Thomas Mair. *Sentencing remarks of Mr Justice Wilkie*. https://www.judiciary.uk/wp-content/uploads/2016/11/sentencing-remarks-r-v-thomas-mair.pdf

Rawlings, P. (2003). Policing before the police. In T. Newburn (Ed.), *Handbook of policing* (1st ed., pp. 41–65). Willan Publishing.

Raynor, P. (2014). Consent to probation in England and Wales: How it was abolished and why it matters. *European Journal of Probation*, *1* (6), 296–307.

Raynor, P., & Vanstone, M. (2007). Towards a correctional service. In L. Gelsthorpe & R. Morgan (Eds.), *Handbook of Probation* (pp.59–89). Routledge.

Reiner, R. (2010). *The politics of the police* (4th ed.). Oxford University Press.

Richards, G., Fright, M., & Davies, N. (2023). Institute for government: Performance tracker 2022: Police. https://www.instituteforgovernment.org.uk/performance-tracker-2022/police

Ritchie, J. H., Dick, D., & Lingham, R. (1994). *The report of the inquiry into the care and treatment of Christopher Clunis*. HMSO.

Roach, K. (1999). Four models of the criminal process. *Journal of Criminal Law and Criminology*, *89*(2) 671–716.

Robinson, G. (2002). Exploring risk management in probation practice: Contemporary developments in England and Wales. *Punishment & Society*, *4*(1), 5–25.

Rosenbaum, H. J., & Sederberg, P. C. (1976). Vigilantism: An analysis of establishment violence. In H. J. Rosenbaum & P. C. Sederberg (Eds.), *Vigilante politics* (pp. 3–29). The University of Pennsylvania Press, Inc.

Rotman, E. (1994). Beyond punishment. In A. Duff & D. Garland (Eds.), *A Reader on Punishment*. Oxford University Press.

Rousseau, J. J. (1968). *The social contract*. Penguin Books.

Rowbottom, J. (2013). To punish, inform, and criticise: The goals of naming and shaming. In J. Petley (Ed.), *Media naming and shaming: Drawing the boundaries of disclosure* (pp. 1–18). I. B. Tauris & Company Ltd.

Rumgay, J., & Munro, E. (2001). The lion's den: Professional defences in the treatment of dangerous patients. *Journal of Forensic Psychiatry*, *12*(2), 357–378.

Rutherford, M. (2010). *Blurring the boundaries: The convergence of mental health and criminal justice policy, legislation, system and practice*. Sainsbury Centre for Mental Health.

Saare, R. (2001). Beyond 'What Works'. A 25 year jubilee retrospective of Robert Martinson's famous article. *Australian and New Zealand Journal of Criminology*, *34*(1) 38–46.

Salter, M. (2013). Justice and revenge in online counter-publics: Emerging responses to sexual violence in the age of social media. *Crime, Media, Culture*, *9*(3), 225–242.

Savage, S. (2007). *Police reform: Forces for change*. Oxford University Press.

Savage, S. P., & Charman, S. (2010). Public protectionism and Sarah's Law: Exerting pressure through single issue campaigns. In M. Nash & A. Williams (Eds.), *Handbook of public protection* (pp. 434–453). Willan Publishing.

Scott, P. (1977). Assessing dangerousness in criminals. *British Journal of Psychiatry*, *131*, 127–142.

Scott, D. (2007). The changing face of the English prison: A critical review of the aims of imprisonment. In Y. Jewkes (Ed.), *Handbook of Prisons* (pp. 49–72). Routledge.

Scottish Council on Crime. (1975). *Crime and the prevention of crime*. HMSO.

Senior, P. (2013). Editorial. Probation: Peering through the uncertainty. *British Journal of Community Justice*, *11*(2–3), 1–8.

Sentencing Council. (2020a). *Sentencing Code*. https://www.sentencingcouncil.org.uk/sentencing-and-the-council/sentencing-code/

Sentencing Council. (2020b). *Sentencing offenders with mental disorders, developmental disorders or neurological impairment*. https://www.sentencingcouncil.org.uk/sentencing-and-the-council/about-sentencing-guidelines/about-published-guidelines/offenders-with-mental-health-conditions-or-disorders/

Shahi, A. (2012). In defence of a 'racist'. *Open Democracy*. https://www.opendemocracy.net/en/opendemocracyuk/in-defence-of-racist/

Shaw, J., Hunt, I. M., Flynn, S., Meehan, J., Robinson, J., Bickley, H., Parsons, R., McCann, K., Burns, J., Amos, T., Kapur, N., & Appleby, L. (2006). Rates of mental disorder in people convicted of homicide: National clinical survey. *British Journal of Psychiatry*, *188*, 143–147.

Shawcross, W. (2023, February). *Independent review of prevent*. House of Commons.

Shearing, C., & Wood, J. (2003). Nodal governance, democracy, and the new "denizens." *Journal of Law and Society*, *30*(3), 400–419. http://www.jstor.org/stable/1410537

Shute, S. (2004). The Sexual Offences Act 2003 (4) New Civil Prevention Orders: Sexual Offences Prevention Orders: Foreign Travel Orders: Risk of Sexual Harm Orders. *Criminal Law Review*, 29004, 417–440.

Siddique, H., & Syal, R. (2023). Calls for more prison funding drowned out by tough talk on sentencing. *The Guardian*.

Silke, A. (2001). Dealing with vigilantism: Issues and lessons for the police. *Police Journal*, *74*, 120–133.

Sjoberg, G., & Miller, P. J. (1973). Social research on bureaucracy: Limitations and opportunities. *Social Problems*, *21*(1), 129–143.

Skett, S., & Lewis, C. (2019). Development of the offender disorder pathway: A summary of the underpinning evidence. *Probation Journal*, *66* (2), 167–180.

Skolnick, J. (1995). What not to do about crime. *Criminology*, *33*, 1–14.

Sky News. (2023, January 17). https://news.sky.com/story/met-police-reviewing-over-1600-cases-of-alleged-sexual-offences-and-domestic-abuse-involving-its-staff-12788452

Sky News. (2023, May 2). Brixton: Man arrested on suspicion of murder after woman, 31, stabbed to death by stranger. https://news.sky.com/story/brixton-man-arrested-on-suspicion-of-murder-after-woman-31-stabbed-to-death-by-stranger-12871380

Sky News. (2023, August 27). Whole-life sentences will become default for sexually motivated or sadistic murders, PM says. https://news.sky.com/story/whole-life-sentences-will-become-default-for-sexually-motivated-murders-pm-says-12948105

Sky News. (2024, April 24). Nottingham attack families traumatised by 'barbaric' police WhatsApp messages about killings. https://news.sky.com/story/amp/nottingham-attack-families-traumatised-by-barbaric-police-whatsapp-message-about-killings-13121763

Smith, D. (2005). Probation and social work. *British Journal of Social Work*, *35*, 621–637.

Smith, N. R. (2017). New times demand old magic: Necklacing past and present. In M. Pfeifer (Ed.), *Global lynching and collective violence: Vol. 1. Asia, Africa, and the Middle East* (pp. 156–184). University of Illinois Press.

Solomon, E., & Silvestri, A. (2008). *Community sentences digest*. Centre for Crime and Justice Studies.

South East Coast Strategic Health Authority Kent County Council Kent Probation Area. (2006). *Report of the independent inquiry into the care and treatment of Michael Stone. South East Coast Strategic Health Authority Kent County Council Kent Probation Area*.

Sparks, R. (2000). Perspectives on risk and penal politics. In T. Hope & R. Sparks (Eds.), *Crime, risk and insecurity*. Routledge.

Spencer, A. (2007). Rethinking imprisonment in Scotland: The dilemma for prison reform and the challenges beyond. http://www.gov.scot/resource/doc/1102/0056826.pdf

Spokes, J. (1988). *Report of the committee of inquiry into the care and after-care of Miss Sharon Campbell*. Department of Health and Social Security, HM Stationery Office.

Stark, C., Patterson, B., & Devlin, B. (2004). Newspaper Coverage of a Violent Assault by a Mentally Ill person. *Journal of Psychiatric and Mental Health Nursing, 11*(16), 635–643.

Stone, A. (2012). Swansea University bans Fabrice Muamba tweet student Liam Stacey. *The Independent.* https://www.independent.co.uk/news/uk/home-news/swansea-university-bans-fabrice-muamba-tweet-student-liam-stacey-7778520.html

Stone, M. (2007). Violent crimes and their relationship to personality disorder. *Personality and Mental Health, 1*(2), 138–153. https://doi.org/10.1002/pmh.18

Storr, W. (2013). The heretics: Adventures with the enemies of science. *Picador.*

Sturge, G. (2023). *UK Prison Population Statistics.* House of Commons Library, 2023, September 8, No 04334. http://www.gov.scot/resource/doc/1102/0056826.pdf

Sulitzeanu-Kenan, R. (2008). Mental state of inquiry: Tragedy, policy and accountability in the case of the Ritchie Inquiry. *American Society for Public Administration*, 2–29. https://openscholar.huji.ac.il/sites/default/files/raanansulitzeanukenan/files/sulitzeanu-kenan_2008.pdf

Symonds, T. (2023). Most probation services are over capacity leaked data reveals. *BBC News.* https://www.bbc.co.uk/news/uk-64344284

Syval, R. (2023). One in 10 prisons in England and Wales should be shut down, watchdog says. The Guardian. https://www.theguardian.com/uk-news/2023/sep/25/one-in-10-prisons-in-england-and-wales-should-be-shut-down-watchdog-says

Tan, Y. H. (1996). Change in probation officers' qualifications. *The Independent.* https://www.independent.co.uk/news/people/change-in-probation-officers-qualifications-1319091.html

The Bradley Report. (2009). *Lord Bradley's review of people with mental health problems or learning disabilities in the criminal justice system.* Department of Health.

The Economist. (2022). *Too many British prisoners are still serving indefinite sentences.*

The Guardian. (2023a). Police win battle with NHS over not attending mental health calls. https://www.theguardian.com/uk-news/2023/aug/17/met-police-mental-health-calls-nhs-mark-rowley

The Guardian. (2023b). *Prison places in England and Wales are bust says governors' union chief.*

The Guardian (2024a). *Prisoners could be let out 60 days early to relieve crowded jails in England and Wales.*

The Guardian. (2024b). Nottingham attacks ministers urged to consider new homicide category. https://www.theguardian.com/law/2024/mar/25/nottingham-attacks-new-homicide-category-urged

The Guardian. (2024c). *Justice not served: Families anger over Nottingham stabbing sentence.*

The Sun. (2018). *Inspirational British Muslims.* https://www.thesun.co.uk/news/6491043/muslim-campaigner-celebrates-british-muslims/

The Telegraph. (2023). Police fail to solve a single burglary in half of neighbourhoods in last three years. https://www.telegraph.co.uk/news/2023/06/04/police-fail-solve-burglary-half-neighbourhoods-three-years/

Thomas, T. (2004). When public protection becomes punishment? The UK use of civil measures to contain the sex offender. *European Journal on Criminal Policy and Research, 10*(4), 337–351.

Thomas, T. (2008). The sex offender register: A case study in function creep. *The Howard Journal of Criminal Justice, 247*(3), 227–237.

Thomas, T., & Marshall, D. (2021). *The sex offenders' register: Politics, policy and public opinion*. Routledge.

Thompson, E. P. (1977). *Whigs and hunters: The origin of the Black Act*. Penguin Books.

Thompson, E. P. (1993). *Customs in common: Studies in traditional popular culture*. The New Press.

Thompson, J. B. (2005). The new visibility. *Theory, Culture & Society, 22*(6), 31–51. https://doi.org/10.1177/0263276405059413

Tidmarsh, M. (2020). The probation service in England and Wales: A decade of radical change or more of the same? *European Journal of Probation, 12*(2), 129–146. https://doi.org/10.1177/2066220320947243

Tidmarsh, M. (2023). Gendering in a 'caring' profession: The demographics and cultural dynamics of the feminisation of the probation service in England and Wales. *Probation Journal, 0*(0), 1–21. https://doi.org/10.1177/02645505231221240

Tippett, A. (2022). The rise of paedophile hunters: To what extent are cyber-vigilante groups a productive form of policing, retribution and justice? *Criminology and Criminal Justice*. https://doi.org/10.1177/17488958221136845

Tonry, M. (1994). Proportionality, parsimony and interchangeability of punishments. In A. Duff & D. Garland (Eds.), *A reader on punishment*. Oxford University Press.

Tonry, M. (2004). *Punishment and politics: Evidence and emulation in the making of English crime control policy*. Willan Publishing.

Townsend, M. (2023, February 12). UK counter-terrorism report author accused of basing conclusions on 'handful of cases. *The Guardian*.

Trottier, D. (2014). Police user-led investigations on social media. *Journal of Law and Information Science, 23*(1), 75–96.

Trottier, D. (2016). *Social media as surveillance: Rethinking visibility in a converging world*. Routledge.

Trottier, D. (2017). Digital vigilantism as weaponisation of visibility. *Philosophy & Technology, 30*, 55–72. https://doi.org/10.1007/s13347-016-0216-4

Tyrer, P., Duggan, C., Cooper, S., Tyrer, H., Swinson, N., & Rutter, D. (2015) The lessons and legacy of the programme for dangerous ad severe personality disorders. *Personality and Mental Health, 9*, 96–106. https://doi.org/10.1002/pmh.1293

Tyrer, P. (2021). The origins of the DSPD programme in England. In G. Ikkos & N. Bowas (Eds.), *Mind, state and society, social history of psychiatry and mental health in Britain, 1960-2010*. Cambridge University Press.

UK Parliament. (2023). *Prevent independent review*. The Secretary of State for the Home Department, Hansard, Vol. 727, 8 February, 2023.

US Dept. of Justice. (2023, July). Sex offender registration and notification in the United States. Case Law. *Summary*. https://www.ojp.gov/library/publications/sex-offender-registration-and-notification-united-states-case-law-summary-1

Vannier, M. (2021). *Normalising extreme imprisonment: The case of life without parole*. Oxford University Press.

Vanstone, M. (2004). *Supervising offenders in the community: A history of probation theory and practice*. Ashgate Publishing Ltd.

Vanstone, M., & Priestley, P. (Eds.). (2016). *Probation and politics: Academic reflections from former practitioners*. Palgrave Macmillan.

Von, H., & Ashworth, A. (1996). Protective sentencing under section 2 (2)(b) the criteria for dangerousness. *Criminal Law Review*, 175–183.

Walker, N. (1997). Harms, probabilities and precaution. *Oxford Journal of Legal Studies*, *17*(4), 611–620.

Walters, A. (2015). Rebels in pink: The Gulabi Gang's gender revolution in India. https://www.cbc.ca/amp/1.2943497

Walters, R. (2007). *Deviant knowledge: Criminology, politics and policy*. Willan Publishing.

Walton, K., & Penfold, R. (2022). Paedophile hunters and the road to injustice. In E. Johnston (Ed.), *Challenges in criminal justice* (pp. 164–179). Routledge.

Warmington, J. (2022). Luka Magnotta's grisly murder shocked Canada 10 years ago. *The Toronto Sun*. https://torontosun.com/news/local-news/warmington-luka-magnottas-grisly-murder-shocked-canada-10-years-ago

Wells, T. (2018, March 28). *How John Worboys' victims triumphed against their sick attacker in court – and The Sun struck a blow for press freedom*.

Wexler, L., Robbennolt, J. K., & Murphy, C. I. (2019). #metoo, time's up, and theories of justice (Vol. 1, pp. 45–110). University of Illinois Law Review.

Whitehead, P., & Statham, R. (2006). *The history of probation*. Shaw and Sons.

Williams, A. (2015). *Forensic criminology*. Routledge.

Williams, A. (2023). Lurking with paedophile hunters: Understanding virtual ethnography and its benefits for policing research. In J. Flemming & S. Charman (Eds.), *Routledge international handbook of police ethnography* (pp. 406–423). Routledge.

Williams, A., & Thompson, B. (2004a). Vigilance or Vigilantes: The Paulsgrove Riots and Policing Paedophiles in the Community, Part 1: The Long Slow Fuse. *Police Journal*, *77*(2), 99–119.

Williams, A., & Thompson, B. (2004b) Vigilance or Vigilantes: The Paulsgrove Riots and Policing Paedophiles in the Community, Part 2: The Lessons of Paulsgrove. *Police Journal*, *77*(3), 119–205.

Wong, J. (2022). Sharing terrorism intelligence: Insights from the UK law enforcement agencies. *Journal of Policing, Intelligence and Counter-Terrorism*, *17*(2). https://doi.org/10.1080/18335330.2021.2016898

Wood, M., Rose, E., & Thompson, C. (2018). Viral justice? Online justice-seeking, intimate partner violence and affective contagion. *Theoretical Criminology*, *23*(3), 375–393. https://doi.org/10.1177/1362480617750507

Woodcock, J. (1994). *Report of the inquiry into the escape of six prisoners from the special security unit at Whitemoor prison, Cambridgeshire, on Friday 9th September 1994*. HMSO.

Woolf, Lord Justice. (1991). *Prison disturbances April 1990: Report of an inquiry*. HMSO.

Worrall, A. (1997). *Punishment in the community: The future of criminal justice*. Longman.

Zedner, L. (2007). Pre-crime and post-criminology? *Theoretical Criminology*, *11*(2), 261–281. https://doi.org/10.1177/1362480607075851

Index

Aarvold inquiry, 38
Academic literature, 29
Acquisitive crime, 18
Active Risk Management System (ARMS), 86–87
Actuarial methods, 30
Acute Childhood Experiences (ACEs), 132–133
Advisory Council on the Penal System, The (1978), 22–23, 64–65
Alex Chalk, 68–69
Alison Moss, 170–171, 173–174
Anglioni Inquiry Report, The, 31
Anthony Rice, 157–158, 174–175
Anti-Social Behaviour, Crime and Policing Act 2014, 54–55
Apostrophe laws, 39
Assessment tools, 51–52
Automatic process, 9

Blame; blaming, 17, 156–157, 215–216
Borstal system, 73
British governments, 63
British politics, 42
Butler Inquiry, 22–23

Calocane case, 114–115
Category 1 and 4, 2–3, 149–150
Certificate of Qualification in Social Work (CQSW), 96–97
Charity Act, The (2006), 145–146
Charivari (see Rough music)
Child Sex Offender Disclosure Scheme, 40, 203–204
Chris Grayling, 105–106
Christopher Clunis, 119–120
Civilian-led policing, 185, 191, 204
Civilian-led public protection (CLPP), 185–186, 205, 207, 216–217

calling Hue and Cry, 189–194
case study, 199–205
digital vigilantism, online activism and, 194–198
informal justice and public protection, 194
vigilantism, 186–189
Clare's Law, 40
Classical vigilantes, 189–190
Clunis case, The, 120–121
Coalition Government, 105, 145–146
Collaboration, 52–56
Commentators, 23
Community Rehabilitation Companies (CRCs), 105, 167
Community/communities
  agenda, 145–146
  participation, 193
  penalties, 95
Conceptualisation, 196–197
Concerted indiscipline, 66–67
Conner Marshall, 155–156
Conservative and Labour politicians, 45, 130
Conservative Home Secretary Leon Brittan Parole Policy, 42
Conservative Party, 44, 93
Conservatives, The, 69–70
Containment of long-term prisoners, 64–67
Contemporary thinking, 17–18
CONTEST strategy, 143–144
Core criminal justice agencies, 5–6
Counter-Terrorism Act, The (2015), 145–146
Crime and Disorder Act (1998), 53–54
Crime and Security Act 2010, 55
Crime Sentences Act (1997), 47–48, 93–94

Crime Sentences bill, The, 47
Crime Sentencing and Courts Act 2022, 42–43
Crime Week, 74
Criminal justice
 agencies, 126
 measures, 42
 system, 107
Criminal Justice (2003), 46
Criminal Justice Act (CJA), 148–149
Criminal Justice Act (1972), 98–100
Criminal Justice Act (1991), 5, 7, 10–11, 93–94, 101, 108–109
Criminal Justice Act (2003), 26–28, 52, 56, 71–72
Criminal Justice and Court Services Act (2000), 5–6, 8, 56, 101
Criminal Justice and Immigration Act (2008), 48–49, 52–53
Crown Prosecution Service (CPS), 115–116
Cultural change, 5–6
Cyber hue and cry, 194–195
Cyber rough music, 194–195

Daisy's Law, 40
Damien Bendall, 174–175
Damien Hanson, 157–158, 174–175
Dangerous and Severe Personality Disordered programme (DSPD programme), 126–131
Dangerous offenders, 25, 28, 38–39, 63–64
 population, 15, 30
Dangerous people, 17
Dangerousness, 15, 19–20, 25, 28, 30, 51
Dangers, 17–19
David Cameron, 60–61
David Carrick, 31, 88–89
Deviant knowledge, 194
Dietrich case, 197–198
Digilantes, 195–196
Digilantism, 195–196, 205, 207
Digital vigilantism, 194, 205, 207

and civilian led public protection, 194–198
Disordered offenders, 213–214
Domestic abuse, 17–18, 83, 193
Domestic violence protection notice order, 55
Dominic Raab, 61, 71, 77
Don't Fuck with Cats, 185
Douglas Hurd, 26, 66
Dynamic security, 67

Elliott White, 174–175
Embodied death, 43–44
European Court of Human Rights (ECHR), 41–42
Exceptional sentences, 15–16, 22–23
Exploitative law-passing strategy, 39–40
Extremism, 142

Failures of public protection, 210–211
Family Law Act, 55, 1996
Fear, 19–20, 22–23
Female genital mutilation protection orders, 55
Fishmongers' Hall, 138–140
Forced marriage protection orders, 55
Formulaic approach, 9

Governmental bodies, 12–13
Governments, 70, 77, 213
Graham Young (St Albans Poisoner), 156–157
Green Paper (2010), 103

Harm, 5, 139–140, 213–214
Harper's Law, 40
Hashtag campaigns, 198
Her Majesty's Prison and Probation Service (HMPPS), 101, 130–131, 156–157
Her/His Majesty's Inspectorate of Probation (HMIP), 215–216
Home Office, 46, 145–146
Homicide, 121
Hue and cry system, 191–192

Index   243

Human Rights, 3–4, 129–130
Human Rights Act, 78–79, 126–127
Humane containment, 66–67

Imminence, 23, 28, 32, 150
Imprisonment for Public Protection (IPP), 48–49
Incapacitation, 61
Incarceration, 62
Inclusion criteria, 22–23
Independent inquiries, politics of, 170–174
Independent Office for Police Complaints (IOPC), 88–89, 114–115
Independent Reviews, 161, 215–216
Indeterminate Sentences for Public Protection (IPP), 25–26, 62, 71–72, 138–139
Informal criminal justice (ICJ), 193–194
Informal justice, 194
Informal public protection (IPP), 48–49, 186
Innocent victims, 137
Inquiries, 38
Internal reviews, 159, 161–162, 174
International Personality Disorder Examination (IPDE), 128
Internet and communication technologies (ICT), 196–197
Internet technologies, 216–217
Intimate partner violence (IPV), 197–198

Jack Straw, 10–11, 96–98, 126–127, 149–150
Jack the Ripper, 17–18
Jade's Law, 40
John Major, 96
John Worboys, 74–75, 79
Joint Extremism Unit (JEXU), 143
Jonathan Zito, 119–122
Jordan McSweeney, 174–175
Joseph McCann, 157–158, 161, 174–175

Joshua Jacques, 174–175
Judge, The, 23–24
Justice Committee, 107
Justifications, 201–202
Justin Russell, 165, 167, 170

Kenneth Clarke, 103, 105

Labour Party, 78
Labour's Offender Management Act (2007), 156–157
Law and Order, 45, 79
Legal Aid, Sentencing and Punishment of Offenders Act (2012), 48–49
Legislation, 39–40, 46–47
  controlling monsters, 49–52
  Criminal Justice Act, 44–47
  new labour, 47–49
  registration and collaboration, 52–56
  tone and trends of public protection legislation, 40–44
Leon Brittain, 26
Leroy Campbell, 157–158, 170–171, 174–175
Liberal regime, 66–67
Life imprisonment, 43–44, 63, 75–76
Long-term prisoners, containment of, 64–67
Low-level offenders, 9

Management of sexual offenders and violent offenders (MOSOVO), 85–86
Manchester Evening News, 23–24
Manslaughter, 7–8, 46
Margaret Thatcher, 65–66
Marketisation, 107–108, 169–170
Mechanical solidarity, 189
Megan's Law, 6, 39
Mental abnormality, 21–22
Mental health, 114–115
Mental Health Act (1983), 113–114
Mental Health Act (2007), 130
Mentally ill, 213–214

Mentally ill and personality disordered offenders
  crown prosecution service, 115–116
  making disorder illness, 119–125
  offender personality disorder pathway, 130–133
  police (in)action, 114–115
  responding to rare events, 125–130
  scale of problem, 118–119
  trial and judge's comments, 116–118
#metoo movement, 198, 205, 207
Metropolitan Police Service, 82–83
Michael Howard, 45, 47, 98
Michael Stone, 20, 122, 125–126
Micro-analysis, 179
Ministry of Justice (MoJ), 105
Ministry of Justice Business Plan, The, 105
Modern police of England, 81–82
Monster predator, 50
Multi-agency public protection arrangements (MAPPA), 5, 8, 56, 139, 148, 151
Multi-agency working (MAW), 5
Murder, 82–83
Murder investigations teams (MITs), 80–83
Muslim Civil Society, 145–146

National Association of Probation Officers (NAPO), 78–79
National Audit Office, The (NAO), 108–109
National Offender Management Service (NOMS), 101, 156–157
National Police Chiefs' Council (NPCC), 6–7, 52, 88–89, 204
National Probation Service (NPS), 167
National Secular Society and the Countryside Alliance, The, 142
Negative sentiments, 178–179
Neo-liberalism, 104–105
Neo-vigilantes, 189–190
New Labour, 47–49

News of the World (NoW), 5–6
Non-molestation orders, 55
Nothing Works, 97–98, 210–211
Notifications, 157–170

Offence eligibility, 158–170
Offender Assessment System (OASys), 150, 159
Offender Disorder Pathway, 134
Offender Group Reconviction Score (OGRS), 150
Offender Management Act (2007), 104–105
Offender management process, 173–174
Offender personality disorder pathway, 130–133
Offender Rehabilitation Act (2014), 104–105, 108–109, 159
Online activism, 205–207
  and civilian led public protection, 194–198
Online child abuse activist groups (OCAGs), 201–202, 204–205, 207, 216–217
Orders, 10–11
Organisations, 209
Outmoded rehabilitation model, 98

Paedophile hunters, 199–200, 205, 207
Paedophiles hunting, 199–205
Parliament, 37–38
Parole, 43–44, 71–72
  assessment process, 21
  process, 78, 80, 123–124
Parole Board, 10, 12–13, 48–49, 71, 73, 79–80, 214–215
  controlling, 76–77
Payment-by-results (PBR), 105–106
Penal optimism, 73
Penal pessimism, 98
Penal welfarism, 73
Persistent and prolific offending (PPO), 104–105
Person on probation (PoP), 155–156
Personal evil concept, 63–64

Personality disordered offenders, 119
  crown prosecution service, 115–116
  making disorder illness, 119–125
  offender personality disorder pathway, 130–133
  police (in)action, 114–115
  responding to rare events, 125–130
  scale of problem, 118–119
  trial and judge's comments, 116–118
Peter Williams, 174–175
Planning & Preparation, Engage and Explain, Account, Closure and Evaluation model (PEACE model), 86–87
Police, 5–7
  (in)action, 114–115
  police-defined public protection, 83–90
  and public protection, 80–82
  service, 5–6, 12–13, 211–212
Police, Crime Sentencing and Courts Act (2022), 42–43, 55, 149–150
Police Domestic Abuse Disclosure Scheme, 40
Police Foundation, 89–91
Politicians, 43–44, 59, 204–205
Politics, 37–38
  of independent inquiries, 170–174
Positive sentiments, 178–179
Post-TR, 174–183
Potentially dangerous offender (PDO), 56
Pre-sentence reports (PSRs), 48–49, 94–95
Pre-TR, 174–183
Predatory offenders, 50
PREVENT, 143–145
  review of, 146–148
Preventing Violent Extremism Pathfinder Fund (PVEPF), 144–145
Prevention, 17, 50
Preventive sentences, 15–16
Prison Reform Trust (PRT), 41, 67–68

Prison Security Classifications, 64–65
Prison Service, the, 12–13
Prisoners, 65–66
Prisons, 59, 67
  system, 131
Prisons Strategy White Paper, 61
Privatisation, 104–105
Probation, 11, 100–101
  officers, 11
Probation service, 48–49, 56, 93–94, 99–100
  bring on revolution, 102–109
  history, 98–100
  protecting public, 101–102
  from punishment to protection, 98–101
  shifting service, 94–98
Probation Service, The, 10–11
Probation Service Act (1993), 96–97
Procedural death, 43–44
Professional change, 210
Professional curiosity, 182–183
Professional knowledge, 10
Proportionality principle, 15–16, 44–45
Proportionate sentences, 44–45
Protection from Harassment Act 1997, 55
Protective sentences, 15–16
Pseudo-official channels, 186
Psychopathy Checklist–Revised (PCL-R), 128
Public protection, 5, 83, 89–91, 101–102, 183, 194, 209–210
  area, 56
  measures, 4, 37–38
  policy, 7–8
  process, 5–6, 12
  system, 16
  task, 211–212
  teams, 82–83, 140–141
  vacuum, 205
  windsock of, 71
Public protection agencies, 12–13, 72–73

containment of long-term prisoners, 64–67
controlling Parole Board, 76–77
dangerous offenders, 63–64
murder, 82–83
Parole, 71–72
place and purpose, 59–63
police and, 80–82
police-defined public protection, 83–90
prisons, 59
shifting in wind, 74–76
superdangerous, 78–79
tough talk, more prisoners, 67–70
Public protection legislation, 3, 50–51
tone and trends of, 40–44
Public safety, 90–91
Punishment, 8–9
Punitive demands, 59
'Punitive Victims' Rights, 39

Quality assurance, 161
Quantification, 28

Radicalisation, 146
Rape, 15, 31
Registration, 52–56
Rehabilitation, 94–95
Rehabilitation revolution, 102
Remission, 73
Research Information and Communications Unit (RICU), 145–146
Residents against Paedophiles (RAP), 52–53
Restraining order, 55
Revolving-door' offenders, 159
Right Care, Right Person (RCRP), 88
Risk, 28, 50–51, 213
assessment tools, 51–52
decisions, 212–213
management, 6–7
Rituals, 188
Robert Peel, 81–82

Rough music, 192, 200
RSOs, 86–87

Safeguarding, 83–84
Sarah's Law, 40
Secure hospitals, 128
Security; Secure, 62
Self-preservation, 190–191
Sentencing Code, 26
Serious acquisitive crime (SAC), 18
Serious Crime Act (2015), 199–200
Serious further offence (SFO), 155–156, 210–211
Serious further offending
offence eligibility, 158–170
politics of independent inquiries, 170–174
Pre-TR *vs.* Post-TR, 174–183
SFO's, notifications and reviews and inquiries, 157–170
supervised individual eligibility, 158
Serious offending, 63–64, 174–175
Seriousness, 27–28, 32
Severity, 32
Sex Offender Order (SOO), 53–54
Sex Offender Register (SOR), 24–25, 52, 84–85
Sex offenders, 5–7
Sex Offenders Act (1997), 52–54, 84–85, 149–150
Sex Offenders Act 2003, 52–53
Sexual Harm Prevention Order (SHPOs), 55
Sexual Offences Act (2003), 199–200
Sexual Risk Order, 54–55
Shaky ideological house of cards, 102–109
TR proposed allocation for different offender groups, 106
Skimmington (*see* Rough music)
Slavery and trafficking prevention and risk order, 55
Social media applications, 199–200
Social work
ethos, 11

training process, 10–11
Stalking protection order, 55
Statute of Winchester, 191–192
Stranger crime, 81–82
Superdangerous, 78–79
Supervised individual eligibility, 158
Sutherland v Her Majesty's Advocate, 201–202

Tariff setting procedures, 42
Terror, UK government response to, 142–146
Terror-related offenders
  dealing with terrorism-related offenders, 138
  Fishmongers' Hall, 138–140
  MAPPA, 148–151
  nature of problem, 140–142
  review of PREVENT, 146–148
  UK government response to terror, 142–146
Terrorism, 142, 214
  dealing with terrorism-related offenders, 138
  Fishmongers' Hall, 138–140
  MAPPA, 148–151
  nature of problem, 140–142
  review of PREVENT, 146–148
  UK government response to terror, 142–146
Terrorism Act (2000), 141–142
Terrorism-related offenders, dealing with, 138
Terrorism-related offending, 138–139
Terrorist, 138–139
Themes, 55
Threat, 29

Tony Blair, 37–38, 45, 104–105
Tony's Law, 40
Transforming Rehabilitation revolution, 11

UK government response to terror, 142–146
Unconditionally dangerous, 21
University of Cambridge, 138–139
US frontier vigilantism, 190–191
US preventive legislation, 52
Usman Khan, 138–139, 143

Valdo Calocane, 7–8, 213–214
Vectis, 64–65
Victims, 7–8
Vigilante groups, 189–190
Vigilante ideology, 190–191
Vigilantism, 186–189
  brief history of, 189–194
Violence, 17–18
Violence-prone offender, 22–23
Violent Crime Reduction Act (2006), 52–53
Violent crimes, 68–69
Violent offender order (VOO), 55
Violent offenders, 8

Wayne Couzens, 9, 26, 88–89
Web 2.0, 193–194
Web 3.0, 193–194
White Paper, 46
Whole life tariff, 26
Windsock, 71
Woolf Report, 67–68
Worry group, 8–10

www.ingramcontent.com/pod-product-compliance
Lightning Source LLC
Jackson TN
JSHW061300070125
76712JS00004B/25